The Presidential Campaign
of Barack Obama

In the early twenty-first century, race still occupies a dominant role in American politics. Despite this truism, presidential candidate Barack Obama was uniquely poised to transcend both race and party as the first African American to have a realistic chance of winning the presidency. Previous contenders running in the traditional mode of the civil rights movement based their appeal primarily on African American voters. Obama, on the other hand, ran a deracialized campaign in an effort to appeal to voters of different backgrounds and political parties.

Clayton examines how race in American politics has changed over time and offers an explanation for why Obama's candidacy offers a different roadmap for the future. *The Presidential Campaign of Barack Obama* provides students of politics, inside and outside of the classroom, a unique opportunity to explore the institutional and structural challenges an African American faces in becoming the president of the United States. This guide to major issues in black politics and the ins and outs of the 2008 campaign provides the necessary contours for understanding how the highest elected African American official won office.

Dewey M. Clayton is Professor in the Department of Political Science at the University of Louisville. He is the author of *African Americans and the Politics of Congressional Redistricting* and numerous scholarly articles.

The Presidential Campaign
of Barack Obama

A Critical Analysis of a Racially
Transcendent Strategy

Dewey M. Clayton

Routledge
Taylor & Francis Group

NEW YORK AND LONDON

First published 2010
by Routledge
270 Madison Avenue, New York, NY 10016

Simultaneously published in the UK
by Routledge
2 Park Square, Milton Park, Abingdon, Oxon OX14 4RN

Routledge is an imprint of the Taylor & Francis Group, an informa business

© 2010 Taylor & Francis

Typeset in Adobe Garamond
by Keystroke, Tettenhall, Wolverhampton
Printed and bound in the United States of America on acid-free paper
by Walsworth Publishing Company, Marceline, MO

Library of Congress Cataloging in Publication Data
Clayton, Dewey M.
The presidential campaign of Barack Obama : a critical analysis of a racially
transcendent strategy / Dewey M. Clayton.
    p. cm.
    Includes bibliographical references.
    1. Presidents—United States—Election—2008, 2. Political
campaigns—United States. 3. Obama, Barack. 4. United States—Politics
and government—2001–2009. I. Title.
JK5262008 .C53 2010
324.973'0931—dc22
2009038465

ISBN 10: 0–415–99734–8 (hbk)
ISBN 10: 0–415–99735–6 (pbk)
ISBN 10: 0–203–88395–0 (ebk)

ISBN 13: 978–0–415–99734–8 (hbk)
ISBN 13: 978–0–415–99735–5 (pbk)
ISBN 13: 978–0–203–88395–2 (ebk)

To my parents,
Christine and Dewey,
who continue to be my greatest source of inspiration

Contents

Tables

Preface

The election of Barack Obama was not just one of the most fascinating and historic campaigns in this country's history; it was also the triumphant convergence of a man for his time, a message for the moment, and the march of history into a new millennium, a new era. All previous forty-three presidents of the United States had been white males. Barack Obama, born of an African father from Kenya and an American mother from Kansas, became number forty-four, representing both a cultural mélange and cultural shift change in American, even global, politics.

From the primary season to the general election, Barack Obama's candidacy was an unlikely one. Given America's racist past, some contended the country wasn't ready to elect an African American as president. Others argued the one-term senator and former community organizer was too young and inexperienced and needed to wait his turn. But Obama proved his keen political instincts and outlined a bold and innovative strategy to win first the Democratic primary, then the presidency. He overcame the formidable name recognition and war chest of Hillary Rodham Clinton, a second-term senator whose husband had served two terms as president and had been elevated to iconic status in many Democratic communities—especially the black community. In the general election, he faced a war hero and political maverick in John McCain. I argue, in this book, that Obama was uniquely situated to overcome the obstacles and the odds to offer America a message of hope and racial reconciliation.

Obama did not run as an African American candidate but as a candidate who happened to be African American. Throughout most of the campaign, he downplayed his ethnic background, while at the same time using his race and relative youthfulness to reach out to entire new subsets of voting blocs. His campaign increased turnout particularly among voters younger than 30, connecting with them by using new media—primarily the Internet—to create a new movement of supporters who organized, mobilized, and turned out at the polls. Obama attracted not only young voters, but also Hispanics and African Americans of all ages in record numbers. He executed a fifty-state strategy that aggressively pursued the vote in states his Democratic predecessors had written off; Obama put these states—including some in the Old Confederacy—back into play for the Democratic Party.

Money, called the mother's milk of politics, was also the sustenance for Obama's groundbreaking campaign. But where and how he hauled in record amounts of campaign cash created a whole new paradigm for successful campaigns. Obama's unique coalition of liberals, independents and disaffected Republicans mixed main street dollars with Wall Street wallets, infused with an unprecedented and uninterrupted flow of cash from contributors via the Internet. Obama has ushered in a much more democratic election process, open to all of the people, whether rich or poor, black, white, brown, or red.

But Obama himself—the man and the message—was the overriding factor in his victory. He ran a thrilling campaign full of substance as well as symbolism. He offered hope to a country that had been bitterly divided by race and partisanship since its inception. He spoke with a new voice and a new message about a new way to fix what many felt was a broken nation. His promise of hope and racial reconciliation resonated across regions and races.

At a time when many Americans hungered for leadership and solutions and yes, change, Barack Obama emerged with that message and America listened. Long before his resounding victory, Barack Obama believed America was ready for him. This is the story of how it happened.

Acknowledgments

There are several individuals I wish to acknowledge in being indispensable to me in completion of this work. As my graduate assistant, Brandon Hubbard helped me with general ideas and his Internet skills proved invaluable with the completion of my tables. Erica Williams, as a graduate student this past year, took an independent study course each semester with me on Barack Obama. She provided incredible insight into many aspects of the election campaign, transcribed numerous tape recordings and took issue with some of my arguments. Chris Lucas, as a recent graduate, was extremely helpful in conducting research on aspects of my book. All three gave me insight into the use of the Internet in the election and how young Americans viewed the candidates and the election. Barbara Reichardt provided excellent copyediting and invaluable constructive criticism. Graduate student Carolyn Morgan helped me tie this project together and was very efficient and an immense help. Lastly, I thank Kimberly Drury for proofreading, and being extremely understanding.

THE HISTORICAL NATURE OF AFRICAN AMERICANS RUNNING FOR POLITICAL OFFICE, COALITION POLITICS, AND OBAMA'S WINNING COALITION

Introduction

To America in general, Obama brings hope, change, opportunity; hope that we can end that war, hope that we can invest in children's education, that we can invest in the seniors that built this country, so that they can pay their rent and live a decent life. That will be the same for black Americans, Asian Americans, and white Americans alike. Obama will bring this country and the world together, and not without challenges. That is what is needed.[1]

Rep. Carolyn Kilpatrick (D-MI)

*T*he *Presidential Campaign of Barack Obama: A Critical Analysis of a Racially Transcendent Strategy* examines one of the most profound presidential elections in the history of this country. This book offers an in-depth look at the extraordinary political journey and meteoric rise of one individual, Barack Obama, from the state legislature in Illinois, to the Senate in Washington, D.C., and finally to the presidency of the United States. My main focus is to demonstrate that Barack Obama, as a Democrat, was uniquely poised to transcend race and party and was the first African American candidate with a realistic chance of winning the presidency in the United States. So, a central theme of this book is how Obama, as an African American, won election in conservative America of 2008.

The main argument for this work is that Barack Obama's candidacy provides a new paradigm for candidates of color to transcend race at the presidential level. One of the big questions to emerge from Obama's election is whether his administration will have a markedly different impact on the lives of African Americans than a white president's administration. Another question that needs thorough examination is what, if anything, has happened to create a political climate in America that has allowed an African American to become the nominee of a major political party and subsequently win the general presidential election. A goal of this book is to show the maturation of the American political process whereby Americans examine candidates based not on the color of their skin but on their stance on the issues and choose the most qualified person. As the book progresses, the reader will be able to discern how race in American society has changed over time, and that although racism is still prevalent, it no longer is an impediment to achieving the highest office in the land.

Barack Obama's candidacy provides an excellent case study of the changing order in American politics for he is the first African American to gain the nomination of his party and then the presidency of this country. When Reverend Jesse Jackson, an African American, ran for president in 1984 and again in 1988, political observers stated that he was unable to transcend race. When Reverend Al Sharpton, another African American, ran in 2004, people felt he was too polarizing a figure. Both of these men came out of the civil rights movement of the 1960s and 1970s. Obama did not grow up as part of this civil rights movement. He was too young to sit-in in Greensboro, North Carolina, to travel as a Freedom Rider from Washington, D.C., to New Orleans, Louisiana, or to march from Selma to Montgomery, Alabama, to gain the right to vote. However, he benefited from the movement's courage, determination, and unwavering belief in the American ideal that all people are created equal. In 2008, Barack Obama was uniquely qualified to offer the American people a new paradigm for politics in the twenty-first century. This paradigm is based on the building of a new coalition of African Americans, Latinos, young people, and first-time voters, and the use of a new technology—the Internet—to organize and mobilize this new coalition, and to mount the most successful fundraising campaign of any presidential candidate in the history of this nation.

Overview of the Book

Part One examines the historical nature of African Americans running for political office in America. It begins with a chapter that explores the history of African American politics in America from Reconstruction to the present. It also discusses Barack Obama and his unique background that made it possible for him to make such a historic presidential bid. Chapter 2 examines descriptive and substantive representation. Will an Obama administration have a markedly different impact on the lives of African Americans than a white president's administration? In this chapter, I analyze the history of racially polarized voting in America. In this country, white voters have traditionally voted only for white candidates while black voters have voted only for black candidates, when possible. Because of this, minority candidates have often been at a disadvantage when running in a majority white district. Obama sought the presidency by running a deracialized campaign. I discuss the concept of deracialization and the implications of running this style campaign on his ability to govern.

Chapter 3 investigates coalition politics in America and how Obama was able to put together a winning coalition of different races, ethnicities, and age groups to win a majority of the vote. I explore the demographic trends in America and discuss what they say about the electoral landscape in the future. In Chapter 4, I examine Obama and the different demographic groups that made up his winning coalition: the white vote, the Latino vote, the black vote, and the youth vote. This election was remarkable on many levels. In the Democratic primary, the two frontrunners were both firsts: Hillary Clinton was the first female major contender for her party's nomination and Barack Obama was the first African American to be a major contender for his party's nomination. Because of this, I also focus on the intersection of race, class, and gender in the election in this chapter.

Part Two takes a more in-depth look at the dynamics of the campaign process itself. Chapter 5 is titled "The Clinton Factor: Hillary and Bill." Hillary Clinton was the frontrunner at the beginning of the 2008 presidential campaign. She had huge name recognition, a substantial campaign chest, more political experience than Barack Obama, and her husband had been president of the United States for eight years. That said, how was it that Barack Obama was able to out-campaign, out-organize, and out-spend Hillary Clinton to win the Democratic nomination? South Carolina became a pivotal primary, and I examine what impact Bill Clinton had on the campaign trail and that primary in particular. Focusing on Obama's campaign for the White House in Chapter 6, I scrutinize some of the major events that emerge. First, I examine the nomination process and key decisions made by the Obama camp, such as going to Iowa to get an upset primary victory and the Super Tuesday strategy. I also look at the Rev. Wright factor and Obama's Father's Day speech. Lastly, I analyze the general election. Obama's opponent, Senator

John McCain, was behind in the polls after the Democratic Convention in August 2008. McCain's surprise pick of Governor Sarah Palin of Alaska to be his vice presidential running mate shored up his base and injected new momentum into his campaign, but in the end failed to convert Independent voters and female Democratic supporters of Senator Hillary Clinton to the Republican cause. Moreover, the choice of Palin called into question McCain's political judgment.

In Chapter 7, I explore how Obama was able to tap into computer technology to run a brilliant grassroots campaign. By using the Internet, and his webpage, and an array of social networking sites such as MyBarackObama, MySpace, Facebook, and Twitter, Obama raised an incredible amount of money and organized a vast army of volunteers in all fifty states. I conclude in Chapter 8 that Obama's bold and innovative strategy positioned him to accomplish what no African American in this country had achieved: capture the presidency of the United States and in the process change forever how presidential campaigns in this country will be conducted.

African American Politics in America

When the United States of America was founded in 1776, the majority of African Americans were enslaved. As such, they had no political rights—no right to vote and no right to political representation. Ironically, this nation, founded on the principles that "all men are created equal and endowed by their creator with certain unalienable rights," refused to acknowledge that these rights pertained to the African American slave population. The founding fathers looked upon slavery as an economic and political issue, not as a moral one. In fact, the right to vote was originally bestowed only on white, male property owners. Poor white men, all women, and the majority of African American men were denied the right to vote in the first half-century of the republic. Furthermore, the Constitution, America's blueprint for democracy, sanctioned the institution of slavery. Slavery was a contentious issue at the Constitutional Convention at Philadelphia in 1787, with Northern and Southern delegates in disagreement over whether slaves should be counted for purposes of taxation and representation. To resolve this dispute, the framers settled on the Three-Fifths Compromise, which stated that each slave would count as equal to three-fifths, or 60 percent, of a free white person in determining representation in the House of Representatives and in apportioning direct taxes.[2] The issue of slavery, however, was not resolved and almost tore this nation apart, when in 1860 and 1861 a total of eleven Southern states seceded from the Union and called themselves the Confederate States of America. On January 1, 1863, President Abraham Lincoln issued the Emancipation Proclamation, which ended slavery in the "states under rebellion."

Civil War Amendments

At the end of the Civil War in 1865, the Union had held and Congress set out to bestow full citizenship rights on all African Americans. To accomplish this, Congress proposed and subsequently ratified a series of amendments to the U.S. Constitution. In 1865, Congress ratified the 13th Amendment, which outlawed slavery; in 1868, Congress ratified the 14th Amendment, which gave African Americans citizenship rights; and in 1870, Congress ratified the 15th Amendment, which gave black males the right to vote.[3] These three amendments, collectively known as the Civil War Amendments, gave hope to African Americans during this time period known as Reconstruction, that America would finally make good on its promise of equality for all of its citizens. Passed by Congress in 1867, the Reconstruction Act stationed Northern military troops in the South and allowed many African Americans to exercise social, political, and economic rights for the first time.[4]

African Americans gained substantial political power during this period. Blacks held elective office in state legislatures throughout the South. Moreover, they served as lieutenant governors in several states, and one black, P. B. S. Pinchback, briefly served as governor of Louisiana. Additionally, between 1869 and 1901, two blacks served in the U.S. Senate and twenty in the U.S. House of Representatives.[5]

Reconstruction

The electoral victories enjoyed by African Americans during the Reconstruction Period did not last long. The disputed presidential election of 1876, settled by the Hayes-Tilden Compromise, spelled the death knell for African American electoral success in the South. In that election, the Republican candidate, Rutherford B. Hayes, struck a deal with Samuel Tilden, the Democratic candidate, in which the Republicans pledged to withdraw federal troops from the South if Hayes were allowed to become president. As a result of the agreement, the political power of African Americans declined precipitously.

White Southerners, who had not stopped their intimidation against blacks during this period, were now unimpeded in their efforts to reclaim their supremacy throughout the South and relegate African Americans to inferior second-class citizenship status.[6]

Southern whites resented African Americans voting and holding public office and exercising political power. They had begun to form secret societies to intimidate blacks through illegal means. Historian John Hope Franklin noted that for ten years after 1867 white terrorist organizations such as the Ku Klux Klan, the Knights of the White Camelia, and other white hate groups sprang up throughout the South with the sole purpose of maintaining white supremacy and keeping blacks in their place.[7]

Concurrently, the U.S. Supreme Court had begun issuing a series of court decisions that limited the effect of the 15th Amendment's guarantee of the right to vote.[8] According to Franklin,

> In 1875 several indictments under the Enforcement Act of 1870 charged defendants with preventing Negroes from exercising their right to vote in elections. In *United States v. Reese* the Court held that the statute covered more offenses than were punishable under the terms of the Fifteenth Amendment and was, therefore, unconstitutional. In *United States v. Cruikshank* the Court declared that the Fifteenth Amendment guaranteed citizens not the right to vote but only a right not to be discriminated against by the state on account of race, color, or previous condition of servitude.[9]

Franklin asserted, "As far as the Court was concerned, the South was free to settle its problems as best it could."[10] Then, in 1896, the Supreme Court issued its opinion in *Plessy v. Ferguson* (163 U.S. 537) in which it enunciated for the first time the doctrine of "separate but equal." This narrow interpretation of the 14th Amendment's equal protection clause by the Court was widely viewed throughout the land as giving legitimacy to separating American society by race and creating a system of racial apartheid in the American South.[11]

Tactics Used to Disenfranchise African Americans

In addition to threat and intimidation, whites began using an array of other devices to deny blacks their constitutional rights. By 1900, most Southern states had revised their state constitutions to disenfranchise African Americans.

For example, Mississippi, which had a majority black population in 1886, was the first to limit the suffrage for blacks. The state held a constitutional convention in 1890, for the sole purpose of denying blacks the right to vote. According to Franklin, "A suffrage amendment was written that imposed a poll tax of two dollars; excluded voters convicted of bribery, burglary, theft, arson, perjury, murder, or bigamy; and also barred all who could not read any section of the state constitution, or understand it when read, or give a reasonable interpretation of it."[12] South Carolina followed Mississippi by disenfranchising blacks in 1895. It held a constitutional convention in 1894 that contained a suffrage provision that when adopted, called for two years' residence, a poll tax of a dollar, the ability to read and write any section of the constitution or to understand it when read aloud, or the owning of property worth three hundred dollars, and the disqualification of convicts.[13]

Efforts by Southern states to hold state conventions to revise their state constitutions continued throughout much of the South. Louisiana added a new device, the "grandfather clause" that was written into its state constitution. It called for an addition to the permanent registration list of the names of all male persons whose fathers and grandfathers were qualified to vote on January 1, 1867. No Negroes, at that time, were qualified to vote in Louisiana. This pattern continued and by 1910, blacks had been effectively disenfranchised by constitutional provisions in North Carolina, Alabama, Virginia, Georgia, and Oklahoma.[14] Southern states began employing such tactics as the grandfather clause, literacy tests, poll taxes, the white primary (excluding blacks from the primary election but not the general election),[15] and racial gerrymanders (the drawing of electoral district boundaries to exclude members of a race)[16] to disenfranchise blacks. These laws often were referred to as "Jim Crow" laws.

The term "Jim Crow" refers to the practice of segregating black and white people in the American South and discriminating against blacks. Even as blacks left the South and migrated to the slums and ghettos of the Northern cities, they still faced discrimination, but they now had the right to vote. According to historian George Davis, "much of the out-migration of blacks from the South . . . had increased so significantly by 1915 that it was referred to as the 'great migration.'"[17]

Many blacks left the rural South and migrated to Northern cities looking for better social conditions and economic opportunities. Employment was often limited and blacks could only find the most onerous and menial jobs. Black women easily found employment as household servants. Housing was also a problem because most cities passed segregation ordinances restricting blacks to usually one section of the city. Louisville, Baltimore, Richmond . . . all passed segregation ordinances in 1912 and 1913. According to Franklin, "The extreme congestion that resulted from the restriction upon the choice of residence and the occupancy of small, unsanitary homes by large families led, naturally, to poor health and a high mortality rate."[18]

Second Reconstruction

Jim Crow remained the order of the day for the first half of the twentieth century in the American South. The North was viewed as the promised land, primarily due to economic opportunity in factories of the cities of the Northeast and Midwest, coupled with the wretched social climate for blacks in the South and the low pay of tenant farming. Blacks experienced prejudice and racism in the North, generally referred to as "de facto segregation."[19] De facto segregation can be defined as segregation existing as a result of residential patterns without legal restraints.[20]

However, World War II had a profound effect on black Americans, especially on blacks who had served in the war. Many returned home from World War II with a renewed determination to no longer tolerate second-class citizenship status. Organizations such as the National Association for the Advancement of Colored People (NAACP) began to lobby Congress and the president more vigorously for equality. President Harry Truman helped contribute to this climate. He appointed a biracial committee to inquire into the condition of civil rights and to make recommendations for their improvement. John Hope Franklin noted that "The report, *To Secure These Rights*, strongly denounced the denial of civil rights to some Americans, and it called for a positive program to strengthen civil rights including 'the elimination of segregation, based on race, color, creed, or national origin, from American life.'"[21](President Harry Truman signed an executive order integrating the Armed Services in 1948.) In the presidential election of 1948, the Democratic Party supported a strong civil rights plank in its campaign platform (many Southern Democrats were angered by this attack on their "Southern" way of life and they bolted from the party and supported Strom Thurmond's Third-party candidacy for president).

The Army adopted a hiring policy in 1949 that opened all jobs to qualified personnel without regard to race or color and change was beginning to take hold in America. In 1954, just five years later, the U.S. Supreme Court struck down the doctrine of "separate but equal" in the landmark case *Brown v. Board of Education* (347 U.S. 483). In 1964, just ten years after the *Brown* decision,

Congress passed the Civil Rights Act of 1964 (CRA of 1964) that outlawed segregation in public schools and all areas of public accommodation such as hotels, restaurants, movie theaters, and employment. The Act marked a turning point in prohibiting *de jure* (state imposed) segregation in the country.[22] However, one area that the CRA of 1964 failed to address adequately was voting. Many of the tactics Southern states had devised to disenfranchise blacks had been declared unconstitutional by the U.S. Supreme Court: the grandfather clause (1915), white primaries (1944), racial gerrymandering (1960), and poll taxes (1964). Still, a majority of Southern blacks were denied the right to vote by violence and literacy tests.

One year later, in 1965, Congress passed the Voting Rights Act (VRA), which suspended literacy tests and allowed blacks the right to register to vote and to vote. These two pieces of legislation, the Civil Rights Act of 1964 and the Voting Rights Act of 1965, were significant accomplishments of the modern-day civil rights movement in America—a struggle by African Americans to gain full citizenship rights that had been guaranteed by the 14th and 15th Amendments to the U.S. Constitution.[23]

The Voting Rights Act has had a tremendous effect on African American political empowerment particularly in the South. African American voter registration levels increased dramatically once blacks were allowed to register to vote throughout the South. Furthermore, the gap between white and black registration levels has narrowed substantially.[24] Table 1.1 compares black voter registration rates in seven Southern states in 1965 and 2006. One can see the enormous impact the VRA has had on African Americans in the South. Black voter registration levels throughout the South have almost reached parity with that of white voters and in some instances exceeded it. For example, in Mississippi in 1965, only 6.7 percent of African Americans were registered to vote; however, by 2006, 72.2 percent of African Americans were registered to vote, an increase of more than tenfold. The gap between black and white voter registration levels in Mississippi in 1965 was 63.2 percent, but in 2006, the gap was −2.2 percent. The black percentage of registered voters was actually higher than the white percentage in 2006.

As African American levels of voter registration increased throughout the South, black political power increased as well. African Americans began seeking political office in the South in unprecedented numbers, so much so that historian C. Vann Woodward referred to the period as the Second Reconstruction, "where blacks began to match the precedents in local, state, and national office that they had achieved during the Reconstruction Period."[25]

TABLE 1.1 VOTER REGISTRATION RATES, 1965 vs. 2006

	1965			2006		
State	Black	White	Gap	Black	White	Gap
Mississippi	6.7	69.9	63.2	72.2	71.0	–2.2
North Carolina	46.8	96.8	50	62.2	72.3	11.1
Alabama	19.3	69.2	49.9	71.4	75.0	3.6
Louisiana	31.6	80.5	48.9	67.5	75.5	8
South Carolina	37.3	75.7	38.4	70.2	63.9	–6.3
Georgia	27.4	62.6	35.2	61.3	68.8	7.5
Virginia	38.3	61.1	22.8	53.8	71.0	17.2

Sources: Bernard Grofman, Lisa Handley, and Richard G. Niemi, *Minority Representation and the Quest for Voting Equality* (New York: Cambridge University Press, 1992); Pew Center On the States: Current Population Survey.

Formation of the Congressional Black Caucus

In spite of the political gains by African Americans at the local and state levels in the South after 1965, black political success at the national level throughout the country was abysmal at best. In fact, by 1966 there were only six blacks serving in the U.S. Congress. By 1969, that number had increased to nine, which was the largest contingent of blacks ever serving in Congress at the same time, and in that year the black representatives formed the Congressional Black Caucus (CBC). According to Congressman William Clay, Sr. (D-MO), a founding member (1969–2001), the CBC was created to represent the interests of all black Americans.[26] Another founding member, Shirley Chisholm (D-NY), who served from 1969 to 1983, was also the first black woman to serve in Congress. According to political scientists Hanes Walton and Robert Smith, authors of *American Politics and the African American Quest for Universal Freedom*,

> The CBC was created as an outgrowth of the black power movement's call for racial solidarity and independent black organization.

In addition to its role as an internal House legislative caucus, the CBC also plays an external role by forming coalitions with interest groups outside the Congress and operating as one of the two or three major African American interest organizations in Washington. The work of the caucus includes such activities as lobbying the president, presenting various black legislative agendas and alternative budgets in floor debates, and holding its annual legislative weekends.[27]

African Americans Seeking the Highest Office in the Land

Having already established herself as a trailblazer, Chisholm ran for president of the United States in 1972 as a Democrat. She was the first African American to run for the presidential nomination of a major political party in this country. Chisholm's goal was never to win but to make a strong showing and to prove that a woman and a black could run for president. She stated that

> I ran because someone had to do it first. In this country everybody is supposed to be able to run for President, but that's never been really true. I ran because most people think the country is not ready for a black candidate, not ready for a woman candidate. Someday . . .[28]

Chisholm won the New Jersey primary with 66.9 percent of the vote. She ran well in the states of Florida, Massachusetts and North Carolina, garnering 4 percent, 23 percent, and 9 percent, respectively.[29] She went to the Democratic National Convention with only 28 delegates; however, she received 151 votes on the first roll call vote at the convention. While many saw Chisholm's campaign as largely symbolic, she helped pave the way for other African Americans to make a bid for the presidency in spite of facing numerous obstacles and limited financial resources.[30]

In 1984 and 1988, Rev. Jesse Jackson ran for president, also as a Democrat. Jackson, who had formed Operation PUSH (People United to Serve Humanity) in Chicago in 1971, had put together the Rainbow Coalition, a multiracial organization consisting of blacks, whites, Hispanics, and Native Americans to fight poverty and other issues nationwide.[31] Jackson was not considered to be a serious candidate in his first bid in 1984. However, he did better than most political observers expected by finishing third in the

Democratic primaries. He received 18.2 percent of the total vote, and won five primaries and caucuses. Jackson was largely seen as a black candidate unable to transcend race, but his campaign helped to redefine the parameters of American politics.

In 1988, Jackson again made a run for the presidency. This time he was better organized and financed. He ran a remarkably competitive race in the Democratic primaries in spite of the political naysayers, winning eleven primaries and four caucuses. For a brief period of time, Jackson was even considered the frontrunner after winning 55 percent of the vote in the Michigan Democratic caucus, which gave him the lead over the other Democratic candidates in the total number of pledged delegates. Jackson ran on a liberal platform which included: creating a Works Progress Administration (WPA)-style program to rebuild America's infrastructure, reducing the defense budget substantially, giving reparations to descendants of black slaves, ratifying the equal rights amendment, and reversing tax cuts for the richest 10 percent of Americans.

He attempted to build a rainbow coalition of minorities including African Americans, Hispanic Americans, Asian Americans, Native Americans, and working-class whites. However, Jackson eventually lost the nomination to Michael Dukakis. Jackson's supporters had hoped that he would gain the number two spot on the ticket but, to the disappointment of his supporters, he was not selected. Nonetheless, Jackson had a significant impact on increasing the number of African Americans registered to vote and increasing African American turnout at the polls in 1984 and 1988.[32]

In 1996, retired General Colin Powell was courted by the two major political parties to run for president. Powell had long enjoyed high popularity in the United States after military successes in the U.S. invasion of Panama in 1989 and Operation Desert Storm in 1991. Powell's name was being mentioned as a potential Democratic vice presidential nominee in the 1992 U.S. presidential election, or even potentially replacing Vice President Dan Quayle as the Republican vice presidential nominee. Powell eventually declared himself a Republican and began to campaign for Republican candidates in 1995. His name was being mentioned as a possible opponent of Bill Clinton in the 1996 U.S. presidential election but Powell declined, saying "he lacked the kind of passionate commitment to politics that sustained his bond of trust with the public across 35 years of Army service."[33] Powell defeated Clinton fifty to thirty-eight in a hypothetical matchup proposed to voters in the exit polls conducted on election day in 1996. Certainly, there was precedent for Powell as a general to become president. This nation has a long history of its military generals becoming president. Powell, however, declined to run.[34]

In 2004, U.S. Senator Carol Moseley Braun, a Democrat from Illinois, and civil rights activist, Baptist minister Rev. Al Sharpton, both African Americans, ran in the Democratic primaries for president. Carol Moseley Braun represented Illinois in the U.S. Senate from 1993 to 1999. She was the first, and to date, the only, African American woman elected to the U.S. Senate, the first African American senator to be elected as a Democrat, and the first female senator from Illinois. From 1999 until 2001, she was the U.S. Ambassador to New Zealand.

Rev. Sharpton is a civil rights activist and radio talk show host. Although he enjoys great respect among African Americans, many whites consider him controversial. In 1991, Rev. Sharpton founded the National Action Network to increase voter education and poverty services and to support small community businesses. Neither mounted a successful campaign nor emerged during the primary season as a viable candidate. However, Moseley Braun was endorsed by the National Organization for Women and the National Women's Political Caucus, something that Shirley Chisholm did not accomplish.[35]

On August 22, 2003, a poll taken by the Pew Foundation found that of Democratic voters who had heard of Moseley Braun, 46 percent stated there was a chance they would vote for her. On the other hand, 70 percent of Democrats who knew about Rev. Sharpton said there was no chance that they would vote for him.[36] A CNN/Gallup poll of black voters conducted in September and October of 2003 found that only 12 percent supported Moseley Braun, while 24 percent favored Rev. Sharpton. According to political scientists Paula McClain, Niambi Carter, and Michael C. Brady, "Black Americans appeared more willing to support a Black man unfavorable to 70 percent of the party faithful than a Black woman with the skills and credentials to move forward issues of concern to Blacks."[37]

The lack of success by all of the African American candidates who ran for president before Barack Obama made his candidacy particularly instructive. Obama's appeal and his campaign were premised on his ability to transcend race. He deemphasized his race throughout his presidential campaign. Moreover, he ran for president as a post-racial candidate.

Background

Barack Obama was born on August 4, 1961, in Honolulu, Hawaii, to Barack Obama Sr. of Kenya, a black African, and Stanley Ann Dunham, a white woman from Kansas. The two met when they were both students at the University of Hawaii and separated when he was two years old and later divorced. Obama's father returned to Kenya and his mother remarried Lolo Soetoro and the family moved to Indonesia until Obama was age 10. He returned to Hawaii and lived with his maternal grandparents while attending Punahou School from fifth grade to high school graduation. An automobile accident in Kenya claimed the life of his father when Obama was 21 and his mother lost her battle with cancer when he was 34.[38]

Obama began his college career at Occidental College in Los Angeles, but transferred to Columbia University in New York City after only two years. It was during those two years at Columbia that Obama lived a rather monastic life and immersed himself in the writings of Friedrich Nietzsche, Herman Melville, Toni Morrison, and the Christian Bible.[39] This was an intellectual growth phase for Obama. He received his Bachelor of Arts degree in political science from Columbia University in 1983. Obama remained in Manhattan and began working for a business firm that published newsletters on global business and offered consulting to American businesses operating overseas. "He wrote and edited and researched articles on international business and finance for multinational corporations."[40] Although successful, Obama was not satisfied with this line of work.

According to journalist David Mendell, who wrote a book about Obama published in 2007 called *Obama: From Promise to Power*, Obama began "toying with the idea of becoming a neighborhood activist who would help empower the poor."[41] He started doing some part-time community organizing in Harlem and started looking for a regular community organizing job. Nothing turned up until one day he got a call from Jerry Kellman, a community organizer in Chicago who had placed an ad in a trade magazine because he was looking for new recruits for an organizing drive he was going to initiate in a poor black neighborhood on Chicago's South Side.[42] Kellman, notes Mendell, "was Jewish and he and his associate had difficulty gaining the trust of black residents."[43] This was the break Obama was looking for. He moved to Chicago, where he was hired as a community organizer on Chicago's far South Side. Chicago offered a different kind of education for Obama. "For a mixed-race young man," noted Mendell, "it was his first deep immersion into the African American community that he had longed to both understand and belong to."[44] Obama quickly learned that the church played a large role in the lives of the people he was organizing, so he began meeting black ministers on the South Side. This was his introduction to Reverend Jeremiah Wright. Obama found that community organizing was difficult and often frustrating. Ultimately, Obama felt that he would be a better community organizer if he went back to school, obtained his law degree, and gained access to the halls of political power in Chicago.[45]

After working in Chicago for three years, Obama entered Harvard Law School. He was elected the first black president of the *Harvard Law Review* and his election received national attention. During Obama's tenure as law review president, the Law School was grappling with issues such as affirmative action and the hiring of black faculty. Obama took on the role of negotiator and conciliator between differing groups—skills he would rely on in a future political career. He received his J.D. degree in 1991; however, he never published any articles as a member of the *Harvard Law Review* or as its president. After graduation, Obama returned to Chicago where he began a civil rights law practice, and taught as a senior lecturer of constitutional law at the University of Chicago—a nationally recognized conservative law school located in the Hyde Park section of Chicago. In 1992, Obama was named Executive Director of Project Vote in Illinois, a voter registration program that targets low-income minority communities throughout Cook County. It is credited with registering 150,000 out of 400,000 previously unregistered blacks in the state. That effort helped to elect Carol Moseley Braun to the U.S. Senate from Illinois and to elect Bill Clinton as president in 1992.

In 1992, he married Michelle Robinson, an African American who was from the South Shore, a working-class enclave on Chicago's South Side. Obama had first met Michelle as a summer intern in 1989 at a law firm in Chicago. She graduated from Princeton University and Harvard Law School. In the summer of 1991, Valerie Jarrett was deputy chief of staff for Mayor Richard Daley. She recruited Michelle Robinson to the mayor's office as a city planning official. Today, Valerie Jarrett is a close friend of the President and First Lady, serves as a senior adviser to the Obama Administration, and is one of his closest confidantes.[46] The Obamas have two daughters, Malia and Sasha.

Black Political Power in Chicago

Barack Obama returned to Chicago after graduating from Harvard Law School, and moved into the Hyde Park area of the city. Hyde Park was founded in the mid-1800s as a suburban resort town for Chicago's affluent and has had a profound political history. The First Congressional District, which includes much of the area, is the historical seat of black political power in the United States. Oscar DePriest became the first African American elected to Congress in the twentieth century, representing the First Congressional District of Illinois (the South Side of Chicago) as a Republican. For three consecutive terms (1929–1935), he served as the only African American in Congress. William L. (Boss) Dawson, the second African American elected to Congress in the twentieth century, represented the First Congressional District for twenty-seven years from 1943 to 1970. Harold Washington, a resident of Hyde Park and the first black mayor of Chicago, represented the district from 1983 to 1987, prior to becoming mayor. Carol Moseley Braun came to Hyde Park with University of Chicago connections. She received her law degree from the university and served one term in the U.S. Senate from 1993 to 1999. Moreover, three African American presidential candidates came out of Hyde Park: Barack Obama, Carol Moseley Braun, and Rev. Jesse Jackson.[47]

Political Career

Obama ran for the Illinois State Senate in 1996. The incumbent, Alice Palmer, had decided to run for Congress and she gave Obama her blessings as her successor. However, when Palmer lost in a special election, she decided to reclaim her seat in the state legislature as a candidate in the 1996 primary. Obama would not withdraw from the primary, and moreover, the Obama campaign staff had Palmer removed, as well as all other candidates, from the primary because of legal challenges to petition signatures. *Chicago* magazine journalist James Merriner said this about Obama's strategic maneuvering: "Obama's aggressive political tactic in that race gets cited often as a sign that, for all his elite connections, he could play hardball, Chicago style."[48] As Obama put it later, "I know politics. I'm skinny, but I'm tough."[49] Obama was reelected to the Illinois Senate in 1998.

In 2000, however, Obama decided to run for the U.S. Congress. His opponent was four-term incumbent and former Black Panther Party member Bobby Rush.[50] Obama lost badly, by a margin of two to one. According to

Fourth Ward alderman Toni Preckwinkle, who supported Obama, "He got beat badly, partly because he wasn't a very good candidate, and partly because the weekend before the election, President Clinton did radio spots for Bobby."[51] Adding insult to injury, during the course of the campaign Rush had accused Obama of not being "black enough."[52] However, Obama won reelection to the state senate in 2002, running unopposed.

In January 2003, Obama formally announced his candidacy for the U.S. Senate. Neither the Republican incumbent (Peter Fitzgerald) nor his Democratic predecessor (Carol Moseley Braun) chose to run, which launched wide-open Democratic and Republican primary contests. Obama enlisted political strategist David Axelrod to help orchestrate his campaign. Early on, Obama was behind in the opinion polls that favored multimillionaire businessman Blair Hull and Illinois Comptroller Dan Haynes among the total of seven candidates in the primary. The crafty advertising campaign orchestrated by David Axelrod aided Obama's candidacy by showing images of the late Mayor Harold Washington and an endorsement by the daughter of the late Senator Paul Simon. Obama emerged with 52 percent of the vote in the March primary.[53]

His opponent in the general election was Jack Ryan, a white candidate, who dropped out of the race when sex scandal allegations arose. Alan Keyes, conservative political activist, was named as a last minute replacement. In late summer 2004, Keyes accepted the Republican Party's nomination for U.S. Senate. In the November general election, Obama received 70 percent of the vote to Keyes' 27 percent. With that victory, Obama became the only African American in the U.S. Senate, and only the third African American U.S. senator since Reconstruction.[54]

Northern Illinois University political scientist and director of the Harold Washington Institute for Research and Policy Studies Robert Starks, who has written about the meteoric rise of Barack Obama, credits Obama with making the right career decision at every turn. Moreover, according to Starks, "The contacts that Obama made at Harvard served him well upon returning to Chicago, entering a civil rights law practice, and working as an adjunct professor . . . at the University of Chicago."[55]

Ironically, those contacts began to pay off when Obama ran for Congress against Bobby Rush in 2000. Although Obama's bid ended in defeat, it was here, according to writer James Merriner, Obama began laying the groundwork for phenomenal future fundraising successes.[56] In his congressional bid against Rush, Obama raised only $509,000. Rush outraised Obama by almost

$300,000 in that 2000 primary. By the end of the race, Obama was $60,000 in debt. But along the way, Obama began attracting big name contributors in Chicago such as Penny Pritzker, heiress of the Hyatt Hotels chains. Pritzker gave $1,000 to Obama's 2000 campaign, the legal maximum at the time. Obama's finance chairman had been Martin Nesbitt, president of an off-airport parking company partly owned by the Pritzker family. Nesbitt is also vice president of the Pritzker Realty Group, headed by Penny Pritzker. In 2002, Nesbitt arranged for Pritzker to meet with Obama and his wife. Pritzker would become finance committee chair for Obama's 2004 campaign for the U.S. Senate, which raised nearly $15 million. Pritzker subsequently became the finance chair of Obama's presidential campaign. It was in 2000, asserts Merriner, that Obama first parlayed his Harvard and legal connections into vast campaign contributions.[57]

Obama's Bold and Innovative Approach to Capturing the Presidency

Obama's candidacy provides a paradigm for candidates of color to transcend race at the presidential level. Obama has done this by changing the face of the American electorate. The cornerstone of Obama's strategy for winning the White House was to run a deracialized campaign. Obama and his advisers decided early on that he was not going to win the presidency by playing up his race. "The thing is, a black man can't be president of America, given the racial aversion and history that's still out there," stated Cornell Belcher, an Obama pollster who is African American.[58] Shelby Steele, a conservative fellow and author at the Hoover Institution at Stanford University stated, "I underestimated the hunger in America for what Obama represents—racial transcendence, redemption. He's that wonderful opportunity to prove that we're not a racist society."[59] And yet Obama represents a new style of African American politician: post-civil rights era and not as polarizing to white voters as some members of the civil rights era such as Rev. Jesse Jackson or Rev. Al Sharpton. Obama does not approach white America with an attitude that "you owe us something," which in turn does not translate into a sense of racial guilt.

Use of the Internet as a Fundraising Mechanism

Howard Dean was the first politician to run for president who used the Internet as a powerful fundraising tool. However, the Obama campaign took this medium to astronomical heights. Jesse Unruh, Speaker of the California Assembly from 1961 to 1968, once said that "money is the mother's milk of politics."[60] One of the reasons Barack Obama was able to run a competitive presidential campaign in the primaries and caucuses and then in the general election was his ability to raise incredibly vast sums of money from literally thousands of individual donors. Obama's use of the Internet served a twofold purpose: it allowed him to secure thousands of small campaign contributions well within the campaign finance limitations and to mobilize a vast cadre of grassroots volunteers.

One of the new features of the Obama campaign was his use of social networking sites such as Facebook and MySpace. He was extremely successful with Facebook, which is widely used by college students and younger Americans. Obama has even designed his official campaign website to look like Facebook. In fact, one of Obama's key strategists, Charles Hughes, is a Facebook co-founder and was recruited for the campaign to create MyBarack Obama.com. For a candidate to be successful at raising money, he must prove that he is a viable candidate. For Obama, early successes generated a flood of small campaign contributions, which allowed him to be extremely competitive throughout the primary season and the general election. Thousands of young voters joined Obama's Facebook website, which became a public expression of support. Moreover, since most of the young voters were familiar with the Facebook and MySpace social networking sites, it was a perfect way to get young voters connected and excited about the political process. Furthermore, supporters were able to meet and organize in addition to contributing money to the campaign.[61]

Community Organizing

One key strategy to Obama's successful run for the presidency was the building of a grassroots organization of campaign staff, offices, and volunteers in almost every state in the nation. Obama had been a community organizer in Chicago and he felt that a bottom-up approach was key to winning the White House. Technology played a key role in Obama's ability to run a grassroots populist campaign. In fact, Obama took a page out of the Republican playbook from

2004. In an article for BBC News, journalist Steve Schifferes stated that, according to Michael Turk, the Bush-Cheney e-campaign director in 2004, "the Republicans were able to mobilize their supporters in every precinct around the country, using technology which predicts voter preferences on the basis of commercial data on car ownership, magazine subscriptions, and the like."[62] The Obama campaign utilized this data mining technique to identify voters across the country. So, according to Robert Starks, "From the very outset, Team Obama, consisting of more than 500,000 people spread out all over the country, were tuned into the regular messages that were sent and broadcast via the campaign's official website, YouTube, MySpace, Facebook, and Twitter."[63] Obama's ability to organize effectively in almost every state gave him a huge advantage over his opponents.

A New Man and a New Message

Obama's appeal has been mostly about the man and his message. His charisma tends to transcend across racial lines. Journalist Jann Wenner wrote, "The similarities between John Kennedy and Barack Obama come to mind easily: the youth, the magnetism, the natural grace, the eloquence, the wit, the intelligence, the hope of a new generation."[64] Obama's message combines symbolism with substance and appeal that crosses racial, gender, and age lines. Being relatively unknown prior to delivering the keynote address at the Democratic National Convention in 2004, Obama's campaign for the presidency has been nothing short of phenomenal. His message of hope has been particularly attractive to many young and first-time voters who have been turned off by "politics as usual." People believed Obama when he offered them a new message and it was delivered by a new face.

Obama first ran for elective public office in 1996, where he won a seat in the Illinois Senate and served two terms from 1997 to 2000. In 2000, Obama ran for the U.S. House of Representatives but was defeated by four-term incumbent Congressman Bobby Rush. In 2002, Obama was reelected to the Illinois Senate. In 2004, Obama ran for the U.S. Senate from the state of Illinois. That year, Obama was chosen by John Kerry's campaign manager, Mary Beth Cahill, to deliver the keynote address at the Democratic National Convention in Boston, Massachusetts, in July 2004. He was only the third African American to deliver such a speech at a major political party convention.

In his first national appearance, Obama electrified the convention hall as well as the American public. He exclaimed that there is no black America and no white America—only the United States of America. The overarching theme of his speech was that there is only one America. Obama told the audience that "In no other country on earth is my story even possible."[65] He recounted how his father was raised in a small village in Kenya and got a scholarship to study in a magical place called America, and how his mother was born in a town on the other side of the world in Kansas, and how while studying here his father met his mother. But after relaying to the audience how improbable it was that a "skinny kid with a funny name" would even have the honor of addressing the convention, Obama then spoke about "our" nation coming together and uniting as Americans. He exclaimed,

> The pundits like to slice and dice our country into Red States and Blue States; Red States for Republicans, Blue States for Democrats. But I've got news for them too. We worship an awesome God in the Blue States, and we don't like federal agents poking around in our libraries in the Red States. We coach Little League in the Blue States and yes, we've got some gay friends in the Red States. There are patriots who opposed the war in Iraq and patriots who supported the war in Iraq. We are one people, all of us pledging allegiance to the Stars and Stripes, all of us defending the United States of America.[66]

Moreover, Obama discussed the role of government in solving all of our problems. Obama stated, "Children can't achieve unless we raise their expectations and turn off the television sets and eradicate the slander that says a black youth with a book is acting white."[67] According to journalist Amy Sullivan of *Time* magazine, "It was a powerful message, particularly from a black politician, and it established for white listeners that Obama was not from the strident, divisive school of politics of Jesse Jackson or Al Sharpton."[68] Obama ended the speech with an inspirational message of choosing hope over fear. Moreover, asserted Obama, "Hope is God's greatest gift to us, the bedrock of this nation; the belief in things not seen, the belief that there are better days ahead."[69] The crowd went wild. Many in the convention hall, particularly in the Illinois delegation, had tears in their eyes. The speech was brilliant both stylistically and substantively. This was Obama's first appearance on the national stage. Many point to that speech as the "defining moment" when Obama opened up a direct path to the presidency of the United States of America. The speech turned Obama into a "rock star" overnight. He won his U.S. Senate race in the fall of 2004. In 2006, Obama was the hottest commodity in American politics and he traveled the country campaigning and helping to raise money for fellow Democrats running for national office in the midterm elections. Interestingly enough, the crowds at these fundraisers began growing exponentially in number and everyone, particularly the media, was becoming fascinated with Barack Obama. Also, in 2006, some of Obama's closest advisers were telling him that now was the time for him to run for president—that one only has a small window of opportunity. After the 2006 midterm elections, Democrats took control of both houses of Congress. Then on February 10, 2007, Barack Obama announced his candidacy for president of the United States of America. So, in the remarkable span of only twelve years, Barack Obama embarked on a meteoric ascension from a little known community organizer in Chicago to the highest political office in the land.

Theoretically, this book causes us to reexamine how one runs a successful campaign for the presidency of the United States. Obama has created a whole new paradigm on how to campaign, how to organize, strategize, fundraise, get out the vote, build coalitions, and use modern technology to connect with voters in the twenty-first century. It also forces us to reexamine the role of race in American politics and how changing demographics may make the traditional style of campaigning a thing of the past.

2

Descriptive and Substantive Representation

I think it's [Barack Obama's election as president] going to have an effect on black politics. It's going to give more opportunities for African Americans to get elected in white districts as I am a Caucasian being elected in a black district. We see people picking up different issues and getting beyond race politics.[1]

Rep. Steve Cohen (D-TN)

Most scholars examining black electoral success begin with a discussion of representation theory. According to political scientist Hanna Pitkin, representation can be divided into four categories: formal, descriptive, symbolic, and substantive.[2] The concept of representation lies at the core of democracy. Formal representation is based on the consent of the governed. Descriptive representation describes the extent to which legislators accurately reflect the characteristics of their district or state. An examination of characteristics of members of Congress by age, race, gender, education, and occupation shows that their characteristics are by no means parallel to that of the general population. Therefore, the representative must focus on symbolic representation.

Symbolic representation is the ability of a legislator to understand constituent needs and empathize with their concerns. The extent to which the representative acts upon this symbolism is described as substantive representation.[3] The U.S. Congress has not been descriptively representative of African Americans. Of the more than 11,000 persons who have served in Congress, only 112 have been African American (107 in the House of Representatives, five in the Senate).[4]

From the year the first Congress met in 1789, until 1870, no African American served in Congress. During the Reconstruction Period and Post-Reconstruction Period, between 1865 and 1901, twenty-two blacks were elected to Congress. Two of them were elected to the Senate and twenty were elected to the House of Representatives. When Congress passed the Reconstruction Act of 1867, slightly more than 90 percent of the black population in this country resided in the South. The states of Alabama, Florida, Louisiana, Mississippi, and South Carolina had majority black populations at that time.[5] Reconstruction did not begin or end at a particular time. However, most scholars point to the Hayes-Tilden Compromise as sounding the death knell for Reconstruction.[6] Rutherford B. Hayes assumed the presidency after a controversial election against Samuel Tilden. Federal troops stationed in the South were subsequently withdrawn and the South began to revert to its antebellum ways by passing laws and changing its state constitutions to deny blacks the political and social rights they had briefly enjoyed (see Chapter 1). When George H. White from North Carolina left his seat in Congress in 1901 as the lone black in Congress, he found it useless to remain in a legislative body where he no longer had the support of his white colleagues from his home state. The state had already gerrymandered its congressional districts so that no blacks could be elected to Congress, and it passed a constitutional amendment denying blacks the right to vote.[7] It would not be until 1928 that another African American, Oscar DePriest, would be elected to Congress from Chicago.

Literature Review

The literature on representation theory is extensive. Political scientist Robert Dahl contends that to have a healthy democracy representatives must be held accountable through elections; those who are unresponsive may be dismissed by their constituents in subsequent elections.[8] To do this, each citizen must have an effective opportunity to vote in a system where all votes are counted equally.[9] Economist and political scientist Joseph Schumpeter critiques the classical theory of democracy that assumes voters will make rational decisions on voting for representatives, thus laying the foundation for proper policy-making initiatives.[10] Schumpeter contests the idea of average people having the capacity to make meaningful decisions about public policy. He posits that the electorate should choose between a number of elites for elected officials.[11]

Two major debates in representation theory are descriptive versus substantive representation and the delegate versus trustee type of representation. Descriptive, or proportional, representation says that representatives should look like but not necessarily act for the constituency.[12] Moreover, Carol Swain asserts that the constituency and representative does not have to be descriptively synonymous for adequate substantive representation.[13]

Ideally, political representation should resemble the citizenry in which it serves.[14] The concept of descriptive representation can be characterized as passive in that it does not describe the action of a legislative body, but rather its demographic make-up, which opens descriptive representation to criticism. Both proponents and opponents of descriptive representation contend that proper representation is predicated upon its resemblance to the population. There is a distinction between representation and decision making, or governing. Descriptive representation is critical to African Americans' ability to acquire and maintain political power through representation.

According to political scientist Michael Dawson, African Americans have a lot of group consciousness that sets blacks in America apart from any other racial group.[15] This linked fate that Dawson articulates is critical to the idea of descriptive representation because in this context descriptive representation seems to be sufficient under the assumption that African American politicians will actually represent the group's interest because of a shared fate. However, the purpose of descriptive politics has been undermined by African Americans that serve not as representatives of the African American community but purely out of self-interest.[16]

In the case of Barack Obama as an African American running for president, the idea of group politics induces a need to ask such questions as "is he black enough?" Being black enough is not to be taken in a literal sense, but rather in a figurative sense. The literal question will translate, in politically correct terms, to: does Barack Obama view his fate as being linked to that of the larger group of African Americans to accurately represent African Americans on descriptive terms? Furthermore, according to Pitkin, descriptive representation is constrained by an element of passivity politics where a representative cannot act for the constituents, but stands in for them like a delegate.[17]

In a setting where race has played a historical, social, economic, and political role, acquiring public office has a substantial "symbolic" meaning for members of a historically excluded group. Political office holding confers a certain "status" on group members, as a cohort that has obtained a level of political status. Political office holding decreases feelings of political alienation and increases feelings of political efficacy among group members.[18] This, however, is more than any legislation could offer. Unfortunately, the same logic, with reverse consequences, is expected to apply to members of the historically dominant group. The loss of political office translates into a decline in political influence, and is reflected in a loss of "status" and accompanying lower levels of electoral participation.

Substantive representation, however, says that a representative should act on behalf of the constituency. Within substantive discourse, there is a debate about whether a representative should act as a delegate, voting as the constituency prefers, or as a trustee, voting as the representative feels is best. Some scholars contend that the representative should act as both (politico) depending on the context or the level of salience of the issue. On lower salient issues, the representative should act as a trustee.[19] With respect to African American constituencies, a pertinent question is, will public policy reflect the concerns of minority interests when minorities are in office? One approach to the substantive discourse contends that policies of interest to black constituencies actually get on the agenda; however, another approach posits that an African American presence has little influence on policy outcomes. Therefore, policies consistent with black interests make it on the agenda for discussion, but rarely result in an outcome of satisfaction to blacks.[20]

The policy-making process is essential to substantive representation and serves as a necessary measure for how well Congress responds to the people. Descriptive representation, however, does not necessarily lead to the initiation and favorable outcomes of policy in the black interest, but black elected officials are more likely to support black policy than whites causing descriptive representation to lead to substantive representation.[21]

In the case of Rev. Jesse Jackson's 1984 and 1988 presidential campaigns, for example, perceived reasons for much of Jackson's support in the African American community was blind racial loyalty. However, Jackson's position on salient issues of policy affecting blacks corresponded with the attitudes of his constituency. According to Dawson, African Americans believed that he (Jackson) possessed the personality traits, or charisma, for political leadership.[22] Some issues that were salient to blacks during Jackson's campaigns were education, employment, health care, and responsiveness of the political system.[23] Overwhelming support by African Americans for Jackson on the surface was descriptive, but in the context of linked fate, this descriptive representation would yield substantial gains.

Descriptive representation may be a prerequisite for substantive representation but does not always translate into substantive representation. Such was the case with the 1991 appointment of Clarence Thomas to replace Thurgood Marshall on the U.S. Supreme Court. In spite of his conservative record and lack of experience, many black leaders were reluctant to publicly criticize him because it would perpetuate the stereotype of black intellectual inferiority.[24] However, they knew that the appointment of Thomas would be detrimental to the advancements made in the area of civil rights. Because blacks and other minorities have traditionally been excluded from political representation in America, many blacks feel that any representation is better than no representation.

While examining representation literature, one might ask if blacks represent black constituencies differently or better than whites. Political scientist Katherine Tate, in examining the issue of representation of blacks in Congress, asks the question, "Does race matter?"[25] According to Swain, race is not a significant factor in a representative's ability to represent his or her constituency when party and region are taken into account.[26] Moreover, she asserts that whites have, on numerous occasions, been shown to represent black constituents better than some black representatives have. However, more comprehensive and detailed studies have disproven Swain's argument, notably Lublin, Whitby, Canon, and Tate.[27] In *The Color of Representation: Congressional Behavior and Black Interests*, political scientist Kenneth Whitby "found that racial differences in congressional voting are more likely to show up when bills are amended than on the final roll-call votes studied by Swain."[28] In an examination of congressional voting behavior from 1973 to 1992, Whitby discovered that "race matters even after controlling for party and region."[29] Moreover, political scientists Hanes Walton, Jr., and Robert C. Smith assert that Whitby, in general, "found that the policy payoffs in the form of more effective anti-discrimination policies in education, employment, and housing, are more likely to come from black than white representatives."[30] In *Race, Redistricting, and Representation: The Unintended Consequences of Black Majority Districts* (1999), political scientist David Canon found that

> race matters in Congress, not just in terms of substantive voting
> but also in various forms of symbolic representation. For example,
> black members of the House are more likely than whites to make

speeches concerning race (50.8 percent of the speeches by blacks compared to 12.8 percent by whites); more likely to sponsor and introduce bills dealing with race (42 percent for blacks, 5 percent for whites); more likely to hire blacks for top staff positions (72.3 percent compared to 6.7 percent); and more likely to raise race issues in their press releases and newsletters (24.6 percent compared to 12.6 percent).[31]

Lastly, political scientist Katherine Tate in her book, *Black Faces in the Mirror: African Americans and Their Representatives in the U.S. Congress*, supports the research of Whitby and Canon by finding that black members are the most reliable and consistent supporters of substantive black interests in Congress.[32] Nonetheless, there is some merit to Swain's argument. For example, Louisiana's initial majority black district went into effect in January 1985 with a 58 percent black majority but continued to elect its white incumbent, Lindy Boggs, until her retirement in 1991. Currently, there are only two whites in Congress that represent majority black congressional districts. One is Representative Steve Cohen (D-TN), a white, who represents the 9th congressional district which is 60 percent black. Cohen, who first won election in 2006, was reelected in 2008, but not before a bitter primary fight. Oddly enough, Cohen's toughest challenger in the primary was a black female and former aide to Harold Ford, Jr., who was Cohen's predecessor. The race was marred by a series of negative advertisements by the black challenger, which featured various racial campaign appeals to black voters in an attempt to discredit Cohen. Harold Ford, Jr., denounced the ads, as did Barack Obama. Robert Brady (D-PA), who is white, represents a black-plurality district (majority-minority), the 1st. It is 45.9 percent black, 15 percent Hispanic, and 4.9 percent Asian. Rep. Joseph Cao (R-LA) is the first native Vietnamese ever elected to Congress. He represents a district that is majority black (64 percent African American).

Racially Polarized Voting

The election of Barack Obama as the 44th president of the United States is truly an extraordinary accomplishment. Representation lies at the heart of democracy but African American success in the political arena has been mixed. This is because much of the black electoral success has occurred in majority-minority electoral districts. Walton and Smith assert that more than 8,000 black elected officials in the United States are elected from majority black places or majority-minority (blacks and Latinos) local, state, or federal legislative districts.[33] Of the forty-two congressional districts represented by blacks in the U.S. House of Representatives, four are majority white and the rest are either majority black or majority-minority. Conversely, they assert that only a few African Americans have been elected as governors or to the U.S. Senate, elections that would require them to run statewide.[34] Indeed, since ratification of the 17th Amendment to the U.S. Constitution (giving states the popular vote for the election of senators) by Congress in 1913, only three African Americans have ever been elected to the U.S. Senate: Edward Brooke from Massachusetts who served from 1966 to 1978; Carol Moseley Braun who was elected in 1992 from Illinois, but defeated for reelection in 1998; and Barack Obama who was elected from Illinois in 2004 and served until he was elected president of the United States in 2008. Moreover, only two African Americans have been elected governor: L. Douglas Wilder of Virginia in 1979 and Deval Patrick of Massachusetts in 2006. In 2008, David Patterson, the lieutenant governor of New York, succeeded to the governorship of that state when the incumbent governor, Eliot Spitzer, resigned. Only four of the Senate nominees were successful (Edward Brooke twice in Massachusetts, and Carol Moseley Braun and Barack Obama once each in Illinois). Of the twelve nominees for governor, only two were successful (L. Douglas Wilder and Deval Patrick). Walton and Smith attribute the lack of winning U.S. Senate or state governorships to two things: racism and the perception among some whites that blacks are too liberal for their conservative ideological inclinations.[35] They quote Alan Gerber who laments:

> African American members of Congress rarely seek higher office. Prospects for winning statewide are discouraging. No African American has moved from the House to the Senate or to the governor's mansion. The liberal voting record that African American representatives typically compile does not provide a strong foundation for winning statewide elections and there remains some resistance to voting for African Americans for higher office.[36]

It was not that qualified black candidates were not running. Tom Bradley, the African American mayor of Los Angeles, California, ran a highly competitive race for governor in 1982.

The term *Bradley effect* originated with this gubernatorial race. Bradley, a Democrat, ran against George Deukmejian, a white Republican. Public opinion polls leading up to the election consistently showed Bradley with a lead in the race. Bradley, however, lost in a very close election. Post-election results showed that a smaller percentage of white voters actually voted for Bradley than those who stated they planned to vote for him, and voters who were categorized as "undecided" voted for Deukmejian.[37]

However, some politicians and political analysts argue that the "Bradley effect" never really existed. According to David Bositis, Senior Research Analyst at the Joint Center for Political and Economic Studies,

> The Bradley effect should be called the Wilder effect. Bradley actually got more votes on election day at the polls. Now, the other candidate was Armenian, and this was the first election in California where they allowed no excuse absentee ballots. There was an organized effort to get Armenians to vote absentee. There were a couple hundred thousand that voted for the other candidate and that's how he won.[38]

Democrat Harvey Gantt, a former black mayor of Charlotte and the first African American student to be admitted to Clemson University in South Carolina in 1963, ran against archconservative Republican incumbent Jesse Helms in 1990 for a U.S. Senate seat in North Carolina. When pre-election polling showed the race tightening up considerably in the weeks before the election, the Helms campaign ran an anti-affirmative action advertisement. The ad showed two white hands holding a pink slip with a voice-over saying,

> You needed that job, and you were the best qualified. But they had to give it to a minority because of a racial quota. Is that really fair? Harvey Gantt says it is. Gantt supports Ted Kennedy's racial quota law that makes the color of your skin more important than your qualifications. You'll vote on this issue next Thursday: For racial quotas, Harvey Gantt; against racial quotas, Jesse Helms.[39]

Helms' opponent considered the advertisement racially motivated and Helms won in a close election.

In 2006, a significant number of African Americans from both major political parties ran in governor and the U.S. Senate races across the country.

In the Senate race in Maryland, Lieutenant Governor Michael Steele was the Republican Senate nominee. In Tennessee, former Congressman Harold Ford was the Democratic nominee for the U.S. Senate. And, in Mississippi, Erik Fleming, a state representative, was the Democratic nominee for the U.S. Senate. All three Senate candidates lost to their white opponents. Harold Ford's Senate race in Tennessee received the most national attention. With public opinion polling showing the race tightening up just weeks before the election, the Republican National Committee ran an advertisement linking Democratic candidate Harold Ford with a white Playboy Bunny at a Playboy party. Some supporters of Ford felt the advertisement played on Southern white fears that Ford, a single black male, if elected senator, might date their daughters.

Three African Americans won their party's nomination for governor in 2006. Kenneth Blackwell, Ohio's Republican Secretary of State, ran for governor in Ohio; Lynn Swann, former professional football player, ran for governor as a Republican in Pennsylvania; and in Massachusetts, Deval Patrick, the former Assistant Attorney General in the Clinton administration, won the Democratic nomination for governor. Patrick won his race; the other two candidates lost theirs. According to Walton and Smith:

> The most extensive study of blacks running for higher office in the United States finds that the presence of a black Democrat on the ballot increases black turnout by 2.3 percent (the presence of a black Republican has no effect on black turnout), while the presence of a black of either party increases white turnout by 2.2 percent . . . And both white Democrats and Republicans are less likely to vote for their party's nominee when she or he is black . . . These barriers are especially high for black Republicans since they can expect little or no increased turnout among blacks and less support from their fellow white partisans.[40]

The outcomes of the 2006 gubernatorial and U.S. Senate races with black candidates running are particularly instructive. Deval Patrick won 56 percent of the vote in his governor's race in Massachusetts, 51 percent of the white vote and 89 percent of the black vote in an ultra-liberal Northeastern state. Harold Ford won 95 percent of the black vote, but only 40 percent of the white vote in a largely conservative Southern state. Erik Fleming won roughly 35 percent of the vote, which matches the black proportion of the state's population. (No exit polls were conducted in Mississippi because the election was considered noncompetitive.)[41] Fleming ran against a popular Republican opponent, former U.S. Senate Majority Leader Trent Lott. One can glean from these elections in 2006 that the electorate remains racially polarized.

Moreover, noted journalist Rachel Swarns, "In 2007, about 30 percent of the nation's 622 black state legislators represented predominantly white districts, up from about 16 percent in 2001, according to data collected by the Joint Center for Political and Economic Studies."[42] Most African American elected officials continue to represent predominantly black districts but the trend is changing. Political scientist Zoltan L. Hajnal, whose book about white experiences with black mayors was titled *Changing White Attitudes toward Black Political Leadership*, noted that "There's a fair amount of experience out there among white voters now, and that has lessened the fears about black candidates."[43] Swarns states that "Political analysts believe that experience with black leadership may have helped some white voters who supported Obama in the primaries and general election."[44] And although much of the successes of African American elected officials has occurred at the local level and has not transferred to any substantial statewide successes, it may be a harbinger of things to come. David Bositis has stated that, "State legislative seats are often stepping stones to higher positions, and these new politicians . . . may well become the next generation of black governors, Congressional leaders and more."[45]

Racial Campaign Appeals

Even if you come from a district like mine, where 58–59 percent of the vote is African American, you will lose about 25 percent of the vote if you run a racially charged campaign. Not only will you lose all of the white folk, but you will lose 25 percent of the black folk, too. So, nobody wants to be a part of a racially charged campaign or any other racially charged efforts in this country.[46]

Rep. James Clyburn (D-SC)

Both Harvey Gantt's U.S. Senate race in 1990 and Harold Ford's U.S. Senate race as recently as 2006 reflect a racial campaign appeal on the part of their white opponents. In *Controversies in Minority Voting*, racial campaign appeals as defined by two sociologists, Paul Luebke and Jerry Himmelstein, are explored.[47] Luebke offers the following definition, "Racial appeal occurs in a campaign if one candidate calls attention to the race of his opponent or his opponent's supporters or if media covering a campaign disproportionately call attention to the race of one candidate or of that candidate's supporters."[48] Political scientist Bernard Grofman states that "One example of a racial campaign appeal would be when a white candidate uses a picture of his black opponent in his own campaign material."[49]

Himmelstein points out how themes identified as racist in earlier historical contexts are still being used in political campaigns in the South in sanitized forms that avoid overt references to race by using code words and other concealed messages that appeal to lingering feelings of white anti-black sentiment. Notes Himmelstein,

> Overt appeals to segregationist sentiments are no longer practiced by politicians who expect to win . . . Black voter strength and perhaps some degree of cultural change in the etiquette of race relations seem to have sanitized the language of political rhetoric . . . In a society so recently and so dominantly obsessed with race . . . one important way political leaders have walked the line between divergent audiences is through the use of code words . . .[50]

Moreover, Himmelstein states that a code word communicates an implicit meaning to part of a public audience but allows the speaker deniability of that meaning by reference to its denotative explicit meaning.[51] Modern-day politicians continue to use code words to appeal to the prejudices and fears of voters. Richard Nixon abandoned the Republican Party's antislavery roots when in 1968 he appealed to white voters using racially coded language such as "B-U-S-I-N-G." Jimmy Carter, the Democratic nominee in 1976, used the term *ethnic purity* in depicting white ethnic enclaves and neighborhood schools.[52]

Is Obama the End of Black Politics?

I think not. Black politics is not "a" person. African American politics is over two hundred years old. Starting from Nat Turner, we are just in a different era. I'm happy young people are engaged. These people are going to start having children soon. They are going to want better schools and jobs. I don't think this is the end of African American leaders. It's the beginning of a broader coalition, young and old. I'm 63, I'm looking forward to the day that I don't have to work eighteen hours a day. I'm good for twelve and I want the healthy people to step up to their responsibility.[53]

Rep. Carolyn Kilpatrick (D-MI)

As a new generation of African American candidates has begun seeking political office, some have butted heads with their elders causing a generational divide. In an article that appeared in *The New York Times Magazine* in August 2008, journalist Matt Bai reflected on this when he quipped,

> For a lot of younger African-Americans, the resistance of the civil rights generation to Obama's candidacy signified the failure of their parents to come to terms, at the dusk of their lives, with the success of their own struggle to embrace the idea that black politics might now be disappearing into American politics in the same way that the Irish and the Italian machines long ago joined the political mainstream.[54]

Moreover, notes Bai, "For almost every one of the talented black politicians who came of age in the postwar years, like James Clyburn and Charles Rangel [two African American Members of Congress occupying leadership positions in the 111th Congress], the pinnacle of power, if you did everything right, lay in one of two offices: City Hall or the House of Representatives. That was as far as you could travel with a mostly black constituency."[55] Furthermore, asserts Bai, "Until the 1990s, even black politicians with wide support among white voters failed in their attempts to win statewide, with only one exception (Edward Brooke, who was elected to the U.S. Senate from Massachusetts in 1966)."[56]

The new black politicians are seeking a broader political resume. They are highly intelligent, trained at the finer universities and not seminaries, and, notes Bai, "they are just as likely to see themselves as ambassadors to the black community as they are to see themselves as spokesmen for it, which often means extolling middle-class values in urban neighborhoods . . ."[57]

Evidence of this generational divide and some tension that exists came about when Democratic presidential nominee Barack Obama gave a Father's

Day speech at an African American church on Chicago's South Side, where he chided black fathers for abdicating their responsibilities. Shortly after the speech, an open microphone on cable television's Fox News picked up Rev. Jesse Jackson saying in effect that "he wouldn't mind personally castrating his party's nominee."[58] Some political observers considered this an example of a presidential candidate scoring points with white Americans at the expense of black ones—something that Rev. Jackson refused to do over the course of two presidential campaigns. To add further drama, Rev. Jesse Jackson's 43-year-old son, who is a congressman from Illinois and co-chaired Obama's national campaign, released a statement saying that he was "deeply outraged and disappointed" with his father's comments.[59] Moreover, some saw this as a "Sister Souljah moment" for Obama—a reference to President Bill Clinton's chastisement of rapper Sister Souljah for exhorting violence in her lyrics to score points with white America.

Journalist and PBS correspondent Gwen Ifill has written a book titled *The Breakthrough: Politics and Race in the Age of Obama*, where she asserts that the black political structure formed during the civil rights movement is giving way to a new generation of men and women who are the direct beneficiaries of the struggles of the 1950s and 1960s.[60] In a discussion of the new black politicians, Ifill interviews Rev. Al Sharpton, who is considered to be a part of the black leadership that came out of the civil rights struggles of the 1960s. Ifill notes, "Sharpton acknowledges the difference between his approach and strategies developed by the new generation of black politicians banging their heads against the ceiling of power politics. They are almost all middle class, college educated, and comfortable in multiracial situations. They are not the 1960s stereotype of a civil rights leader."[61] Ifill argues that the new breed of black politician has come of age in a period that has moved beyond the mass protests of the 1950s and 1960s. Additionally, she states that the new black politician feels that black politicians need to move beyond the traditional civil rights paradigm. In an interview Ifill conducted with Michael Steele, an African American and current chairperson of the Republican National Committee, Steele exclaims, "This generation is less interested in having a seat at the lunch counter and more interested in owning the diner."[62]

Rep. Artur Davis (D-AL) represents a majority black district in Alabama that includes Birmingham and has been in Congress since 2003. He first met Obama while the two were in law school at Harvard and said he knew then that Obama was going places. Davis, who has announced that he will run for governor of Alabama in 2010, questions if the term "new" is fitting with the recent success of younger politicians who happen to be black. He noted that

> I am always dubious of generational analyses because the whole purpose of generational analysis is to suggest that age is predictive of political approach. That's not always the case. In fact, it's often not the case. There are a number of older black politicians that were paving this ground many years ago. For example, the kind of campaign Tom Bradley ran in 1982, which ultimately led to his governor run. It was a moderate centrist campaign that had enormous biracial appeal . . . Doug Wilder was 59 when he ran for governor of Virginia in 1989, where he focused on his centrist credentials and received significant white support from conservative white Virginians. If generation were the only predictor of political approach, how do you explain 60+-year-old Tom Bradley and 59-year-old Doug Wilder? What about Harvey Gantt? On the other hand you have younger political figures like Kwame Kilpatrick [the former young mayor of Detroit] who very much copied the model of a traditional black machine politician.[63]

Some of these new black politicians do not want to be seen as simply black leaders. When Corey Booker, the Ivy League educated mayor of Newark, New Jersey, was asked whether he considered himself a leader of the black community, he responded, "I don't want to be pigeonholed. I don't want people to expect me to speak about those issues."[64] This type of approach has caused some in the black community to worry that an Obama presidency "might actually leave black Americans less well represented in Washington rather than more so—that, in fact, the end of black politics, if that is what we are witnessing, might also mean the precipitous decline of black influence."[65]

It has been a struggle for blacks to gain access to political power in this country. Now that Barack Obama has been elected as the 44th president of the United States, some are beginning to ask, is this the end of black politics? Of the forty-two congressional districts occupied by African Americans, four are majority white, and the others are either majority black or majority-minority.[66] So, the political realities of the successful black politician who wants to win office statewide is that he must appeal to a broader base of Americans beyond African Americans.

Structural and Institutional Hurdles that Obama May Face in Attempting to Address Systematic Inequality in America

Backroom barbershop philosophy holds that black people are able to gain leadership positions the same way one can move into white neighborhoods, when the housing stock decreases, maintenance increases, and past abuse and mismanagement by whites makes it virtually impossible for new homeowners to do anything.[67] When black mayors began to win election to City Hall across America, federal funding dried up, white flight to the suburbs drastically decreased city budgets, and corruption was the norm in city politics. As city budgets declined and cities could not provide many basic services, the black mayors were blamed for the failure. Such was the case with Mayor David Dinkins in New York City. In the case of President Barack Obama, he has become the nation's chief executive in the midst of two ongoing wars, a deepening global recession, a rising healthcare cost, high unemployment rates, and a crumbling infrastructure. For the first time ever, middle-class families are at the end of a recovery without regaining lost ground from a previous recession. Unemployment increased from 4.4 percent in March 2007 to 8.5 percent in mid-2008. As our gross domestic product (GDP) increases, income remains stagnant due largely to inflation. According to the Economic Policy Institute's *State of Working America 2008/2009*, workers reported record numbers of output with no increase in income.[68]

In an interview for this book, Rep. Carolyn Kilpatrick (D-MI) was asked what challenges Obama would face trying to address systemic inequality in America. She was quite candid when she replied,

> The federal budget is $3 trillion. Two trillion dollars goes to the entitlements, and the main three are Medicare: health care for 43 million seniors; Medicaid: low income, disabled, and children's health care; and veterans. Our committee handles one trillion. The deficit and loss of manufacturing revenue will leave this country with less than that to work with. Cities will be challenged as well as higher education. One of the first things that he has to do is end the wars in Iraq and Afghanistan. Iraq being first and Afghanistan will be a bit harder. Over $900 billion have been spent in Iraq since March 2003. The structural problems will be the dollars that he has to work with. Secondly, will be health care. We've got to do something.[69]

Thus, to serve the American people effectively, Obama needs to address some intractable problems at a time when federal resources are limited. Social and political institutions set the context for individual and group behavior and are meant to provide the resources individuals need to survive; however, some societal institutions are plagued with exploitation, political exclusion, and unequal access to resources.[70] Not only does Obama have to focus on structural change, but also he must work within the structures of government to implement such change.

According to Article 1, Section 8, of the U.S. Constitution, Congress has the power of the purse, which means that before any financial transactions can take place in the federal government, they must be approved by Congress.[71] Legislation is generally initiated through committees, which have jurisdiction over various policy areas. Therefore, most of the legislation President Obama proposes must be approved by Congress. Given the Democratic majority in both houses of Congress presently, one would see this as an ideal time for the president to get Congress to sign off on most of his legislative agenda. In addition to having majorities in both houses of Congress, the president currently has very high approval ratings.

Political scientist and presidential scholar Richard Neustadt, in his book *Presidential Power*, states that "Presidential power is the power to persuade."[72] And, notes Neustadt, a popular president is more persuasive than an unpopular one.[73] Members of Congress who know that a president is extremely popular back home have more incentive to cooperate with a president's program. A technique common to the modern presidency is the energy presidents devote to mobilizing public support for their programs. According to political scientist Kenneth Janda, "A president uses televised addresses (and the media coverage surrounding them), remarks to reporters, and public appearances to speak directly to the American people and convince them of the wisdom of his policies."[74] Moreover, presidential scholar Samuel Kernell asserts that "scholars have coined the phrase 'going public' to describe situations where the president 'forces compliance from fellow Washingtonians by going over their heads to appeal to their constituents.'"[75] Rather than bargain exclusively with party and committee leaders in Congress, the president "rallies broad coalitions of support as though undertaking a political campaign."[76]

President Barack Obama has been extremely skillful at utilizing this strategy since he became president. He has held numerous press conferences in his first year in office to explain his legislative agenda. He has continued to operate his official campaign website barackobama.org even though he is now the president. He also has the official whitehouse.gov website and has launched a new website usaservice.org, where citizens can sign up and get involved in community service. Obama is using his former campaign website to deliver video messages and podcasts to Americans every week. Moreover, unlike his predecessors, President Obama and the First Family have been seen around Washington on numerous occasions. According to the *New York Times*, Obama can be seen catching a basketball game between his hometown Chicago Bulls and the Washington Wizards.[77] The Obamas have attended two events at the Kennedy Center for the Performing Arts (once to see the Alvin Ailey Dance Troupe—with daughters in tow—and once to attend a musical tribute to Senator Edward Kennedy). Furthermore, Obama has appeared on "The Tonight Show," with Jay Leno, to discuss his economic package, making him the first sitting president to appear on a late night comedy show. According to presidential historian Michael Beschloss, "the notion of presidential engagement with Washington has typically meant 'going to parties in Georgetown or making friends on Capitol Hill, in other words, engaging with the permanent political establishment here.'"[78] Beschloss stated that "The Obamas know that it's different. As the first African-American couple in the White House, they want to reach beyond the prosperous, predominantly white corridors of Washington."[79] Furthermore, according to journalist Rachel Swarns, "Political analysts assert that the images of Obama hooting and hollering during a basketball game, eating a hot dog at Ben's Chili Bowl and watching the ballet with his wife and daughters—pastimes routinely broadcast to a national audience—may humanize a politician who is sometimes viewed as too cerebral and too distant."[80] Dee Dee Myers, a former press secretary for President Clinton, was quoted by Swarns as saying, "The outings allow Mr. Obama to project 'an accessible glamour' and to convey a message of hope during bleak economic times."[81]

All of this may help to increase a president's popularity with public opinion—a resource that modern presidents can utilize. According to Janda, Berry, and Goldman, "Presidents closely monitor their approval ratings, or 'popularity,' which is a report card on how well they are performing their duties."[82] A president's popularity is typically highest in his first year in office. This time frame, often referred to as the "honeymoon period," gives the president a great opportunity to use public support to move much of his legislation through Congress.[83]

But, these are sobering times. In March 2009, President Obama submitted his executive budget of $3.5 trillion to Congress. The budget called for expanded government activism and tax increases on affluent families and businesses. Moreover, one war would end, as troops leave Iraq, while another would ramp up in Afghanistan. President Obama is already calling on Americans to make extreme sacrifices as a result of an era of profound irresponsibility that engulfed both private and public institutions in this country. As an example of a president using his popularity to accomplish his legislative agenda, Obama's $3.5 trillion budget was approved by both the House and Senate with the president's specifications largely intact.

The Concept of Deracialization

In a conference paper written by political scientists Byron D. Orey and Boris E. Ricks, they assert that the concept of deracialization has been defined by political scientists Joseph P. McCormick and Charles E. Jones as "conducting a campaign in a stylistic fashion that defuses the polarizing effects of race by avoiding explicit reference to race-specific issues, while at the same time emphasizing those issues that are perceived as racially transcendent, thus mobilizing a broad segment of the electorate for purposes of capturing or maintaining public office."[84] "Moreover," assert McCormick and Jones, "a deracialized political strategy affects the issues candidates stress, their mobilization tactics and the style of their campaigns."[85] In utilizing a normative approach, they argue that black candidates should emphasize issues that appear to be race-neutral to avoid giving white voters the impression that they are only interested in representing blacks.[86]

According to Orey and Ricks, the final component of McCormick and Jones' model is political style. Orey and Ricks summarize this style by asserting, "The success of black candidates in attracting white support depends, in part, on their ability to project a nonthreatening image . . . Black candidates, for example, should avoid associating themselves with people that white voters will view as racial partisans."[87] Others have noted that a deracialization strategy is only pragmatic politics given the current demographics in the country. Political scientist Ron Walters, who served as adviser to both of Rev. Jesse Jackson's bids for the presidency, has argued that "the available political jurisdictions that are majority black are drying up. So, to increase the number of black elected officials, they will have to come from majority white districts. You cannot run there in the same way as in a majority black district and be successful."[88]

Orey and Ricks cite a case study by political scientists Charles E. Jones and Michael Clemmons of L. Douglas Wilder as the nation's first black elected governor. In determining whether Wilder ran a deracialized campaign for the Virginia governorship, they examined Wilder's public appearances between June 19 and September 4, 1989. They found that Wilder appeared before the public eighty-four times, and after dividing the groups Wilder spoke to as predominantly black or predominantly white, they found that only ten of these appearances were before predominantly black audiences.[89] Political scientist Alvin Schexnider, who analyzed Wilder's deracialization strategy as far back as his 1985 campaign to become lieutenant governor, found that Wilder "did not present himself to the Virginia electorate as a black candidate in 1985, rather Wilder focused on his legislative record and issues that appealed to all voters—economic, educational, and environmental."[90]

Political scientist Katherine Underwood conducted a systematic analysis in examining campaigns of Latino candidates for the city council elections in Los Angeles, California. Using the deracialization concept, she found that "Latino candidates were able to build cross-racial support by running deracialized campaigns."[91] Moreover, University of Florida political scientist Sharon Wright who specializes in African American political behavior examined the 1991 mayoral election in Memphis, Tennessee, by focusing on the impact of a candidate's campaign strategy. She found classic racially polarized voting where the black candidate, Willie Herenton, received roughly 98.5 percent of the black vote and 1.5 percent of the white vote. Conversely, the white candidate, Richard Hacket, attracted 98.5 percent of the white vote and 1.5 percent of the black vote.[92] Orey even argues that the media should be used as a contextual variable when examining the deracialization construct. Using content analysis as a methodology, he found that "the print media helped to create a racialized environment, even when the black candidate attempted to run a deracialized campaign."[93]

Implication of Running a Deracialized Campaign on Obama's Ability to Deliver Goods to the Black Community or Advance a Civil Rights Agenda

[R]unning a deracialized campaign has its upside and downside. The upside is that we won and diffused the issue of race on a national scale. The downside is that some settings will imply that racism has now disappeared in America, which we know is not true.[94]

Rep. William Lacy Clay (D-MO)

African Americans comprise 11.3 percent of the national voting age population; therefore, it was virtually impossible for Obama to win the presidency with only the support of black voters. According to the conflict and accommodation thesis, he must deemphasize the role of race to accommodate multiple races to build a winning electoral coalition. Just as blacks are no longer the largest minority in this country (Hispanics now number 15 percent of the total U.S. population), there are no states with a majority black population. A U.S. presidential election is not a national election, but rather a series of state elections. In the event of one black-majority state, according to the thesis, the campaigning style is projected to be different.

When Rep. James Clyburn (D-SC), Majority Whip in the U.S. House of Representatives, was asked what he thought were the implications of running a deracialized campaign on President Obama's ability to deliver the goods to black communities or advance a civil right agenda, he was rather candid:

> Very few people that support the civil rights community are unrealistic . . . Most people are realistic enough to know that in this country, to win the presidency, you must understand that with more than two people in the race, you may get elected. With black people being 12 percent of the population, you will not get elected with 12 percent of the vote. If you do not run a deracialized campaign, chances are you will not get elected.[95]

However, opponents of deracialization argue that deracialization is an approach that fails to push for more extensive policy changes that would be of greater benefit to the black constituency. Candidates cannot easily switch to a redistribution and race-focused governing agenda after having only stressed more moderate appeals during the election campaign. Moderate black candidates have generally pursued policies of fiscal conservatism and central business development rather than a more redistributive agenda. According to opponents, deracialization is a denial of the historical context of black politics, which is a group struggle for race-specific empowerment in order to exercise some degree of independence and self-determination. If campaign behavior is a predictor of governance style and governance behavior, then deracialization serves as an aberration to the essence of black politics. These scholars conclude that deracialization strategies will cause black politics to degenerate, rather than to mature.[96]

Given the racial composition of the United States, the conflict and accommodation thesis suggests that it is in the best interests of the Obama campaign to run a deracialized strategy.[97] To do this, developing biracial and multiracial electoral coalitions are mandatory to gain racial crossover voting. In doing so, Obama must not alienate and mobilize those against him, thus keeping them home instead of at the polls. Likewise, he must attract those voters that are turned off by racialized and negative campaigning strategies.

The fact that an African American has been elected president of the United States only forty years out of "Jim Crow" is remarkable. But, is that proof of change? Will Obama's blackness alleviate issues of concern to blacks such as lack of adequate health care, the achievement gap in elementary and secondary education between whites and nonwhites, high incarceration rates among young African American males, and double digit unemployment rates in the black community? Or, does Obama mark an end to one phase of the black struggle for freedom and the beginning of another? What role does symbolism play with this Obama victory? The black community is asking these questions after this country has elected its first African American president.

The Obama administration is projected to impact black lives just as much, if not more, than the monumental achievements of Franklin D. Roosevelt, who implemented the New Deal, John F. Kennedy, who restored hope with his Fair Deal but whose life was cut short by an assassin's bullet, and Lyndon B. Johnson, whose Great Society programs and "War on Poverty" continued the work of Kennedy and who signed the Civil Rights Act of 1964 and the Voting Rights Act of 1965 into law.

According to Erica Williams, an M.A. student at Louisville, the University of Louisville's Pan-African Studies professor Ricky Jones (2008) states that the "mania" or optimism generated by the Obama campaign can have an adverse effect on his administration if he is unsuccessful in delivering policy change or economic improvement.[98] And, Williams also contends that it is possible that since Obama represents proof that America has now entered a "post-racial" era, some programs designed to benefit African Americans and other minorities such as affirmative action may lose their appeal.[99]

3

Obama's Winning Coalition

When I first started this campaign, I was reluctantly with John Edwards
. . . But as time went on it became apparent to me that not only was John
Edwards not going to win but . . . that Barack Obama had the organization
and he had the vision and he had the charisma and he had the fundraising
prowess and he had everything that one would want in a presidential
candidate.[1]

Rep. G. K. Butterfield (D-NC)

Barack Obama assembled a diverse coalition on his way to winning the
presidential election in 2008 the likes of which the Democratic Party had
never seen. Obama was able to tap into the energy and pulse of a new
generation of voters who were disenchanted with politicians of the past and
were looking for someone who shared their energy and enthusiasm. Obama's
emerging coalition of American voters included young people, Hispanics and
other minorities, and white upper-middle-class professionals. That "coalition
of the ascendant" (a phrase coined by political analyst Ronald Brownstein),
added to a huge majority of the African American vote, gave Obama a
resounding victory over Republican John McCain for the presidency.[2]
According to Simon Rosenberg, president of DND, a Democratic group that
studies electoral trends and tactics, "Democrats [are] . . . surging with all the
ascending and growing parts of the electorate. He [Obama] is building a
coalition that Democrats could ride for 30 or 40 years, the way they rode the
FDR [Franklin D. Roosevelt] coalition of the 1930s."[3] Whether this actually

happens remains to be seen, but the rise of this new coalition does tend to parallel some of the major demographic trends in the country. This nation is becoming increasingly multiracial. According to political scientist Scott Page, "Given the growth of the Asian and, particularly, the Hispanic share of the population, most demographers predict that whites will no longer comprise a majority by 2050."[4] Obama's victory was the most decisive for either party since Ronald Reagan's in 1980 and the largest for any Democrat since Lyndon Johnson defeated Barry Goldwater in 1964. Obama's gains came behind parallel coalitions centered on minorities and better-educated whites who are often the most comfortable with the country's increasingly diverse and racial-ethnic mix.

According to political scientist Gerald Pomper, "minority voters had the greatest effect on the election result. African Americans and Latinos affected the outcome both by increased turnout, as they voted in larger numbers than in 2004, and by more marked support of the Democratic candidate."[5] Moreover, notes Pomper, Latinos are already the largest minority group in the nation, and their share of the electorate will grow considerably as the children of recent immigrants, often first-generation Americans, become eligible to vote.[6] "The total effect of ethnic minorities . . . was to add more than seven million votes to Obama's tally . . . nearly three-fourths of the Democrats' overall gain in votes," stated Pomper.[7]

Although minority votes played a substantial role in Obama's victory, he would not have won the election but for his support from white voters, the largest demographic in the electorate. Rather than showing racial hostility toward the black candidate, white support for the Democrats actually increased. Obama ran strongly among white voters, garnering 43 percent of their vote, but the majority of whites continued to vote Republican as they had done for the last forty years. However, Obama ran better with white voters than recent Democratic candidates who ran for president, all of whom were white.[8]

According to Pomper, "strong opposition to Obama was limited to a few demographic groups . . . and party loyalties largely overrode racial defections."[9] Moreover, "There was considerable opposition to Obama in the white working class, as expected, but this opposition cannot be attributed simply to racism, since these 'Reagan Democrats' have also been voting for years against the party's white candidates." Obama actually did better with the white working class than Kerry in 2004, by five points, to gain a 41 percent share of their votes.[10]

On November 4, 2008, Hispanics preferred Obama to McCain by better than two to one and simultaneously increased their share of the vote from 8 percent in 2004 to 9 percent. Asians and other minorities, although just 5 percent of voters, gave Obama nearly two-thirds of their votes.[11]

According to Brownstein, one trend to watch is the vast "millennial" generation now stampeding into the electorate.

> In 2004, John Kerry, the Democratic nominee, carried 54 percent of voters younger than 30; amid disillusionment with President Bush and the Iraq War, on November 4, 2008, Obama beat McCain among voters under 30 by 2-to-1. Moreover, even among white young people, the Republicans are losing ground. Bush carried 55 percent of whites under 30 in 2000 and 2004. However, Obama won 44 percent of these young white voters.[12]

The next major demographic of Obama's coalition was white voters with college or post-graduate educations, many of them professionals. Brownstein stated that "Obama won 47 percent of those well-educated whites, a higher percentage than Kerry, Gore, or Clinton. He carried 52 percent of college-educated white women . . . and 42 percent of college-educated white men, again better than Kerry, Gore, or Clinton."[13]

Background

Journalist John Judis and political scientist Ruy Teixeira argue in their book, *The Emerging Democratic Majority*, that Obama's victory and the winning coalition that he put together is the culmination of a Democratic realignment that began in the 1990s, was delayed by September 11, 2001, and the attack on the World Trade Center, and resumed with the 2006 election.[14] Moreover, Judis asserts that this "realignment is predicated on a change in political demography and geography."[15]

The new Democratic realignment reflects the shift that began decades ago toward a post-industrial economy centered in large urban-suburban metropolitan areas devoted primarily to the production of ideas and services rather than material goods. Moreover, Judis notes that "Clustered in the regions that have undergone this economic transition are the three main groups that constitute the backbone of the new Democratic majority: professionals (college-educated workers who produce ideas and services); minorities (African

Americans, Latinos, and Asian Americans); and women (particularly working, single, and college-educated women)."[16]

Political scientist and election data specialist Walter Dean Burnham has referred to realignments as America's "surrogate for revolution." Realignments, notes Burnham, "respond to the sharp clashes between interests, classes, regions, religions, and ethnic groups brought about by tectonic shifts in the economy and society."[17] Burnham asserts, moreover, that "Realignments occur because a dominant political coalition fails to adapt to or to contain a growing social and political conflict. A political movement like the Southern civil rights movement can precipitate this sort of conflict."[18] Realignments are not scientifically predictable events like lunar eclipses note Judis and Teixeira; however, they have occurred with some consistency over the last two hundred years—in 1828, 1860, 1896, 1932, and 1980.[19] (See Table 3.1.) In each realignment, a new coalition emerges and forms a majority party "by winning over votes from its rival party and by increasing its sway over its own voters, whose ranks have typically increased through birth, immigration, and economic change."[20]

New Deal Coalition

Franklin D. Roosevelt was able to create a coalition in 1932 centered around anger over the Great Depression that drove a number of groups—industrial workers of the Northeast and Midwest, with ethnic immigrants of Poles, Italians, and Irish, small farmers, blacks, Catholics, and Jews—back into the Democratic Party. Together with the party's existing base of Southern whites, these disparate voting blocs gave the Democrats an enduring majority for

TABLE 3.1 PAST REALIGNING ELECTIONS

Year	Winner	Party	Electoral Votes	Popular Vote Percentage
1828	Andrew Jackson	Democratic	178	56
1860	Abraham Lincoln	Republican	180	40
1896	William McKinley	Republican	271	51
1932	Franklin Roosevelt	Democratic	472	57
1980	Ronald Reagan	Republican	489	51

Source: National Archives: Electoral College Box Scores 1789–1996.

many years to come. According to Walton and Smith, "This coalition of opposites—African Americans and Southern whites—was held together by a common interest in universal material benefits."[21] Blacks and Southern whites were uneasy partners because Franklin Roosevelt avoided taking any stand on race issues, even refusing to support anti-lynching legislation. This coalition gave the Democratic Party seven victories out of nine presidential elections (1932–1948, 1960, and 1964). Roosevelt gained substantial support of black voters who left the Republican Party because of Roosevelt's liberal economic policies which were widely popular after Herbert Hoover's presidency and the Great Depression. Moreover, Republicans were reduced to their loyal business supporters in the Northeast and Midwest, farmers in the Western plains states, and rural white Protestants in the Midwest and Northeast, according to Judis and Teixeira.[22] White working-class voters for decades made up the majority of the Democratic vote as the largest bloc within the New Deal coalition.

To understand Obama's emergent coalition today, one must look at race and politics in the South. Following the Civil War, since the Republican Party was the party of Lincoln that freed the slaves, Southern whites became the party of racial segregation. The New Deal coalition included a Southern white component that, for the most part, denied blacks the right to vote. The interests of integrationist whites were clearly not in accord with segregationist Southern whites. According to political scientist Michael Nelson, "As long as African-Americans did not press a civil rights agenda on the federal government, this fault line remained unexposed and politically insignificant."[23] The political coalition that Franklin D. Roosevelt built began slowly shifting during the New Deal era. Roosevelt's huge popularity nationwide began to decrease the Democratic Party's reliance on Southern support in presidential elections.

According to Nelson, "From 1932 to 1944, FDR had carried every Southern state in all four elections. In 1948, however, Georgia stayed with Truman, but the other four Deep South states—Alabama, Louisiana, Mississippi, and South Carolina—cast their electoral votes for Democratic governor Strom Thurmond of South Carolina, the nominee of the rebellious Southern Democrats who had walked out of their party's pro-civil-rights convention and formed the States' Rights Party, or Dixiecrats."[24] According to researcher Peter Katel, "Support for Jim Crow was entrenched in the South, but so was loyalty to the Democrats, and the Dixiecrats won only about 25 percent of white Southerners' votes."[25]

Just six years later, the U.S. Supreme Court struck down the *Plessy v. Ferguson* (1896) doctrine of "separate but equal" in the landmark decision

Brown v. Board of Education (1954). The *Brown* decision marked a watershed in race relations in this country, particularly in the South, and ushered in the civil rights movement in the American South. Dedicated to the philosophy of nonviolence and led by Martin Luther King, Jr., black Americans began to march and protest for their civil rights throughout the South. Much of their protest was met by violent resistance by Southern whites determined to keep blacks relegated to second-class citizenship status. Blacks and sympathetic whites were threatened daily; many were beaten and some were murdered in random acts of terrorism. For example, in 1963, in Birmingham, Alabama, the commissioner of public safety turned water hoses and police dogs on children marching for freedom. But later that same year, the civil rights movement held a March on Washington for Jobs and Freedom where 250,000 people assembled on the mall in Washington to demand meaningful federal civil rights legislation. The keynote speaker was Martin Luther King, Jr., and he delivered his famous "I Have a Dream" speech where he called on the nation to heal its racial wounds and come together in the spirit of brotherhood and unity. A year later, Congress passed the Civil Rights Act of 1964 which outlawed segregation in employment, public schools, and all areas of public accommodations. The following year, a nation watched in horror as state troopers violently beat a group of civil rights protesters in Selma, Alabama, who were on a symbolic march to the state capitol in Montgomery to protest to the governor the denial of their constitutional right to vote. The governor of Alabama, George Wallace, had ordered the state troopers not to allow the march to proceed. The event, subsequently referred to as "Bloody Sunday," showed America the extent of racial hatred and bigotry in the South. One week later, President Lyndon Johnson went before a joint session of Congress and a televised audience and called on Congress to pass a comprehensive voting rights bill and used the phrase "we shall overcome," the civil rights movement's most powerful theme. Two days later, the president sent the Voting Rights bill to Congress. Later that year, on August 6, 1965, President Johnson signed the Voting Rights Act into law. Martin Luther King, Jr., often exclaimed "that the arc of the moral universe is long but it bends toward justice." Nearly one hundred years after passage of the 15th Amendment to the U.S. Constitution in 1870, which prohibited states from denying citizens the right to vote on account of race, color, or previous condition of servitude, that arc approached its downward turn. Within three years, a majority of African Americans in the South were registered to vote.

Southern White Backlash

Passage of the Voting Rights Act of 1965 came one year after President Johnson's election over Republican Barry Goldwater. Goldwater, a staunch conservative, had opposed the Civil Rights Act of 1964. When Johnson signed the bill into law, he remarked to an aide, "We have lost the South for a generation."[26] The election of 1964 marked a watershed in American politics. Johnson soundly defeated his ultra-conservative opponent carrying 44 of the 50 states and the District of Columbia. Goldwater won only his home state of Arizona and five Deep South states of the Old Confederacy: Alabama, Georgia, Louisiana, Mississippi, and South Carolina—and "he was the first Republican to receive the votes of a majority—55 percent—of white Southerners."[27] This election is instructive for two reasons: Goldwater is considered a pioneer in the modern conservative movement, and second, this was an important transition point for the South. It marked an important step in dismantling the "Solid South" from a Democratic stronghold to a Republican bastion: The South was beginning to undergo a political realignment.

When President Johnson signed the Voting Rights Act into law in 1965, he knew that he was breaking up the New Deal coalition. Many Southerners were increasingly offended by the passage of federal civil rights laws granting equal opportunity and voting privileges to African Americans. Moreover, as the number of African American registered voters in the South began to increase dramatically, many Southern Democrats felt as though the Democratic Party had abandoned their cause and principles. The Republican Party began to appear much more attractive as a party.

In the presidential election of 1968, Republican candidate Richard Nixon campaigned on a platform to attract those disaffected Southern white voters. This strategy, known as the "Southern strategy," was based on "appealing to the fears of whites in response to the growing political power and demands of African Americans."[28] Nixon was not above using code words like "law and order" and "B-U-S-I-N-G" to appeal to blue-collar white voters. The Democratic share of the presidential vote decreased precipitously from 61 percent in 1964 to only 43 percent in 1968.[29]

Johnson's civil rights legislation and "Great Society" programs were significant in the advancement of the cause of African Americans in this country and expanded the role of government in the everyday lives of American citizens. In his 1969 book, *The Emerging Republican Majority*,

Nixon political strategist Kevin Phillips remarked, "This repudiation visited upon the Democratic Party for its ambitious social programming, and inability to handle the urban and Negro revolutions, was comparable to that given conservative Republicanism in 1932 for its failure to cope with the economic crisis of the Depression."[30]

Moreover, during this time frame, the U.S. Supreme Court issued a series of opinions that many conservatives opposed including requirements that white families bus their children to predominantly black schools to achieve racial integration, the outlawing of mandatory prayer in public schools, the lessening of restrictions on contraception, and increased protections for criminal defendants.[31]

Republicans would go on to win all but one of the next six presidential elections. The only Republican loss came in the aftermath of the Watergate scandal that forced Republican president Richard Nixon to resign from office in 1974. As the South realigned, the Democratic Party fought Republican expansion by attracting African American voters. Democrat Jimmy Carter, a Southerner, won the White House in 1976 with the support of 82 percent of black Southerners, though he lost most white Southerners to President Gerald Ford.[32] Alan Greenblatt notes that underlying the Republican success was the splintering of the "New Deal coalition and the GOP [Grand Old Party]'s ability to tap into white working-class votes that had long been denied its candidates."[33]

"The New Deal coalition collapsed for many reasons," note Walton and Smith, "but the major one was racism. Many whites, especially in the South, were unwilling to be a part of a broad material-based coalition if that coalition also embraced the historic quest of African Americans for equality and universal freedom."[34] Ronald Reagan's successful presidential campaigns in 1980 and 1984 moved the South further into the GOP corner. Reagan was so successful at attracting disaffected white Democrats that the phrase "Reagan Democrats" became part of the American lexicon. In 1980, Reagan faced a Southern Democratic incumbent president, Jimmy Carter. He announced his candidacy in New York City on November 13, 1979. Looking to make inroads in the Deep South, he gave his first major speech after the announcement of his candidacy at the Neshoba County Fair in Philadelphia, Mississippi, on August 3, 1980, where three civil rights workers were murdered by the police and the Ku Klux Klan during Freedom Summer in 1964. Furthermore, it was a bitter touch of symbolism for black Americans. Reagan won all of the Deep South states in 1980 with the exception of Georgia, which supported its native son, Jimmy Carter. Reagan's Mississippi speech was noted as crucial in both his presidential election and Republican victory in the South. Speaking to an overwhelmingly white audience, Reagan intoned "I believe in states' rights [racial code words]; I believe in people doing as much as they can at the private level."[35] It was a continuation of the "Southern strategy" invoked by Nixon in 1968 to appeal to the racial fears and anxieties of whites.

By the end of Ronald Reagan's two-term administration in 1988, the Republican Party was clearly the majority party in the South. As a result of the Voting Rights Act of 1965, African American registered voters in the South were increasing dramatically as were the number of African American elected officials. As civil rights laws took effect, it became unacceptable for mainstream politicians to support separation of the races. However, that did not mean the end to racial politics. In 1987–1988, when George H. W. Bush was running for president, his campaign ran a television advertisement accusing his Democratic opponent, Michael Dukakis, of being soft on criminals. According to Peter Katel,

> The controversial ad noted that under a prison furlough program —begun by Dukakis' Republican predecessor—a murderer serving a life sentence without parole raped a woman and slashed her husband after being released for a weekend furlough. The criminal, William "Willie" Horton, was black, and his victim white. Official Bush campaign ads didn't show Horton's face, though at least one commercial and some fliers produced by independent pro-Bush groups did.[36]

Democratic leaders accused the Bush campaign of exploiting racist fears and emotions as soon as the explosive ads hit the airways. Moreover, asserts Katel, "Ensuing news coverage made the campaign's avoidance of Horton's photo irrelevant, because the media frequently showed the image."[37]

And prior to Barack Obama's presidential victory in 2008, Bill Clinton in 1992 had become the only Democratic presidential candidate since the Reagan era to carry any Southern states. He won back a larger share of the working-class white vote by emphasizing issues and moving away from identity politics by pledging to end welfare as we know it.[38] In order to compete for the votes of the Reagan Democrats, in the 1990s, the Democratic Party under Clinton moved steadfastly to the right.

In the presidential election of 2000, George W. Bush lost the popular vote to Al Gore, but interestingly, benefited from the Democratic trends that had

TABLE 3.2 SOUTHERN STATES WON BY BUSH IN 2000

State	Electoral Votes	Popular Votes (Bush)	Popular Votes (Gore)
Alabama	9	941,173	692,611
Arkansas	6	472,940	422,768
Florida	25	2,912,790	2,912,253
Georgia	13	1,419,720	1,116,230
Louisiana	9	927,871	792,344
Mississippi	7	572,844	404,614
North Carolina	14	1,631,163	1,257,692
South Carolina	8	785,937	565,561
Tennessee	11	1,061,949	981,720
Texas	32	3,799,639	2,433,746
Virginia	13	1,437,490	1,217,290

Source: Federal Election Commission: Federal Elections 2004.

been moving voters into the Republican camp. Bush carried every Southern state and the evangelical vote (see Table 3.2). His opponent, Al Gore, a Southerner, had captured a total of 266 Electoral College votes, just four shy of the 270 needed to win the presidency. In spite of the controversy in Florida, if Gore, a Southerner, had just won his home state of Tennessee with eleven Electoral College votes, he would have won the presidency.

Walton and Smith state that since the 1970s and 1980s, the Democratic Party has taken the black vote for granted just as the Republicans did a century ago. Knowing that the Democrats can count on nearly 90 percent of the black vote, "the Democrats pocket it at the outset of the elections, while offering little in the way of policies to address the main concerns of blacks—joblessness and racialized poverty."[39] Moreover, they allege that at the beginning of the twenty-first century in the American party system, black identification with the Democratic Party is nearly total. This is so because "black partisanship is based on their perceptions of each Party's responsiveness to the needs and interests of the black community."[40] In other words, "individual black voters hold a group-based perception of the parties . . . racial identification determines Democratic partisanship."[41]

It is against this backdrop of African Americans as the core Democratic voting bloc that Barack Obama won the Democratic nomination in 2008.

Obama's nomination for president was made possible by two key circumstances. First, the Democratic Party created a commission after the 1968 Democratic Convention to reform the nominating process that had been denying African Americans delegates in proportion to their number of voters. The Commission required the states to take the necessary measures to encourage the representation of minority groups, young people, and women in a reasonable relationship to their presence in the population of the state. Furthermore, each state was charged with creating delegate selection procedures to ensure that all voters in each state would have meaningful opportunities to participate in the election and selection of delegates and alternatives. The effect of these reforms was to remove the delegate selection process from the hands of the party leaders and place it in the hands of the people.[42]

In 1984, when Jesse Jackson first ran for president in the Democratic primary, he was allocated fewer delegates (8 percent) than the actual percentage of voters that he won (18 percent).[43] He argued that this was unfair and undemocratic and pressed for rules changes. The 1984 Convention appointed a Fairness Commission which changed the delegate selection rules to more closely align with the wishes of the voters.

The Rainbow Coalition

Jesse Jackson laid much of the foundation that allowed an African American like Barack Obama to become the first black president in this country. Not only did Jackson's two bids for the presidency in 1984 and 1988 bring about changes in the delegate selection process that allowed Obama to gain the necessary delegates to win the nomination, but the coalition of voters Jackson amassed became the prototype for the type of voters Obama would bring together to form a winning coalition. Walton and Smith assert that Jackson never intended to win the nomination or the presidency. Jackson wanted to exert leverage on the party to

> halt the conservative drift of the party, to inject progressive perspectives on foreign and domestic issues into the campaign debates and party platform, to mobilize the black vote by increasing registration and turnout, to serve as the balance of power in determining the nominee, and to lay the groundwork for the mobilization of a multiethnic rainbow coalition that might in the future become an electoral majority in presidential politics.[44]

The rainbow coalition that Jesse Jackson assembled in 1988 resembled Obama's winning coalition twenty years later in 2008 in terms of race and class. Both candidates started with African Americans as their base and built on that. Walton and Smith state that, "In 1988, college-educated middle-aged blacks were more likely to support Jackson. Second, their white support was drawn disproportionately from the young, well-educated, and high-income group rather than the elderly, less-educated, poor, or working class."[45] Moreover, Walton and Smith acknowledge that the age and race-class bases of both the Jackson and Obama campaigns are similar, the key distinction being the size of Obama's support among educated, middle-class, white Americans. So, there are lessons to be learned from the Jackson presidential campaigns of 1984 and 1988. Obama's Rainbow Coalition was a winning coalition of blacks, young people, well-educated and high-income whites.[46]

However, Obama's election signals a deep change in American politics. David Bositis, a senior research analyst with the Joint Center for Political and Economic Studies, said that "while John McCain got 55 percent of the white vote versus 43 percent for Barack Obama nationally, a majority of white voters in 16 states and the District of Columbia voted for Obama."[47] Obama did better with white voters than John Kerry in 2004 (43 percent to 41 percent).

Obama's Southern Strategy

Demographic changes have been in the making in American electoral politics for some time. The "Southern strategy" perfected by Republican Richard Nixon and utilized by every Republican president since may have run its course. Barack Obama devised a new Southern strategy. He was largely able to do this because of demographic changes that have taken hold in the Old South. In fact, the Old South has given way to the "New South." Virginia, North Carolina, and Florida all voted for Obama. This is due, in part, to the large number of people who have moved into those states from elsewhere and the higher level of education in some of those states.

But Obama's decisive coalition is due to more than just a brilliantly run and highly disciplined campaign. The old Southern strategy was based on the notion that national elections were won by co-opting Southern whites on racial issues. But, as political scientist and expert on Southern politics Merle Black argued, "the Republican Party went too far in appealing to the South, alienating voters elsewhere."[48]

Thomas Schaller, a political scientist, asserts that the Democratic coalition forged under FDR and the New Deal is gone. But instead of trying to recreate the past, he notes in his book *Whistling Past Dixie*, "Democrats should forget about recapturing the South in the near term and begin building a national majority that ends, not begins, with restoring their lost southern glory."[49] He alleges that the South is beyond the Democrats' reach and that race and religion have created a socially conservative and electorally hostile environment for most Democratic presidential nominees.[50] Schaller goes on to argue that the Republicans "have completely marginalized themselves to a mostly regional party."[51] Several Southern states have voted for the presidential winner for decades, states such as Arkansas, Louisiana, and Tennessee. But this was not the case in 2008. *New York Times* journalist Adam Nossiter remarks that, "And Mr. Obama's race appears to have been the critical deciding factor in pushing ever greater numbers of white Southerners away from Democrats."[52] Schaller is not alone in identifying the South's loss of power in presidential elections. In examining Obama's winning formula for the presidency, one clearly sees a loss of deep South states (Alabama, Georgia, Louisiana, Mississippi, and South Carolina) among that formula.

Political scientist Wayne Parent observed, "The region's absence from Mr. Obama's winning formula means it is becoming distinctly less important . . . The South has moved from being at the center of the political universe to being an outside player in presidential politics."[53] Nossiter asserts that one reason this shift became evident in Obama's electoral victory in 2008

> is that the South is no longer a solid voting bloc. Along the Atlantic Coast, parts of the "suburban South," notably Virginia and North Carolina, made history . . . in breaking from their Confederate past and supporting Mr. Obama. Those states have experienced an influx of better educated and more prosperous voters in recent years, pointing them in a different political direction than states farther west, like Alabama, Arkansas, Louisiana, and Mississippi, and Appalachian sections of Kentucky and Tennessee.[54]

Unlike many of his democratic predecessors, however, Obama saw the South as fertile ground for electoral votes and he aggressively courted it. The Obama camp appears to have learned lessons from the past. According to Merle Black, "Democratic candidates have typically written off many Southern states early in the process. But when Democrats give up the South, they need to win 70 percent of the rest of the electoral votes . . ."[55] Obama pursued a new "Southern strategy" in the 2008 presidential election. So, rather than ignoring the South as Democratic presidential nominee John Kerry did in 2004, Obama spent time and poured considerable financial resources into the region. A Kerry campaign aide remarked, "We started out with a pretty broad playing field, with the intention of putting more states in play than had been put into play before . . . At a certain point, we needed to make a decision on whether to continue to compete in states that weren't likely to pay off and drain money from states that could."[56]

Whether it was a lack of resources, or the fact that Democrats just have not made a compelling argument to attract the Southern vote, their success has been abysmal at best. In the presidential elections of 2000 and 2004, the Democrats did not carry one Southern state. And in 2000, the Democratic nominee was Al Gore, a Southerner from Tennessee. According to *New York Times* journalist Robin Toner, "The only times since 1972 that the Democrats have carried more than a third of the Southern white vote, according to exit polls, were when Jimmy Carter or Bill Clinton, both Southerners, were atop the ticket. In 1996, for example, Mr. Clinton got the votes of 36 percent of Southern whites and 87 percent of Southern blacks, and carried 5 of 13 Southern states."[57]

How did Obama execute his Southern strategy? He did so on several fronts. According to officials in Obama's campaign, they actively courted Southern voters, which was apparent by early campaign appearances in North Carolina and Virginia. Although Obama knew these two states combined have only voted Democratic once since 1964—North Carolina in 1976—he nevertheless aggressively pursued both, evidenced by him kicking off his general election campaign in Virginia. Moreover, Obama's deputy campaign manager Steve Hildebrand observed, "If you go in and look at the number of unregistered voters in demographic groups that are important to Barack's candidacy —younger voters, African American voters—the potential is just incredible . . ."[58] Obama's campaign held major voter registration drives in the region and bought television advertising in Florida, Georgia, North Carolina, and Virginia. Obama was able to be competitive where his predecessor was not because of his huge political war chest. The economy and the Iraq War were two major issues that caused parts of the South to be more open to new leadership and a new direction for the country. Obama's decision to bypass public financing and spending limits that accompany it gave him a considerable advantage over his opponent, John McCain, who opted to take the public financing (see Chapter 6). Secondly, Obama's strategy to compete in the South, rather than write it off like many of the Democrats had previously done, had an unexpected consequence. Several states of the Deep South (Alabama, Georgia, Louisiana, and South Carolina) had been written off for years by both the Democrats and the Republicans. The Democrats had written the South off because they simply felt they could not afford to spend valuable resources in those states with little to no payoff, and Republicans had not campaigned heavily there because the South had been a Republican strong-hold for quite some time. However, with the Obama camp spending time and resources in the Deep South, John McCain was forced to spend valuable campaign funding and resources in states that had been in the Republican column for years.

As a battleground state, Florida had been the scene of the disputed vote count in 2000 that ultimately was decided by the U.S. Supreme Court in *Bush v. Gore* (2000) in favor of Republican George Bush. In 2004, Bush defeated Kerry by 51.7 percent to 47.0 percent. Florida was problematic for Obama during the Democratic primary season. The state Democratic Party went against the wishes of the national Democratic Party and moved its primary date up to January 29, 2008. The Democratic National Committee ruled that Florida's delegates would not be able to vote. A compromise was later reached. Because of this, none of the Democratic candidates campaigned in Florida. Obama went into the general election campaign, unlike his opponent, without having campaigned in Florida. Conversely, John McCain won the Republican primary in Florida essentially ending Mitt Romney's campaign.

Second, Florida has a significant Hispanic population, but unlike other areas of the country, the Hispanic population, particularly in South Florida, has largely voted Republican. The media speculated that the substantial Jewish vote in Florida would never vote for an African American whose middle name was Hussein.[59] All signs were pointing to a McCain advantage. But Obama had a secret weapon in Florida which included a huge organizational effort and large sums of money to spend. Obama organized a grand effort to get voters to vote early. A team of 230,000 volunteers engineered a massive get-out-the-vote effort. Field operations organized into 19,000 neighborhood teams.[60] NBC News political director Chuck Todd and elections director Sheldon Gawiser, in their book, *How Barack Obama Won*, state that Obama spent $8 million in television advertising in the state, at a time when McCain was trying to save money.[61] Obama won Florida 51.0 percent to McCain's 48.4 percent. The key to Obama's victory in Florida was the baby boom generation according to Todd and Gawiser. In their analysis, they found that

Not only did Obama swing the 45- to 64-year-old age group 20 points from John Kerry in 2004—one of the single biggest swings in 2008, more than one in three Florida voters was baby boomers, 37%. Forget young voters or minority voters, it was baby boomers who delivered Florida for Obama.[62]

However, Obama did receive significant support from African Americans, 96 percent, voters under the age of 30, 61 percent, and probably the biggest surprise was Hispanics, 57 percent. The Jewish vote went more than three to one for Obama.[63] Much of the Jewish population in Florida consists of senior citizens who relocate to the state during their retirement years. The economic recession did not help the McCain campaign with many voters in this state, in particular.

North Carolina is a state that has trended Republican since passage of the Civil Rights Act of 1964. The state has always been somewhat schizophrenic, with the eastern part of the state exemplifying social conservative values. Other parts of the state, particularly around the Research Triangle Park, which includes major universities—University of North Carolina, North Carolina Central University, North Carolina State University, and Duke University—has always been more progressive. However, the demographics of the state have changed considerably in the last twenty years. Major urban areas in the state have grown in population as white-collar professionals from other states have moved into areas like Charlotte-Mecklenburg County, and the Research Triangle Park. In an extremely tight race, Obama eked out a victory over McCain 49.7 percent to 49.4 percent, with only 14,177 votes separating them.[64]

While the state has a sizable African American population, roughly 23 percent, Obama needed a large share of the white vote to win the election. Obama ran extremely well among African Americans, receiving 96 percent of the vote. He also garnered 74 percent of the 18- to 29-year-old voters. McCain did better than Obama among white voters who made up 72 percent of the total voters. McCain won 64 percent of the white vote as compared to 35 percent for Obama. However, Obama did considerably better than John Kerry in 2004 when he garnered only 27 percent of the white vote compared to Bush's 73 percent. It appears that Obama's huge African American vote, up 10 percentage points from Kerry's 85 percent, coupled with his increase of 8 percent of white voters from Kerry's showing in 2004, provided the margin of victory. Todd and Gawiser state that Obama laid the foundation for his victory during the primary season with a huge effort to register new voters.[65] There was an 809,782 vote increase over 2004 which probably benefitted Obama as well.

Virginia was the third Southern state to go to Obama in 2008 and it too was a battleground state. Virginia, like North Carolina, shared some of the rural-urban schizophrenia. The northern part of the state—just south of Washington, D.C.—has been growing rapidly in population. It tends to be a progressive region of the state. As one goes further south in the state, Virginia tends to be more rural and more socially conservative. Virginia had been a Republican stronghold at the presidential level since 1964. The suburban areas of northern Virginia made the difference in this election. The Obama strategy was to win big in northern Virginia, and limit the GOP damage to the rest of the state.

According to Todd and Gawiser, "In northern Virginia, the strategy was a huge success. From a mere 22,000 vote plurality for Kerry in 2004, Obama won a 234,079 vote majority in northern Virginia."[66] African Americans make up 20 percent of the electorate and Obama received 92 percent of their vote. The white vote constitutes 70 percent of the total vote and McCain won 60 percent of this vote as compared to 39 percent for Obama. Obama's portion was an increase, however, of seven points from John Kerry's 2004 white total vote of 32 percent. The Hispanic vote, which was only 5 percent of the total electorate, went for Obama 65 percent to 34 percent. Obama won Virginia decisively with a 52.6 percent to 46.3 percent margin. Young voters, who made up 21 percent of the total voters, went heavily for Obama 60 percent to 39 percent.

Obama charted a new map for Democrats to follow in future elections. Rather than writing the South off, Obama was smart enough to realize there were votes to be had in Dixie, and he engineered a campaign that went after those votes and came out with enough votes to put three states back in the Democratic column for the first time in many years.

Obama's overall campaign strategy extended beyond the boundaries of the South. His huge campaign chest allowed him to execute a fifty-state assault that changed the traditional Democratic strategy and focused on actively campaigning in more states around the country. Obama's new coalition reflected the increasing diversity of this country. Obama made increases across all demographic subgroups: 61 percent of his supporters were white, 23 percent were African American, and 11 percent were Hispanic.

Minorities had a huge effect on the election results. African Americans and Latinos affected the outcome both by increased turnout, as they voted in larger numbers than in 2004, and by more support for the Democratic candidate. Gerald Pomper stated that "The total effect of ethnic minorities was to add more than seven million votes to Obama's tally, nearly three fourths of the Democrats' overall gain in votes."[67] Moreover, Obama's election victory appears to be the result of a dramatic shift in the political landscape and an astute political strategy that included attracting parts of the South back into the Democratic fold. This new coalition of African Americans, Latinos, young people, and white professionals has a new political worldview that is considered "progressive." It remains to be seen whether this majority coalition that Obama has forged will have party dominance for some time to come.

PART

2

THE DYNAMICS
OF THE
CAMPAIGN PROCESS

Demographic Groups that
Supported Obama

I was supporting Hillary at the beginning of the presidential election but I changed my mind. When I thought about Hillary, I thought about the Clinton years and how good everything was. And then she was a woman and that was exciting to me. When I took a better look at how they were running the campaigns, I liked the way Barack carried himself. That was the guy for me. I moved before Barack secured the nomination.[1]

Nancy Bruner

On November 4, 2008, Barack Obama won the most decisive Democratic presidential election victory in a generation. Obama's victory was historically significant because he attracted a winning coalition of diverse Americans that included educated whites, women, Latinos, African Americans, Asians, and young voters. Obama was able to motivate a broad cross-section of American voters and increase turnout among these voters. Obama achieved only moderate success with working-class voters, who made up the majority of the Democratic Party from Franklin Delano Roosevelt's victory in 1932 until the election of Republican Richard Nixon in 1968. Obama's unprecedented victory created an aura of excitement at home and abroad over a historic bid by an African American.

Less than a half-century ago in many parts of this country, African Americans could not dine in public restaurants, sleep in the public hotels of the cities and motels of the highways, wade in public swimming pools, reside in many neighborhoods, or attend public educational facilities that were reserved for whites only. Signs in stores and entrances to buildings read "Whites Only" and "Colored Only" above the drinking fountains, and in many major department stores, especially in the South, blacks could purchase apparel but only without the established custom available to whites of being able to try them on first before making a purchase. Blacks in most Southern states did not have the right to vote or take part in the political process.

Now, in the first decade of the twenty-first century, an African American sits as the chief of state of the most powerful nation in the world. Though Obama had the overwhelming support of African Americans in his presidential bid, there were many other Americans who enthusiastically supported this historic bid. Rarely has an American political campaign for president generated such excitement, enthusiasm, and energy as this one did. Obama's electoral victory did something else as well: It brought Americans together across racial lines, gender lines, occupational lines, party lines, and generational lines in an unprecedented manner. Obama offered a simplified message of hope and change: two things the American people were hungry for. This chapter will examine the demographic groups that coalesced around one candidate: who were they and what were their motivations?

The majority of voters who supported Obama reflect the increasing diversity in the American population. Given the growth of the Hispanic and Asian populations, demographers predict that by year 2050 whites will no longer be a majority of the population. University of Michigan political scientist Scott Page asserts that "Within 40 years, no single racial group will be a majority. Second, interracial marriage is increasing, and many of those marriages are in the upper income groups, which means that many of our future leaders will be multiracial."[2]

Who Made Up Obama's Winning Coalition

In spite of all the trends pointing to Obama's election representing the possible future of American politics, that future is not here yet. According to NBC political analysts Chuck Todd and Sheldon Gawiser, "While the coalition of voters that supported Obama reflected the increasing diversity of America, and while Obama made gains across all demographic subgroups, the majority of his support came from white voters."[3] Indeed, 61 percent of Obama's supporters were white, 23 percent were African American, and 11 percent were

Hispanic. By contrast, 89.17 percent of McCain's supporters were white, 6.1 percent were Latino, 1.1 percent were black, 1.5 percent were Asian, and 2.0 percent were other. This is a huge potential problem for the Republican Party. "In 1976, only one in ten voters was not white, 10 percent. In 2008, one in four voters was not white, 26 percent. Furthermore, the white vote alone can no longer catapult the Republican candidate to victory."[4]

As the white middle class fled the cities after the *Brown* decision in 1954, they were replaced by blacks, Hispanics, and poor whites who migrated to the cities in vast numbers. By 1970, for the first time in U.S. history, a majority of urban dwellers resided outside the central cities, a trend that had begun fifty years earlier.[5] Ruy Teixeira observes that "Half of all Americans lived in the suburbs in 2000, which is a sevenfold increase from 90 years earlier. The Democratic Party has been making significant inroads into the traditional GOP turf in the suburbs. Meanwhile, the percentage of Americans living in central cities has remained at around 30 percent of the population since 1930, also favoring Democrats."[6]

The electorate in most states, observes Greenblatt, has split along predictable geographic lines. Big cities are primarily Democratic, while rural areas are reliably Republican. According to Greenblatt, "The suburbs have become the most important battlegrounds, the biggest trove of votes nationwide, with enough numbers to sway most statewide elections."[7] Political strategists are keenly aware of the importance of the suburban vote in winning elections. Greenblatt quotes political journalist David Mark: "Suburban and exurban [beyond the suburbs] areas . . . were central to Republican political guru Karl Rove's grand scheme for cementing GOP dominance for decades in the wake of President Bush's 2004 re-election victory."[8] Joel Kotkin, an expert on development and living patterns, stated that "for the past 40 years cities have lost middle-class white people with children who have moved to suburbs seeking better schools, more space and increased security . . . which left cities with what . . . tends to be either minorities, poor people, young people or people without children—all of whom tend to be much more liberal."[9] Ruy Teixeira asserts that "despite the long-standing notion that suburban voters are more conservative than city folks, voters in older, more established 'inner-ring' suburbs are increasingly favoring Democrats."[10] In the 2008 presidential election, 49 percent of the actual vote was cast in the suburbs, and Obama received 50 percent of that vote compared to McCain's 48 percent.

White Voters for Obama

Although minority voters were critical to Obama's presidential victory in 2008, he would not have won without the support of white Americans who made up the largest ethnic group in the election. According to NBC News director Chuck Todd and elections director Sheldon Gawiser, "Obama ran as well with white voters nationwide as any previous Democratic candidate since Jimmy Carter in 1976; Carter garnered 47 percent of the white vote. In 2008, Obama tallied 43 percent of the white vote nationwide as compared to John McCain's 55 percent of the white vote."[11] Obama fared better among white voters than recent Democratic candidates. For example, John Kerry, the Democratic Party nominee in 2004, received 41 percent of the white vote, two percentage points less than Obama received in 2008. This was an amazing percentage given all the hype about racism still being very prevalent and how America (white America in particular) was not ready to elect a black American as president.

The majority of whites, however, continued to vote Republican (see Table 4.1). Strong opposition to Obama was limited to several demographic groups. While much of the opposition came from the white working class, Pomper asserts, "this opposition cannot be attributed simply to racism, since these 'Reagan Democrats' have also been voting for years against the party's white candidates."[12]

Regional differences highlighted a sharp contrast in support or lack of support for Obama. In eight of the eleven Southern states of the Old Confederacy (as well as five other states), Obama received less than 35 percent of the white vote (see Table 4.2). In the Deep South, Obama received less than 30 percent of the vote in each of those states. Racial prejudice may have been a factor in the voting of those residents. However, in many other states, if white voters had racist sentiments, they cast them aside in the voting booth because in eighteen states, a majority of whites voted for Obama over McCain (see Table 4.3).[13]

Race was clearly an issue that was front and center from the start of the campaign. Even though both major party candidates downplayed race throughout the general election, and Obama's intention from the moment he announced his candidacy was to run as a post-racial candidate, race clearly had an effect on the result. There was a media frenzy concerning the manner in which race would manifest itself throughout the campaign. Much of the media hype surrounded the so-called "Bradley effect," whereby white voters when polled would be reluctant to respond that they were not going to vote for an

TABLE 4.1 WHITE VOTING TRENDS IN PRESIDENTIAL ELECTIONS, 1968–2008

Year	Whites As Percentage of Electorate	Whites Voting Democratic	Whites Voting Republican
1968	90+	38	40
1972	90+	31	67
1976	89	48	52
1980	88	36	56
1984	86	34	66
1988	85	40	60
1992	87	39	41
1996	83	44	46
2000	81	42	55
2004	77	41	58
2008	74	43	55

Sources: Roper Center; CNN Election Center; *New York Times*; Earl and Merle Black, *The Rise of Southern Republicans* (Cambridge, MA: Belnap Press of Harvard University Press, 2002).

TABLE 4.2 PERCENTAGE OF WHITE SUPPORT UNDER 35 PERCENT

State	Obama Percentage of White Vote	State	Obama Percentage of White Vote
Alabama*	10	Oklahoma	29
Alaska	32	South Carolina*	26
Arkansas*	30	Tennessee*	34
Georgia*	23	Texas*	26
Idaho	33	Utah	31
Louisiana*	14	Wyoming	32
Mississippi*	11		

Source: CNN: 2008 Presidential Exit Poll.

* Southern states of the Old Confederacy.

**TABLE 4.3 STATES WHERE OBAMA OBTAINED
A MAJORITY OF THE WHITE VOTE**

State	Obama Percentage of White Vote	State	Obama Percentage of White Vote
CA	52	MI	51
CO	55	MN	53
CT	51	NH	54
DC*	86	NY	52
DE	53	OR	60
HI	70	RI	58
IA	51	VT	68
IL	51	WA	59
MA	57	WI	54
ME	58		

Source: CNN: 2008 Presidential Exit Poll.

* District of Columbia, the nation's capital, but not a state.

African American because of fear that they would be perceived as racists (see Chapter 1). Actually, public opinion already had begun to shift dramatically on the question of willingness to vote for a qualified African American candidate for president. Michael Nelson, Rhodes College political scientist and presidential scholar, stated that, "In a February 2007 Gallup poll, 94 percent of voters said they were willing to support a 'generally well-qualified' African American for president, a number that had risen sharply since 1937, when only 33 percent said they would."[14]

Obama began courting white voters as early as 2004 when he had not even declared his candidacy for the president of the United States. As an African American candidate for the U.S. Senate from Illinois, he was selected in 2004 by John Kerry's campaign manager, Mary Beth Cahill, to deliver the keynote address at the Democratic National Convention in Boston, Massachusetts. Cahill had seen Obama speak on previous occasions and she knew that he would energize voters. He was only the third African American to deliver such a speech at a major political party's convention. The speech was absolutely electrifying in its substance and style. Obama asked the crowd, "Do we participate in a politics of cynicism, or in the politics of hope?" Obama exhorted, "And I stand here today grateful for the diversity of my heritage, aware that my parents' dreams live on in my two precious daughters. I stand here knowing that my story is part of the larger American story, that I owe a debt to all those who came before me, and that in no other country on earth is my story even possible."[15]

It was a brilliantly crafted speech, and Obama was not only taking the convention stage that night, but he was also taking the world stage. Obama was doing more than introducing himself to the world and setting the tone for the Democratic Convention that week. He was very skillfully disarming white America and assuring them that he was a different breed of black politician, with a "new face" and a "new message." Moreover, Obama sought to establish himself as a member of the post-civil rights generation of African American politicians who differ from Rev. Jesse Jackson and Rev. Al Sharpton, who may be seen as polarizing to white voters. At one point in the speech, Obama asserted, "Go into any inner-city neighborhood, and folks will tell you that government alone can't teach our kids to learn. They know that parents have to teach, that children can't achieve unless we raise their expectations and turn off the television sets and eradicate the slander that says a black youth with a book is acting white."[16]

Obama was clearly sending a message to white Americans that he was not averse to taking on the issue of personal responsibility in the African American community. In the speech, Obama declared that there is no black America or white America—only the United States of America. He made an appeal to all Americans to unite across racial and party lines. The speech brought the crowd to its feet and heralded a new political superstar. Most Americans would look back at that speech as when they first were introduced to Barack Obama.

Following that keynote address, Barack Obama has been the "superstar" of the Democratic Party. In the fall of 2006, he campaigned across the country in the midterm elections for Democratic candidates running for office. Everywhere he went there were huge crowds in attendance—black, white, brown, young, old, male and female. Many people brought their children to these rallies. In a personal interview with Nancy Bruner, a white female soccer mom from Southern Indiana, she said she took her children to an Obama rally "because she felt that history was being made and she wanted her children to be a part of it."[17] Obama rallies had an aura about them, a feeling of excitement and a sense of togetherness. One thing that stood out at the Obama rallies more than anything else was the diversity of the crowds. The mainstream media became enamored with Barack Obama (the cable networks appeared mixed) early on largely because of his charismatic style and his seeming indifference to identity politics and grievance. Obama's appeal is largely one that connects with people of all stations in life and transcends race and racial stereotypes. People began comparing him to John F. Kennedy because of his style and inspirational message which, like John Kennedy, offered hope for a new generation of Americans.

It was not long before talk began about Obama running for president. According to *Newsweek* journalist Evan Thomas, in his book, *A Long Time Coming*, one of those people was a Washington, D.C., lawyer by the name of Gregory Craig, who had worked with the powerful in Washington since being an aide to Senator Ted Kennedy in the 1980s. As a 63-year-old baby boomer, he remembered his youthful idealism as a student at Harvard in the 1960s and then at Yale Law School. He longed for someone who appeared above the partisan bickering in Washington. He was invited to hear Obama speak initially as a young state senator from Illinois who was running for the U.S. Senate. Craig was immediately taken aback by Obama. He subsequently read Obama's book, *The Audacity of Hope*, then he read his first autobiography, *Dreams from My Father*, and was hooked. In 2005, at another Obama speech, Craig sat next to an old friend, George Stevens; both had been a part of the Robert Kennedy clan. Stevens leaned over to Craig and asked him what he thought of Obama for president. Moreover, he remarked that he had not heard anyone like this since Bobby Kennedy. Craig replied "sign me up" and the two approached Obama after the speech and queried, "What are you doing in 2008?" The calls for Obama continued to grow. At Coretta Scott King's funeral in early 2006, Ethel Kennedy, the widow of Robert Kennedy, remarked to Obama, "The torch is being passed to you."[18]

Although excitement was building for Obama to run, Obama told fellow Illinois senator Richard Durbin that many of his African American friends were advising him not to run, some of them because they were afraid he would be assassinated. In fact, Durbin began lobbying to get Obama put under Secret Service protection. Obama would be the first candidate in history to receive this protection so early in the primary campaign, on April 3, 2007.[19]

On February 10, 2007, Obama announced his candidacy for president of the United States. The Obama campaign maintained that he decided to run for president in December 2006 during a vacation with his family in Hawaii. Others believe it was around the summer of 2006. Northern Illinois University political analyst Robert Starks remarked about Obama, "His decision to run for president in 2007 was a stroke of genius at a time when most observers gave little chance of success to any Democrat because of the perceived invincibility of the Republican Party."[20] But if the Republican Party had been perceived as invincible, by 2006, there appeared a chink in their armor. The Democrats regained control of both houses of Congress as a result of the midterm elections. With a growing opposition to the war in Iraq (Obama had opposed the war as early as 2002 when he gave a speech expressing his opposition), and the increasing unpopularity of an incumbent president, the Democrats appeared to have a real opening for a presidential bid.

Most political pundits stated that Obama's most difficult challenge in his quest for the White House would be winning the white vote. Team Obama approached the campaign with a delicate task: appeal to white voters without alienating black voters. To accomplish this, Obama attempted to run a campaign that transcended race. Indiana University political scientist Marjorie Hershey, who specializes in media coverage of American campaigns, observed that "His [Obama's] advertising portrayed him interacting with a lot of white citizens and a few black citizens, the same way most other presidential candidates advertise themselves. Black faces were not prominent among the supporters standing behind the candidate at campaign events. Photos of Obama's white mother and grandparents appeared in several of his television ads."[21] Unbelievably, as the campaign came closer to the general election, "the campaign ran ads in which Obama spoke directly to the camera for long periods—a 'talking head' approach that may have seemed old-fashioned to some, but could make the darker skin tones of Obama's face more familiar and reassuring to whites unaccustomed to the sight of a black man running for the nation's highest office."[22] Even though we are in the twenty-first century, in this country, fifty-five years after *Brown v. Board of Education* (1954) outlawed racially separate public schools, America is still reluctant to talk openly about race. Hershey further opined, "Although a small percentage of the American people is willing to express overt racism, social psychologists argue that a substantially larger proportion holds racially biased attitudes of which they may be barely conscious: what some sociologists term 'racism without racists.'"[23]

Obama effectively put together a new coalition of voters for the twenty-first century. One major pillar of that coalition was white voters with college or post-graduate degrees, many of them professionals with white-collar occupations. Obama won 47 percent of those highly educated whites. He carried 52 percent of college-educated white women and 42 percent of college-educated white men. These numbers are greater than for Kerry, Gore, or

TABLE 4.4 PERCENTAGE OF EDUCATED WHITE ELECTORATE VOTING FOR DEMOCRATS, 1988–2008

	College Educated	College-Educated Women	College-Educated Men
2008 (Obama)	47	52	42
2004 (Kerry)	44	49	39
2000 (Gore)	44	52	35
1996 (Clinton)	43	49	36
1992 (Clinton)	40	44	36
1988 (Dukakis)	40	47	34

Sources: National Journal Exit-Poll Analysis; National Election Day Exit Poll.

Clinton, as Table 4.4 illustrates. This trend bodes well for the Democrats because over the last ten years, more college-educated suburban whites have been moving in the Democratic column. According to Ronald Brownstein, "Obama ran well in what might be called suburban melting pots: affluent counties that contain large numbers of both well-educated whites and racial minorities."[24] Brownstein asserted,

> He [Obama] posted big gains in diverse suburban counties from Arlington, Fairfax, and Prince William in Northern Virginia to Arapahoe outside Denver (which like its neighbor Jefferson, had not voted Democratic since 1964) to Mecklenburg and Wake, centered on Charlotte and Raleigh, respectively, in North Carolina. In Florida's Orange County, a mélange of Hispanics and better-educated whites, Obama's 86,000-vote advantage improved on Kerry's margin by a factor of 100.[25]

Brownstein further stated that "Obama's victories in these Sun Belt suburbs extended onto new terrain the Democratic breakthroughs that occurred under Bill Clinton in white-collar suburbs across the Northeast, Upper Midwest, and West Coast."[26] Overall, the white shift was limited and the majority of white voters voted Republican as has been the case for forty years.

Obama and the Black Vote

In politics and comedy, it is all about timing. America has had a sordid racial history that has included slavery and racial apartheid, but finally was poised to elect an African American as president when Barack Obama announced his candidacy. Michael Nelson, Rhodes College political scientist and presidential scholar, quoted noted sociologist Orlando Patterson as saying, "Colin Powell's flirtation with a presidential run was a critical turning point in the shift in white attitude."[27] A generation of young Americans had grown up with a popular culture that had regularly showcased African Americans in the role as president. Nelson remarked on how television audiences had watched black presidents govern calmly and well in recent popular television series such as "24" and in movies like *Deep Impact* and *Head of State.*[28] Yet Obama's political ascendancy was nothing short of amazing. His uniqueness (his father black African and his mother white Kansan), both biologically and historically, gave him the opportunity to offer this nation a message of reconciliation.

Ironically, Nelson asserts that according to David Axelrod, Obama's campaign manager, "The biggest race problem we had to start was not with white voters, but with African American voters."[29] Some early public opinion polling showed that black voters initially favored Clinton over Obama. African American voters initially favored Clinton, by 46 percent to 37 percent in a November 2007 *Wall Street Journal*/NBC News poll.[30] The tremendous support from White America for Obama's presidency gave many in the African American community a moment for pause. Cries rang out in the African American community questioning his "blackness."

Obama, though biracial, has clearly chosen to be identified as an African American; he has said that growing up he yearned to be accepted as a black man. In his 2000 U.S. House race against incumbent Bobby Rush (D-IL), Obama was defeated soundly in the Democratic primary. During the campaign, Congressman Rush accused Obama of not being "black enough." Others said he was too young and needed to wait his turn. Some political observers said this was the best thing that could have happened to Obama. Many constituents stated that Obama's speaking style was more like a law professor than a politician. With respect to Obama's loss to Rush, *Chicago* magazine journalist James Merriner wrote, "He found out a lot about himself . . . He just assumed that he had some natural affinity with black voters."[31]

The Civil Rights Legacy

Obama's mother, "to compensate for the absence of black people in her son's life, brought home books on the Civil Rights movement and recordings of Mahalia Jackson."[32] The civil rights movement of the 1950s and 1960s was primarily concerned with breaking down barriers of racial discrimination and allowing all Americans the opportunity to participate in the democratic process. That included the right of African Americans to run for any political office in the country—including the presidency of the United States. In a strange twist of irony, some of the icons of that movement, among them Andrew Young, were initially reluctant to back Barack Obama. Young, who had been a chief lieutenant to Martin Luther King, Jr., during the movement and a fellow member of the Southern Christian Leadership Conference (SCLC), said he'd like Obama to be president in 2016. Young attributed his pessimism to a combination of political loyalty to Hillary Clinton and deep suspicion about what America would allow. Journalist Gwen Ifill discusses this generational rift among African American leaders in her book, *The Breakthrough*. She writes,

> The rift between black politicians born in the 1930s and 1940s and those born in the 1960s and 1970s is a deep one that is often peppered over. The worldview of older politicians, many of them preachers like Young, was defined by limitation. They could not eat at lunch counters. They could not sit where they liked on buses or vote how and for whom they liked. They could not attend the schools they preferred or aspire to the jobs they believed they were qualified to hold. Every time one of those barriers fell, it was power seized, not given. They marched, they preached, and they protested . . . [33]

Moreover, asserts Ifill,

> Their children, who walked freely down the streets where their parents marched, were raised to believe they could do anything . . . They're idealistic enough not to be carrying the luggage of the older generation . . . These true believers did not grow up with Jim Crow laws or lynching trials, and they lived in a world shaped by access instead of denial.[34]

Ifill quotes Christopher Edley, a former Carter and Clinton administration official, who stated, "The prior generation that they replaced defined their position, their mission, their program, in opposition to whites. And in that sense, the new generation defined their position, their vision, their program in a way that is—again that word we're looking for; it's not *nonracial*, it's not *postracial—supraracial*."[35] There are numerous parallels between the civil rights movement of the 1950s and 1960s and the Obama movement today. Both were grassroots organizations that empowered ordinary citizens to mobilize, set goals, develop strategy, raise money and accomplish their goals. Both organizations were based on change and hope for the future as well as a sense of idealism that they could change this country. Furthermore, Andrew Young and John Lewis, both of whom were on the frontlines of numerous bloody conflicts in the civil rights movement, heard many of their elders tell them to wait, not to get out of line, that they were going too fast, that they were pushing too much. Incredulously, they are now expressing some of those same reservations to a new generation of black leaders. Ron Dellums, the 72-year-old former African American congressional representative, had these rather profound words to say concerning the generational rift: "The older people have to work very diligently not to allow themselves to get into a time warp . . . Each generation carries its own baggage, but the challenge of life is to be able to move beyond the baggage to continue to update and refine, to stay in the moment, to stay in the time, to stay focused on the future . . . And I think too many of our older people continue to view the world through the same old lens."[36]

David Bositis, of the Joint Center for Political and Economic Studies, however, had the following musings about Obama's policy direction if he were to win the election:

> Barack Obama is a constitutional lawyer who has strong commitments to civil rights. If he is elected in a landslide, he may be able to do anything he wants. Civil rights are not going to be the top item on his agenda as president. But, that path has a positive to it. A lot of things can be done in regard to civil rights. There's not much opposition because it's not at the top of other people's agenda.[37]

In the same vein as Bositis, Rep. John Yarmuth (D-KY), who was an early supporter of Obama, stated,

> If you don't think this is, in terms of race relations, a huge step, listen to all of my white friends. They would say, "you know he's

half white?" White people are now wanting to step up and claim him. That gives him power to advance the civil rights agenda. He may not have to advance much of the racial aspect right now.[38]

The Congressional Black Caucus

Political scientist Michael Nelson remarks that "The forty-two member Congressional Black Caucus (CBC) initially split down the middle between Obama and Clinton, with older members from the civil rights era, most of them representing majority black districts, supporting Clinton."[39] Many members of the CBC saw Hillary Clinton as the stronger of the two candidates and felt she would be the better candidate to defeat the Republican nominee in the general election. Moreover, asserts Nelson, "To them, Obama was a newcomer whom they did not know nearly as well as they knew the Clintons; nor did they want to support a candidate whom they expected to lose."[40] It was not that Barack Obama was not an attractive candidate but just that after eight years of a Republican president, many blacks were willing to put aside the historic promise of having the first African American in the White House for another historic occurrence: the first woman in the White House as president. Hillary Clinton was very attractive to many African Americans. Her husband, as president for two terms (1992–2000), had been extremely popular with the African American community, so much so that he was dubbed "the first black president." Moreover, Senator Hillary Rodham Clinton, as the Democratic frontrunner, presented a formidable challenge to Senator Obama. Additionally, some African American ministers were opposed to Obama because "he, unlike Clinton, disdained the custom of passing out 'walking-around money' in the guise of primary day get-out-the-vote expenses."[41]

So, the Obama campaign went into the Iowa caucus on January 3, 2008 (the first contest of the primary election season) with extreme caution. Because of America's racist past, many African Americans were still of the opinion that America was not ready to elect a black president. Many black politicians, entertainers, and civil rights leaders supported Hillary Clinton and saw her as the best candidate for black Americans. If Obama could pull off an upset against the frontrunner Hillary Clinton in the first contest of the election season in predominantly white Iowa (a state that is only 2.6 percent black), he could show black leaders and voters that whites would vote for him. Obama won big in Iowa winning 38 percent of the vote. John Edwards came in second with 29.7 percent, and Hillary Clinton finished a disappointing third with 29.5 percent, which damaged her profile as the inevitable nominee. According to Michael Nelson, "Right after Iowa both candidates' internal polls showed Obama garnering support from 75 percent to 80 percent of African American voters."[42] If Obama began increasing his support among African American voters following the Iowa caucus on January 3, 2008, he essentially solidified that base by the South Carolina primary on January 26, 2008. Following the South Carolina primary, one in which former president Clinton campaigned vigorously for his wife, public opinion polls showed Obama now had more support from the African American community than did Hillary Clinton. Obama's support in the African American community would continue to grow throughout the rest of the campaign. In the general election, Obama won 95 percent of the black vote compared to only 4 percent for John McCain.

After the slow support from the CBC, former director of the NAACP Legal Defense Fund and noted civil rights attorney Julius Chambers is confident that the CBC can remain relevant and positively influence the Obama administration. He stated the following about the CBC in an interview: "They can constantly press the president to do things that will advance opportunities for minorities."[43] Rep. G. K. Butterfield (D-NC), also contends, "The CBC will have access to the Obama administration. In politics, access is critically important. For the past eight years, the CBC did not have access."[44] However, Rep. William Lacy Clay (D-MO) is not as optimistic towards the influence the CBC can exert on the Obama administration, given its lukewarm support:

> I'm going to be careful in how I say this. I don't think CBC did themselves any good by the way this campaign got started. Most of the black caucus was not with Obama. They were going with the conventional political wisdom that is usually wrong inside the beltway. They went with the easiest way out, which was to be with Hillary Clinton. They were very disrespectful of Senator Obama who happens to be a member of our caucus. It was one of those moments that was unnecessary that I hated to see. It divided us as a caucus. Any initiatives and agenda that the caucus pushes at this point will be secondary to this administration. If it is in line with what this administration is about then that's well and good. But at this point, I don't think Mr. Obama is giving too much weight to what the black caucus thinks about his agenda. And I don't blame him.[45]

Obama and the Latino Vote

One key factor that allowed Obama to create a new winning coalition was his ability to tap into the growing segments of the American landscape. No demographic is growing faster than the nation's Hispanic population. *Congressional Quarterly* writer Alan Greenblatt cites a U.S. Census analysis by William H. Frey that states that while black and white growth has slowed considerably, by 9 percent and 2 percent respectively, Hispanics have grown by nearly one-third since 2000.[46] In 2050, it is estimated that the Hispanic population will reach 29 percent or roughly one-third of an entire population of 438 million. Fueling this increase in growth is the immigration of Hispanics. According to the U.S. Census Bureau, the Hispanic population is projected to nearly triple, from 46.7 million to 132.8 million during the 2008–2050 period. Its share of the nation's total population is projected to double, from 15 percent to 30 percent. Thus, nearly one in three U.S. residents would be Hispanic. The black population is projected to increase from 41.1 million, or 14 percent of the population in 2008, to 65.7 million, or 15 percent in 2050.[47]

Those numbers have radically changed. Since the 2000 election, the number of Latino citizens of voting age has increased dramatically. Beyond just eligibility, there are now an estimated 15 million registered Latino voters. That is not the only shift in ethnic politics in America. In past elections, the majority of the Hispanic vote was concentrated in California, Texas, Nevada, New Mexico, Arizona, and Colorado. In the 2008 presidential election, aided by the sharp increase in the number of legal and illegal immigrants in the Midwest and Northeast, the Hispanic vote was of national importance.

As the nation becomes more diverse, the most representative institution of government, Congress, and in particular the Senate, has yet to reflect that diversity. Rep. John Yarmuth (D-KY) sees this as a potential structural hurdle for Obama.

> There's a real interesting thing going on in the Senate. If you look at the 10 largest states in America, population wise, they have over 50 percent of the population of the country, and that's not by coincidence, they are very diverse racially. If you look at the ten smallest states, which in total makes up 10 percent of the population but 20 percent of the Senate, [they] are the least racially diverse states. So now you have almost a majority of the Senate that does not look like the majority of America, and as we move along, this is going to be very problematic.[48]

In 2004, Bush received roughly two-thirds of the Hispanic vote. But after his proposal for comprehensive immigration reform was derailed by congressional conservatives early in his second term, the Republican vote among Hispanics dipped to 29 percent in the 2006 House elections. Therefore, the question going into the 2008 presidential election was whether racial politics would affect the Democratic nomination. After the South Carolina primary, blacks almost unanimously moved to support Senator Barack Obama by margins as great as nine to one, while Senator Hillary Clinton enjoyed a two to one advantage among Hispanics. Numerous political observers attributed Clinton's significant support from the Hispanic community to President Bill Clinton's huge popularity with Hispanic voters during his eight years in the White House. "Taken as a group, Hispanics did well economically during her husband's time in the White House," asserts black voting expert David Bositis.[49] Early on in the election season, states Sergio Bendixen, Clinton's Hispanic pollster, "The Hispanic voter . . . had not shown a lot of willingness or affinity to support black candidates."[50] *Congressional Quarterly* writer Alan Greenblatt quotes Stephan Malanga, a senior fellow at the Manhattan Institute, a conservative think tank:

> There have been some schisms between the two groups. Traditionally black areas of the country that have now become majority Hispanic such as South Central Los Angeles and Compton have become majority Latino, and Hispanics have made strong inroads in southern states such as North Carolina and Georgia, bringing change to communities where blacks had gained economic and political power after years of struggle against Jim Crow laws.[51]

Greenblatt also cites a study done by Duke University political scientist and specialist in racial and urban politics, Paula McClain, asserting that "blacks believe Latinos have robbed them of jobs while Hispanics regard blacks as 'slothful and untrustworthy.'"[52]

One of the most notable divides during the Democratic primary season was the gap between African Americans and Hispanics. The relationship between the two groups has not always been friendly. Greenblatt observes that in local elections "there have been examples both of coalitions built between the two groups, and of one constituency's refusal to vote for candidates drawn from the other. In Democratic primary campaigns over the years in New York and Texas, Hispanics have tended to vote for whites over blacks, and blacks have returned the favor when it comes to contests between Anglos and Hispanics."[53] In an analysis done by the Pew Hispanic Center, for the 2008 Democratic presidential nomination, Hispanics voted for Senator Hillary Clinton over Senator Barack Obama by a margin of nearly two to one based on exit polls taken throughout the primary season.[54] The Bush campaign had made significant inroads into the Hispanic vote and Hillary Clinton had clearly attracted more Hispanics than Obama. Thus, heading into the general election, many of the political observers felt Obama's ability to attract Hispanic voters would be problematic. One of the more interesting stories to come out of the 2008 presidential election was the political power now being wielded by the Hispanic population in America.

As the campaign moved into the general election, Senator John McCain seemed positioned to win support among Hispanic voters. During the fall campaign, *New York Times* reporter Larry Rohter wrote the following about McCain: "He had sponsored legislation for comprehensive immigration overhaul in Congress, made a point of speaking warmly about the contributions of immigrants and was popular among Latinos in Arizona, his home state, which borders three battleground states here in the Southwest: New Mexico, Colorado, and Nevada."[55] Both candidates had courted the Hispanic vote with Spanish-language advertising and numerous campaign events in communities with heavily concentrated Hispanics. With only a couple of weeks left before the November election, Gallup polling showed Hispanic support for McCain nationwide at only 26 percent.[56]

The media fixation on the black and brown problem notwithstanding, the Hispanic support appeared to have shifted from Hillary Clinton in the Democratic primaries to Barack Obama in the weeks before the general election. Furthermore, the economy tended to trump all other issues that seemingly would have favored McCain: immigration and social conservatism. In the end, Obama had concentrated on registering many new and young Hispanic voters. Additionally, his message of change seemed to resonate with Hispanics more than other issues. Hispanics, who comprise 9 percent of the electorate (an increase of 1 percent from 2004), overwhelmingly supported Obama in the general election by more than two to one over McCain. Obama received 67 percent to 31 percent of the eligible Hispanic votes.

Intersections of Race, Class, and Gender

Class

To win the Democratic nomination and the general election, instead of relying on strategies of the past, Obama chose to execute a new strategy which was predicated on creating a new coalition of voters. "It's typical for one candidate to appeal to educated elites, as Obama does, while a rival appeals to 'beer track' blue-collar voters, as Clinton does," states Greenblatt.[57] "What Obama has done differently is wed African Americans, who typically vote along with lower income whites in Democratic primaries, to his base among elites."[58] Political analyst David Bositis observed that "This is the first time African Americans have sided with the educated class."[59] Referring to the leading contenders of the 1984 Democratic primary race, Bositis continues, "Obama is Gary Hart, but with the black vote. Hillary Clinton is Walter Mondale but without any black support. Obama's going to be the first nominee who represents the more educated and higher income Democrats."[60]

Obama's victory is the result, in part, of the fact that educated and upper income voters are both growing in number and becoming more Democratic. McCain won white voters with no college degree 58 percent to 40 percent. Obama received 47 percent of white voters with college or post-graduate degrees. Additionally, college-educated white women gave Obama 52 percent of their vote. Obama won white voters with post-graduate education 55 percent to 45 percent. Thus, it appears that education was a salient variable in determining how whites voted in the general election. There seems to have been a direct proportional relationship between the level of education and support for a candidate: As education increased among white voters, they were more likely to vote for Obama. He has also benefited from unusually high levels of support among young voters of all races. Obama received 66 percent (just under two-thirds) of the vote of all voters between the ages of 18 and 29 compared to 32 percent for McCain. That result is partly explained by that age group's increasing diversity, however, Obama won 54 percent of whites in that age category.

Race

With Obama's campaign, one can clearly see the intersection of race and class. Obama received 95 percent of the black vote in his general election victory over John McCain. Black voters of all income and education levels supported

Obama overwhelmingly. Race was probably the biggest issue in the 2008 presidential election. Never before had an African American been a serious contender for a major party nomination. However, Obama attempted to minimize race and focus on class. His policies were designed from the start to focus on the middle class at the expense of the wealthy. This is where there was friction between the old guard and the new guard of African American leaders. The old guard practiced the politics of compensation: what white Americans owe blacks. Obama, as part of the new guard, is saying let us do it another way.

Because of this, the racial politics of the twenty-first century differ from those of the end of the twentieth century. Many whites were immediately drawn to Obama because he represented a new style of black leadership. But many African Americans supported Obama simply because of the shared history of oppression and common struggle for liberation shared by African people all over the world. Identity politics can be defined as political action to advance the interests of a group whose members perceive themselves to be oppressed by virtue of a shared and marginalized identity (such as race, ethnicity, gender, and sexual orientation).

Gender

In the Democratic primary, the two top contenders were a white female, Hillary Clinton, and a black male, Barack Obama. This country had never elected a woman or an African American as president of the United States. ABC News journalist Jennifer Parker made the following observation about the Democratic primary election:

> It's a quandary for Democratic women who, after decades of choosing between a slate of white males on the ballot competing for their party's nomination, must deal with the possibility that for the first time, identity politics—a desire to politically advance women or African Americans—could play a role in their decision-making.[61]

Parker said that even though Democratic women are aware of the historic nature of the campaign between an African American and a woman, those two factors are not more important than the candidates' stance on issues.[62] In an interview between Parker and Kamala Harris, the first elected African

American female district attorney in California history, Harris asserted, "it is insulting to assume women will make their decision simply on the basis of race or gender."[63] Many black women were especially ambivalent about the two candidates because Bill Clinton had been extremely popular with the African American community during his two terms as president. Many blacks remember the economic prosperity enjoyed under Clinton's administration. In an October 2007 interview conducted by journalist Katharine Seelye of the *New York Times* with Clara Vereen, a local beauty shop owner, in Loris, South Carolina, Ms. Vereen exclaimed, "We always love Hillary because we love her husband."[64]

Because Barack Obama was the first African American running as a serious contender for the Democratic nomination, many African Americans supported him. This debate split families and friendships. For instance, Jacqueline Jackson, wife of former presidential candidate Rev. Jesse Jackson, endorsed Clinton in a South Carolina radio spot. Her husband and her son, Rep. Jesse Jackson, Jr., came out in support of Obama. In fact, Rep. Jesse Jackson, Jr., served as Obama's state co-chairman in Illinois. Georgetown University political science professor Clyde Wilcox, who specializes in gender politics, stated that "Issues trump identity . . . Women voters consistently go for someone who will take care of their policies over someone who looks like them."[65]

Obama executed a campaign strategy that brought together a new coalition of voters that crossed race, gender, and class lines, expanded the electorate and engaged over 40 million youth voters. In courting white voters, he had to be careful not to offend black voters and vice versa. Ironically, it took the support of white voters in Iowa, who gave Obama a victory at their caucus, to convince African American voters that Obama was a viable candidate. Young people enthusiastically supported Obama. His campaign had a progressive message and a charismatic style that appealed to them from the beginning. They have grown up with integration and in a much more racially tolerant society. The Latino vote which supported Hillary Clinton in the primary looked to be a huge hurdle for Obama. However, the majority of the Latino vote came home to Obama in the general election. His vision for a new America has transcended time and place. Finally, women were put in a unique position of having a choice between a white female and a black male. White women Democrats who supported Clinton during the primary ultimately supported Obama in the general election. Black females found themselves having to choose between race and gender in the election. Many were Clinton supporters up until the South Carolina primary (see chapter 5). Others remained loyal throughout the primary stage. In the general election, black females over-whelmingly supported Obama. Obama's candidacy reflects America's changing attitude on race and ethnicity.

5

The Clinton Factor:
Hillary and Bill

That Monday before the primary, we had a debate at Myrtle Beach. At that debate I appeared on this show on CNN and Bill Clinton had made some statements that caused some reaction in the black community. He used the term "fairytale" or whatnot to describe Obama's campaign. And I was asked about it. I said that Bill just needs to chill. That statement just kind of caught on. CNN liked it and it just caught on. That frame wrapped itself around everything going forward. After the primary and Obama won so big, Bill Clinton tried to dismiss the win by saying Jesse Jackson won S.C. Then that phrase was placed on that as well . . . Bill just needs to chill. But I didn't comment, not that I can remember, about anything else that Bill said.[1]

Rep. James Clyburn (D-SC), U.S. House Majority Whip

The Democratic primary for the 2008 presidential election would be like none other. This primary election was transformative because the two top contenders, Hillary Clinton and Barack Obama, were both firsts: No woman or African American had ever won the nomination of a major party in the history of U.S. presidential elections.

Hillary Clinton was the former First Lady when her husband Bill Clinton had been president for two terms (1992–2000). Moreover, she had been a high profile First Lady, often regarded as the most openly active First Lady since Eleanor Roosevelt. Bill Clinton had promised during his campaign that if elected, voters would get "two for one," meaning that his wife would take an active role in his administration. She was involved in policy decisions from the beginning of her husband's administration, most notably as chairwoman of the Task Force on National Health Care Reform, which ultimately went down to defeat. In 2000, Hillary Clinton successfully ran for the U.S. Senate in New York after she and her husband had purchased a home there in 1999. Clinton expressed an interest in running for president in 2002 while a first-term senator. She opted not to run for the Democratic nomination in 2004, however, and successfully ran for reelection to the Senate in 2006. On January 20, 2007, Hillary Clinton announced on her website the formation of a presidential exploratory committee and along with it a video announcement that stated, "I'm in and I'm in to win."[2] It was a very low-keyed announcement in comparison to Obama's announcement three weeks later on February 10, 2007, at the Old State Capitol Building in Springfield, Illinois, where Abraham Lincoln delivered his famous "House divided" speech against slavery in 1858; some 15,000 people gathered to hear his announcement.

Clinton entered the race as the early frontrunner. She had a considerable war chest of $14 million left over from her 2006 Senate race. In January 2007, she announced that she was not accepting public financing for both the primary and general elections because of the spending limitations, and that her goal was to raise at least $60 million in 2007. Moreover, Clinton led in the early public opinion polls. Many felt that the country was more inclined to vote for a woman as its chief executive of the country as opposed to an African American. Even political observers felt that the country would elect a woman before an African American. One reason was that white women had been more successful at winning national public office: the 110th Congress (2006–2008) had seventy-three women in the House of Representatives, and sixteen women in the Senate. Moreover, on January 3, 2007, Democrat Nancy Pelosi of California was elected Speaker of the House of Representatives, the first woman to ever hold that position. There were forty-two African Americans in the House of Representatives and only one in the Senate. Furthermore, at that time there were nine women governors and only one African American governor. Women accounted for 51 percent of the population and African Americans accounted for only 12.7 percent. This was seen by some political junkies as a sign that the country was ready to elect a woman as president since they had seen women in the role of chief executive in various states around the country.

Geraldine Ferraro, the first woman to run as a major party vice presidential candidate, stated, "It's more realistic for a woman than it is for an African

American . . . there is a certain amount of racism that exists in the United States—whether it's conscious or not it's true."[3] However, just as many African Americans were not sure if this country was ready to elect an African American president, there were doubts about a woman being able to win the presidency as well. *Newsweek* magazine depicted Barack Obama and Hillary Clinton on its cover for the week of December 25, 2006, to January 1, 2007, with the caption "The Race Is On, But Is America Ready for Either One?"

Campaign Strategy

Hillary Clinton's strong suit from the beginning was to highlight her managerial skills from "Day One." She felt that contrasting her experience next to Barack Obama and John Edwards would give her an edge with the voters in the Democratic primaries. Mark Penn, who had been Bill Clinton's pollster, emerged as the chief strategist for Hillary Clinton. Penn's plan was for Clinton to build a coalition of voters called the "Invisible Americans," similar to Bill Clinton's "forgotten middle class."

In an article in *The Atlantic* by journalist Joshua Green titled "The Front-Runner's Fall," Mark Penn outlines the coalition as follows:

> As this race unfolds, the winning coalition for us is clearer and clearer. There are three demographic variables that explain almost all of the voters in the primary—gender, party, and income. Race is a factor as well, but we are fighting hard to neutralize it. We are the candidate of people with needs. We win women, lower classes, and Democrats (about 3 to 1 in our favor). Obama wins men, upper class, and independents (about 2 to 1 in his favor). Edwards draws from these groups as well. Our winning strategy builds from a base of women, builds on top of that a lower and middle class constituency, and seeks to minimize his advantages with the high class democrats. If we double perform with WOMEN, LOWER AND MIDDLE CLASS VOTERS, then we have about 55% of the voters.[4]

One of the most interesting points to come out of this memo, observes Green, is that "the coalition that she [Clinton] ended up winning a year later, was the one that was described here."[5]

According to *Time* magazine journalist Karen Tumulty, Clinton made several mistakes early on that may have ultimately cost her the election. She ran on a campaign of experience and competence which Tumulty calls "an incumbent's strategy."[6] The Clinton camp misread the mood of the Democratic primary voters, who were looking for change more than experience. Clinton was the early frontrunner and her strategy was a top-down approach. She planned to focus on the big states and let Obama have the caucus states. She expected the Democratic nomination process to be over after Super Tuesday, February 5, 2008.

The first contest of the Democratic primary election was the Iowa caucus scheduled for January 3, 2008. Clinton opted not to make early visits to some of the early primary states like Iowa and New Hampshire. However, polling after Clinton's Senate reelection campaign in November showed her running in third place behind Edwards and Obama. Clinton decided to campaign more vigorously in Iowa. The Democratic candidates were holding a series of debates in the pre-primary campaign. In one October debate, Democratic candidate Chris Dodd of Connecticut called "foul on an answer Clinton gave on whether she supported a New York state proposal to give drivers' licenses to illegal immigrants."[7] Clinton appeared to avoid giving a clear answer, which political reporters pounced on by asking whether she was prone to do what her husband was famous for doing, and equivocate. Journalist Chuck Todd commented, "While her campaign believes the media pounced unfairly, from that point on, the die was cast, and her lead in the polls began to shrink."[8]

Although Clinton spent heavily in Iowa, she came in third in the caucus ($106 million had been spent by her). The Clinton camp had made a crucial error in underestimating the organizational and fundraising strength of Barack Obama in Iowa. A Clinton win in Iowa would have dealt a crushing blow to Obama and probably sealed the nomination for Clinton, who was the frontrunner and the "inevitable" nominee. Obama gained ground as a result of this win and national polling predicted a victory for him in New Hampshire. But after a disappointing third-place finish in Iowa, Clinton held a conference call with her staff. Joshua Green noted the following exchange:

> Mustering enthusiasm, Clinton declared that the campaign was mistaken not to have competed harder for the youth vote and that—overruling her New Hampshire staff—she would take questions at town-hall meetings designed to draw . . . contrasts with Obama. Hearing little response, Clinton began to grow angry, according to a participant's notes. She complained of being out-

maneuvered in Iowa and being painted as the establishment candidate. The race, she insisted, now had "three front-runners." More silence ensued. "This has been a very instructive call, talking to myself," she snapped, and hung up.[9]

Just as the political pundits were beginning to declare Clinton's campaign over and public opinion polling in New Hampshire gave Obama a ten-point margin, something happened on the day before the polls opened on January 8, 2008. In responding to a question at a campaign event, Clinton became emotional and replied, "I just don't want to see us fall backward as a nation."[10] It showed a human side to Clinton, one that the voters had not seen, and the New Hampshire voters, especially women, were thrilled. Cable news television played the clip throughout the day. Clinton narrowly won a surprise three-percentage-point victory in New Hampshire that gave her campaign much needed new life.

Clinton's Double Bind

Although Hillary Clinton was the 25th woman to run for president in the United States, she is the first woman in the history of this country to have had a legitimate chance at becoming a major political party's presidential candidate. Throughout the Democratic nomination contest, she had to deal with the fact that she was a woman, and she had to deal with what has been referred to as the "double bind."[11] Kathleen Dolan, a University of Wisconsin–Milwaukee political scientist and specialist in women and politics, stated, "Generally, work on women candidates has shown that voters favor more 'male' traits in their elected leaders, which may lead them to choose men candidates over women."[12] Because Clinton was a female, her appearance seemed to be part of the equation as to whom the candidate was. However, none of the male candidates running for president in the Democratic primary faced the same type of commentary and criticism about their clothing and appearance. Women running for political office still face double standards, and Hillary Clinton was no different in the Democratic nomination contest in 2008. Men simply run for political office. In contrast, women face a set of preconceived stereotypes surrounding gender.[13] Journalism and Communication professors Chingching Chang and Jacqueline Hitchon note that even as children, boys and girls are socialized into different roles related to political behavior.[14] Young men have been raised to be leaders, whereas the traditional role for young women has been that of a supporter. As a result of this socialization process, the public has differing expectations concerning the role of male versus female candidates.

Women as political candidates are expected to portray the feminine characteristics ascribed to them in their daily roles as mother, daughter, sister, and wife. Senator Clinton was mocked for wearing pantsuits on the campaign trail. Cable news channel MSNBC commentator Tucker Carlson stated this about Clinton: "There's just something about her that feels castrating, overbearing, and scary."[15] The problem, however, is that political candidates are expected to be aggressive, tough, strong, and rational.[16] In contrast, traits such as nurturing and sensitivity are attributed to women; hence, women do not fit the traditional political mold. Susan Carroll, professor of political science and women's studies at Rutgers University and a specialist on women's and gender studies, argues that successful female politicians must possess and portray masculine traits while simultaneously maintaining a traditional feminine persona.[17] In an article examining gender in the 2008 presidential election, Patricia Lee Sykes, a political scientist at American University specializing in democratic theory and gender studies, asserts that Senator Clinton attempted to follow the model of former British prime minister, Margaret Thatcher, dubbed the "Iron Lady," "and present herself as the strong, experienced candidate capable of tackling tough decisions on war as well as law and order."[18] However, states Sykes, "much of the public responded by perceiving her as cold and hardhearted, and polls repeatedly revealed the public searching for a conciliator, not a combatant, to change the Washington partisan battlefield."[19] To soften her image, Clinton showed a bit of emotion the day before the New Hampshire primary when she expressed her deep commitment and concern for the country. This might have won the hearts of some voters in New Hampshire, but it predictably sparked her opponents to question her qualifications for commander in chief.[20]

Clinton found herself caught in the classic double bind: When she appeared tough, she seemed insensitive; when she expressed emotion and compassion, she conveyed weakness.[21] Clinton was the only woman in an initial field of seven candidates, yet she never seemed to use that to her advantage and to constantly remind voters of that strength.[22] Sykes argues that in this election, "the emergence and dominance of domestic issues would have benefited a woman candidate for president if she had been able to exhibit and emphasize feminalist rather than masculinist aspects of her leadership."[23] An example of Clinton's attempt to present herself as masculine and strong as opposed to feminine and weak involved a cover magazine photo shoot. In January 2008, Clinton declined, at the last minute, to do a cover photo shoot for *Vogue* magazine because of her concern that she might appear "too feminine." The magazine's editor in chief, Anna Wintour, responded by writing, "Imagine to my amazement, when Hillary Clinton, our only female president hopeful had to steer clear of our pages at this point in her campaign, for fear of looking too feminine. The notion that a contemporary woman must look mannish in order to be taken seriously as a seeker of power is frankly dismaying."[24]

Clinton's attempts to portray herself as a "foreign policy expert" and readiness to be commander in chief led to one of her biggest campaign mistakes. Clinton had repeatedly stated during the campaign that on a 1996 visit to U.S. troops in Bosnia-Herzegovina that she had come under hostile fire from snipers. However, news file footage showed that she had arrived safely and received a warm greeting. Later, on the campaign trail, she admitted to having been mistaken about the incident. Clinton's credibility suffered with some voters because of this.

In March 2006, actress Sharon Stone expressed reservations about Hillary Clinton's presidential candidacy when she was quoted as saying, "Hillary still has sexual power, and I don't think people will accept that. It's too threatening."[25] In December 2007, Kathleen Hall Jamieson, an American professor of Communication and the director of the Annenberg Public Policy Center at the University of Pennsylvania, stated that there was a considerable amount of misogyny present on the Internet about Hillary Clinton.[26] Throughout the primary season, the media often commented on Clinton's physical appearance as well as clothing. Oddly enough, in our appearance obsessed society, none of Clinton's male counterparts in the Democratic primaries had to endure such scrutiny. Regrettably, in politics, there is still a double standard in how we judge women and men.

Fundraising

As the presumptive nominee, Clinton had created a group of fundraisers called Hillraisers who collected more than $100,000 for her campaign but were asked to raise as much as $1 million each for her campaign. These included high profile people from government, entertainment, sports, and other areas of the public and private sectors.

In April 2007, Clinton announced that she had raised $26 million dollars during the first quarter of 2007, but the Obama campaign matched it, having raised $25 million during the quarter. Obama put Clinton on notice that he, too, was a formidable fundraiser. Clinton raised $27 million for the second quarter, which came up considerably short against the $32.5 million raised by Obama during that same period. Furthermore, the Obama money came from 258,000 contributors, much of it raised through the Internet.[27] According to the Center for Responsive Politics, during the first six months of 2007, about 70 percent of Clinton's funds came from donors giving the maximum $2,300, compared to 44 percent for Obama. This would impact Clinton's ability, but not Obama's, to raise funds down the road. Federal campaign election law limits individual contributions to a maximum of $2,300 per election cycle. After only six months, many Clinton donors were "maxed out" and would not be able to contribute financially to her campaign until the general election. However, since Obama had received thousands of contributions of $10, $15, and $25, he could continue to solicit contributions from the same people without them having reached their maximum limit.

There were other early signs that Obama was a politically viable candidate. During the 1990s, the Clintons had been extremely successful with fundraising and support from Hollywood and the movie industry in America. Hollywood mogul David Geffen, who had once been a supporter of the Clintons, held a fundraiser for Obama and raised more than $1 million. This was another example of how Obama was on par with Clinton in the ability to raise money early in the primary season.[28] When Obama finished law school in 1991, he returned to Chicago and found friends and powerful patrons there, some black and some white, who were willing and able to boost his career. When Obama married Michelle Robinson, he was also marrying into her network of affluent and upwardly mobile African Africans. This network would later prove key to Obama's meteoric rise in state and national politics. Michelle had powerful connections in the black business community, such as the Alliance of Business Leaders and Entrepreneurs (ABLE); this organization was comprised of black CEOs of Obama's generation who were supporters and fundraisers.[29]

South Carolina Becomes a Defining Moment

As the candidates turned their attention to South Carolina, the issue of "race" came to the fore. Roughly half of the Democratic electorate in South Carolina are African Americans. Shortly before the Democratic primary, the campaign turned "ugly." Hillary Clinton, when trying to make a point about presidential leadership and Barack Obama's constant reference to Dr. Martin Luther King, Jr., said, "Dr. King's dream began to be realized when President Lyndon Johnson passed the Civil Rights Act of 1964. It took a president to get it done."[30] Clinton denied any racial intent but the comment angered many civil rights-era blacks. Dr. King had given his famous "I Have a Dream" speech in front of 200,000 people on the steps of the Lincoln Memorial in Washington, D.C., at the March on Washington for Jobs and Freedom on August 28, 1963. One of the stated goals of the march was to urge Congress and the president to pass a comprehensive civil rights bill outlawing discrimination in all areas of public accommodation, among other things. It was the culmination of decades of litigation, protests, marches, demonstrations, boycotts, sit-ins, and other forms of nonviolent civil disobedience to force America to abandon its system of racial apartheid and provide equal citizenship rights for all Americans. Congress passed the civil rights bill and it was signed into law by the president but only after ordinary citizens from all walks of America made it happen.

> So if you are looking for a laboratory where there's a cheap media market and you'd be able to look back on the results to get a good feel for how that candidate will be able to conduct him or herself going forward, South Carolina is your place . . . I promised those people that if they gave South Carolina the first nation's primary, I would not get involved because one of the things that was used against us is that Jim Clyburn is majority whip and if he gets actively involved in the campaign it could not give us a fair stake.[31]

South Carolina representative James Clyburn, as the Majority Whip, was the highest ranking African American in the U.S. House of Representatives; he was also a veteran of the civil rights movement. Clyburn had previously vowed to remain neutral during the Democratic nomination process. However, he told the *New York Times* that "he had been 'bothered a great deal' by the remarks and was rethinking his position."[32] Additionally, the African American radio stations throughout South Carolina were incensed over Hillary Clinton's comments and they became a topic of discussion on black radio.

Because she was behind Barack Obama in public opinion polls, Clinton chose to leave the campaign trail in South Carolina before the primary and campaign in some of the Super Tuesday states. Her husband Bill Clinton stayed behind in South Carolina and continued to campaign for his wife.

Bill Clinton and Barack Obama began engaging in a series of discussions. According to *New Yorker* writer Ryan Lizza, Obama began arguing that "the country's economic troubles are as much Clinton's fault as Bush's—he blames Clinton-era deregulation of the telecommunication and banking industries—and he implicitly accuses Bill Clinton of surrendering to special interests."[33] Bill Clinton responded with comments that were perceived by many as limiting the post-racial significance of the Obama campaign. Although both sides attempted to downplay the rhetoric, Democratic voting became more polarized as a result and Clinton lost much of her support in the African American community. On primary election day, Obama won handily over Clinton, garnering 55 percent of the vote to her 27 percent and 80 percent of the African American vote.

On the day of the primary, Bill Clinton compared Obama's expected win to Jesse Jackson's victory in the 1988 South Carolina primary. These comments were widely criticized as an attempt to minimize the primary results and marginalize Obama as the "black" candidate. Ironically, because of Bill Clinton's popularity in the African American community, Hillary Clinton had felt she could win a portion of the black vote.[34] According to Lizza, an aide to Obama stated that Rep. James Clyburn informed him that "[Bill] Clinton called him in the middle of the night after Obama won that state's primary and raged at him for fifty minutes . . . It's pretty widespread now that African Americans have lost a whole lot of respect for Bill Clinton."[35] To quote Chuck Todd of NBC News, "Bubba was seen as dissing Obama, and this caused the black vote to solidify for Obama in a way that even the Obama campaign didn't expect."[36] Bill Clinton had now become a liability rather than an asset for Hillary Clinton. Democratic stalwarts were asking him to tone down the rhetoric. According to CNN political correspondent Candy Crowley, whether it was supporters inside or outside the Clinton campaign, there was "a huge wave of sentiment that Bill Clinton needs to stop."[37]

One of the most bizarre ironies to come out of the 2008 presidential election is that Bill Clinton appears to have injected race into the presidential campaign leading up to the South Carolina primary. "By injecting himself into the Democratic primary campaign with a series of inflammatory and negative statements, Bill Clinton may have helped his wife's presidential hopes in the long term but at a cost of his reputation with a group of voters, African Americans that have been one of his strongest bases of political support."[38]

According to NBC News political director Chuck Todd, "It was at this point in the campaign that the Democratic electorate started to break into two very formidable coalitions. The Obama coalition was made up of African-Americans, college-educated whites, and young voters. Clinton's coalition was Latinos, women, and non-educated whites."[39] Todd asserted that "Obama's coalition proved to be the winning one for a few reasons, mostly a matter of timing. The primaries in February featured states that were dominated by Obama's while Clinton's coalition really didn't dominate any state primaries until much later when the campaign was all but over."[40]

Super Tuesday

The Clinton camp had planned on winning the nomination by Super Tuesday. This was the day when the largest number of states held their primary elections. Since the early 1970s, many states had moved their primaries or caucuses up to this date so that they could gain attention from the media and candidates. The process, known as front-loading, has allowed the nominee to be selected much earlier in the nomination season. On that date, set for February 5, 2008, twenty-three states and territories held their primaries and caucuses. Mark Penn, Clinton's chief strategist, had argued that "California would put her [Clinton] over the top because she would pick up all the state's 370 delegates."[41] And on Super Tuesday, Clinton won California, New York, New Jersey, and Massachusetts. This was according to the Clinton strategy. However, Obama won more states and actually gained more pledged delegates because of the system of delegate allocation that the Democratic Party used for 2008. Democrats, unlike Republicans, apportion their delegates based on the percentage of primary votes they win, with a minimum 15 percent threshold required in order to get any delegates.[42] Unfortunately, for Clinton, it was the Republicans who in most primaries follow the winner-take-all rule. Both candidates declared victory coming out of Super Tuesday with Obama winning thirteen states and territories to Clinton's ten. However, Clinton expected the race to be over and she had not organized troops in states whose primaries followed—and she was out of money.[43] Clinton even revealed that she had personally loaned her campaign $5 million in January 2009.

The Role of the Media

The role of the media can have a significant impact on any modern political campaign and the 2008 presidential campaign was no different. By December

2007, Clinton's senior advisers had begun complaining that the Obama campaign was receiving much more favorable coverage than Hillary Clinton. According to an article by *Washington Post* columnist Howard Kurtz, some journalists agree. Kurtz quotes Mark Halperin, *Time* magazine's editor-at-large, who lamented about Hillary Clinton:

> She's just held to a different standard in every respect. The press rooted for Obama to go negative, and when he did he was applauded. When she does it, it's treated as this huge violation of propriety. While Clinton's mistakes deserve full coverage, the press's flaws—wild swings, accentuating the negative—are magnified 50 times when it comes to her. It's not a level playing field.[44]

Moreover, remarked Halperin, "Your typical reporter has a thinly disguised preference that Barack Obama be the nominee. The narrative of him beating her is better than her beating him, in part because she's a Clinton and in part because he's a young African American . . . There's no one rooting for her to come back."[45]

To illustrate how life sometimes imitates fiction, "Saturday Night Live," the popular weekend late-night sketch comedy and variety show, played a pivotal role in the 2008 Democratic primary. In late February 2008, as Obama and Clinton were battling for delegates, "SNL" performed a sketch of a Democratic debate lampooning the perceived media bias favoring Barack Obama over Hillary Clinton. The skit showed starry-eyed supporters fawning over Obama. Clinton used the sketch to argue that Obama had not received proper scrutiny and even mentioned the sketch in one of the actual Democratic debates. The media responded by taking a more critical look at Obama. Furthermore, Ben Smith, senior political writer and blogger for Politico.com, wrote that Bill Clinton "suggested that media bias will force Clinton to go negative on Barack Obama."[46] Ultimately, Clinton chose to go negative. One particularly powerful advertisement aired in Texas prior to that state's primary in which Hillary Clinton questioned Obama's readiness to be commander in chief from Day One. The advertisement shows a little girl tucked up in bed, while the presidential candidate answers the phone in the White House. The ad, which has become known as the "3 a.m. phone call," features a voice-over asking: "It's 3 a.m. and your children are safely asleep. Who do you want answering the phone?" The picture then cuts to a bespectacled Mrs. Clinton picking up the White House phone. This advertisement is credited with putting Clinton's primary campaign back on track.

Sykes said that "By gender necessity, Clinton's commercials emphasized her commanding capabilities . . . and her extensive experience in the White House as well as the Senate. The ad is reminiscent of Barry Goldwater's girl-with-a-daisy/mushroom-cloud ad in 1964."[47] Moreover, in an article on gender and negative campaigning, Paul Herrnson, Director of the Center for American Politics and Citizenship at the University of Maryland, and Jennifer Lucas, a Ph.D. student at Maryland, argue that "women who campaign against male opponents who decide to use negative campaigning as part of their strategies may be hurt by voters' perceptions that they are too harsh and the more negative of the two, even when both candidates run negative ads."[48]

The Rhetoric Heats Up

After the Democratic primaries and caucuses in March, there was a six-week stretch with no contests until Pennsylvania on April 22. In mid-March, clips of controversial sermons from Obama's former pastor, Rev. Jeremiah Wright, appeared on YouTube, and the cable news network stations aired them continuously. Obama responded to the controversy by giving a speech in Philadelphia on race (see Chapter 6). Although Obama had a substantial lead in the overall delegate count, Clinton knew she had a large swath of Appalachian voters from Pennsylvania down to Kentucky that were part of her coalition. Clinton appeared to think that she could still win the nomination by raising doubts about Obama's electability, particularly among blue-collar white voters and women. According to Ryan Lizza, Bill Clinton, while campaigning in Pennsylvania, told one white working-class audience, "She's in it for you and she's in it because of you. People like *you* have voted for her in every single state in the country."[49] The implication here was that people who voted for Obama were somehow different.

Wilfred McClay, professor of history at the University of Tennessee at Chattanooga, remarked that Clinton's appeal to working-class white voters in Ohio, Pennsylvania, West Virginia, and Kentucky was further enhanced by crossover votes from Republicans.[50] Clinton received an unexpected boost from conservative talk show host Rush Limbaugh in his attempt to prolong the primaries and divide the Democratic Party. Limbaugh came up with a plan for his listeners to vote for Clinton in their state's primary. This concept, formally known as raiding, consists of voters of one party crossing over and voting in the primary of another party, effectively allowing a party to help choose its opposition's candidate. The theory is that opposing party members vote for the weakest candidate of the opposite party in order to give their own party the advantage in the general election.[51]

Meanwhile, Obama had been speaking to a private group in San Francisco, California, when he stated that "some Pennsylvanians were 'bitter' and would 'cling' to guns and religion, because jobs fell through the Clinton Administration and the Bush Administration."[52] This offended many of the blue-collar voters in Pennsylvania, West Virginia, and Kentucky—states that were yet to hold their primaries. The cable news cycle picked up on these comments and played them repeatedly. Bill Clinton took the offense and the two continued their campaign sparring. The tension reached a head, according to Ryan Lizza, when on the day before the Pennsylvania primary, Clinton lost his "cool" when a radio talk show host asked him about his Jesse Jackson comments. Lizza stated that "Clinton went on a three-minute rant in which he posited the mysterious theory that Obama had played the race card against *him*."[53]

The damage had been done with Obama's comments about "guns and religion." These comments were seen by many as elitist and condescending. The media began doing stories about blue-collar white voters in these states who began telling the media that voting for Barack Obama would be problematic for them. In an article titled "Race on the Trail" that appeared in the *Pittsburgh Post-Gazette* after the West Virginia primary, staff writer Dennis Roddy wrote, "Prior exit polls produced numbers showing voters in a variety of states—including Pennsylvania and Ohio—acknowledging that a candidate's race played a role in their decision-making."[54] By this point, however, Obama's delegate count was insurmountable. According to Rick Pearson, a writer for *The Swamp*, a political blog of the *Chicago Tribune*'s Washington Bureau: "Tired of hearing TV pundits declare 'last call' for her presidential campaign, Sen. Hillary Clinton used a famed bourbon distillery to pronounce her broadcast critics as members of an elite wealthy class that isn't troubled by the costly problems facing average Americans."[55] Clinton won in those Appalachian states of Pennsylvania, West Virginia, and Kentucky. However, it was not enough to overtake Obama's lead in pledged delegates and ultimately superdelegates.

Hillary Clinton began the campaign for president in 2008 as the Democratic frontrunner. She had name recognition having been the First Lady for eight years when her husband was president. She was in her second term as a senator from New York and she had a distinguished career of public service. In politics, timing is everything. Clinton had a high profile as a woman who was qualified and had experience. But voters wanted Obama's message of change over her message of experience. Unlike the Obama campaign, the Clinton campaign was in constant upheaval. Her campaign team was undisciplined in contrast with the Obama team that took a page from George W. Bush's two presidential campaigns, and ran a highly disciplined operation. Clinton made numerous personnel changes throughout her campaign because of the bickering that occurred much of the time. A *New York Times* article stated that as Clinton "flew from town halls to rallies on the road, she did little to stop the infighting back home among advisers who nursed grudges from their White House days."[56] Clinton and Obama both faced stereotyping. The concept of aggressive black masculinity is the lead story on most television news broadcasts on a daily basis. Obama, however, presented himself as a new brand of leadership with progressive ideas that moved beyond the civil rights movement and offered the American electorate a new face and a new style of campaigning, whereas Clinton seemed to get hung up on the gender stereotyping and was unable to break out of the classic double bind.

6

The Campaign for the White House

Three reasons for Obama having the possibility of being a transcendent figure are: 1) He would change the perception of America overnight. 2) He was the only candidate that can truly bring a bipartisan approach to government. 3) No matter how talented Hillary is, if she were elected, her administration would be the same thing we saw with her husband and we now see with Bush.[1]

Rep. John Yarmuth (D-KY)

Barack Obama's decision to run for president of the United States in 2007 was a stroke of genius. Everyone told him he was too young and it was not his time. But Barack Obama is one of the most brilliant political figures of our time, and he is uniquely qualified to lead America. Obama has created a new paradigm on how campaigns will be run in the twenty-first century, as well as a new political rhetoric. At a time when politics in America is filled with cynicism and partisan bickering, Obama sees an optimistic future for Americans and challenges America to be so audacious. In his keynote address at the 2004 Democratic National Convention, he introduced himself to America and spoke passionately about "one America." In a country that continues to judge people based on their race, and the size of their pocketbooks, Obama appeals to America to make good on its promises. One of his most brilliant characteristics is his sense of timing. He knew that America would be ready for him even if the establishment was not. Obama looked to the future when his opponents looked to the past. His campaign slogan embodied it: Change We Can Believe In.

Dynamics of the Nomination Process

Obama's road to the White House started with a small group of advisers that had orchestrated his 2004 Senate election in Illinois: David Plouffe as his campaign manager; David Axelrod as his chief campaign strategist; Robert Gibbs, communications spokesman; Anita Dunn, communications, policy, and research; and Valerie Jarrett, as a senior adviser. When Obama met with his chief operating officer Betsy Myers around the time he was forming an exploratory committee to run for president, he laid down three ruling principles: 1) run the campaign with respect; 2) build it from the bottom up; and 3) no drama. No Drama Obama became the ethos for the campaign.[2] In an interview with Karen Tumulty, Obama stated that his team had the same philosophy: "Because I was not favored, that meant that the people who signed up for this campaign really believed in what the campaign was about. So they weren't mercenaries. They weren't coming in to just attach to a campaign . . ."[3] Valerie Jarrett remarked that when the campaign for the presidency began, Obama announced that he wanted to run a grassroots campaign; he had seen it work as a community organizer and he wanted to take the model and go national. Secondly, Obama ran on a strategy of change. It was a fifty-state strategy based on change and left of center progressive policies, a swift and clean end to the war in Iraq, and economic policies that support a strong middle class. Obama had an organization of tens of thousands of people spread out all over the country who were tuned into regular messages that were sent and broadcast from the campaign's official website, YouTube, MySpace, Facebook, and Twitter. Obama vowed from the start that he would not accept campaign donations from federal lobbyists or political action committees. Moreover, he made a calculated decision not to accept public financing, a decision that he would later benefit tremendously from by being able to raise enough money to mount a fifty-state campaign.

The campaign began in earnest after the 2006 midterm elections. By February 2007, eight major Democratic candidates had opened their campaigns. The primary season was a little less than a year away with the first caucus to be held in Iowa on January 3, 2008, followed by the first primary in New Hampshire on January 8, 2008. As early as October 2007, Hillary Clinton, John Edwards, and Barack Obama were seen as the Democratic frontrunners. Of those three, Hillary Clinton was the favorite. It was easy to see why Clinton was the early frontrunner. She had money, experience, and the most recognizable brand name in Democratic politics in America. In early

TABLE 6.1 GENERAL ELECTION MATCHUPS
(AMONG REGISTERED VOTERS)

Republican Candidate	Percentage	
	Clinton	*GOP Opponent*
Rudy Giuliani	48	50
John McCain	50	47
	Obama	*GOP Opponent*
Rudy Giuliani	43	52
John McCain	48	48

Source: Gallup Organization: *USA Today*/Gallup poll, conducted Feb. 9–11, 2007.

trial heat polls, Clinton led Obama in Democratic primary matchups, but Obama ran nearly as well as Clinton in general election matchups against the leading Republican contenders (see Table 6.1).

David Plouffe, Obama's campaign manager, outlined a simple initial strategy: concentrate on four early states—Iowa, New Hampshire, Nevada and South Carolina. According to Plouffe, "Mission No. 1 was finishing ahead of Hillary Clinton in Iowa. If we hadn't done that, it would have been hard to stop her."[4] Obama had a difficult task against a formidable opponent. Iowa is a state that is 90 percent white. Most political observers assumed that Obama would eventually gain the support of black Americans but the key question was, can he draw voters from other demographic groups? Learning a lesson from the Howard Dean campaign of 2004, the Obama camp knew it had to build a network made up of Iowans rather than supporters brought in from other parts of the country.

Obama Finds His Rhythm

On November 10, 2007, the Iowa Democratic Party held its annual Jefferson-Jackson Dinner in Des Moines. It was an opportunity for all of the candidates to make their case to the party faithful before the caucuses on January 3, 2008. The candidates were not allowed to use teleprompters. Obama memorized his speech and practiced it until it was sharp. The Obama supporters were the largest contingent in the hall. Obama spoke last and electrified the crowd. It was a great speech, not only for style but for substance as well. At one point,

Obama told the story of an incident earlier in the campaign when he faced a small, bored crowd in Greenwood, South Carolina, and a single black woman in the audience revived his spirit by getting the crowd to chant, responsively, "Fired up! Ready to go!" In his book *A Long Time Coming*, Evan Thomas wrote that syndicated columnist "David Broder was watching and understood that Obama had found the Force. The speech became Obama's standard stump speech."[5] Obama closed his speech with the charge, "Let's go change the world." Noted Broder, "There is a jolt of pure electrical energy at those closing words."[6]

All great speeches have a certain rhythm and cadence to them. Obama caught his stride with this speech. As Obama was campaigning in Iowa, the crowds began growing larger and larger. Obama had given an anti-Iraq War speech in 2002 around the same time as U.S. lawmakers were debating whether to give President Bush the authority to launch a war against Iraq.[7] In 2007, Obama would use his anti-war stance as a point of entry into the 2008 presidential election. Unlike Clinton and Edwards, who had voted for the war, Obama had been opposed to the Iraq War from the beginning. Obama's strategy would be to build a coalition in Iowa of anti-war voters, young people, and progressives. According to all reports, Obama was beating Clinton in the operational aspects of the campaign.

The "O" Factor

The Obama campaign announced in mid-November 2007 that Oprah Winfrey would be campaigning for Obama in the early primary states of Iowa, New Hampshire, and South Carolina.[8] Oprah Winfrey is the guru of talk show hosts and her show is seen by viewers all across America. The "O" tour dominated the news for several weeks. They both hailed from Chicago and both had names beginning with "O." Public opinion polls began to show that Clinton was losing some ground in Iowa over Barack Obama and John Edwards.[9]

In December 2007, Oprah appeared with Obama as a warm-up act, and tens of thousands of people began showing up at the rallies. At one rally, Obama recalled how in *The Autobiography of Miss Jane Pittman*, the enslaved Pittman was searching for "the One," the child savior who would lead her people to freedom. Oprah said, "I'm here to tell y'all, he is the one . . ."[10] Her celebrity endorsement and actual campaigning for Obama were huge. Oprah had already accomplished on one level what Obama was attempting to accomplish on another: She had transcended race with her television show geared to women that had been on air for many years. In the United States alone, her show is viewed by roughly thirty million people a week and geared primarily to women. So, many of these voters had to be thinking: If Oprah thinks Obama is OK, then he must *be* OK.

The Iowa campaign was amazing. It would be a true test for Obama and his youth-oriented and technology-fueled organization. With a practice that began in Iowa, the Obama Chicago headquarters "turned over its voter lists— normally a closely guarded crown jewel—to volunteers, who used their own laptops and the unlimited night and weekend minutes of their cell-phone plans to contact every name and populate a political organization from the ground up."[11] Moreover, Howard Dean's 2004 campaign manager was quoted as saying, "The tools were there, and they built on it . . . In a lot of ways the Dean campaign was like the Wright Brothers. Four years later we're watching the Apollo project."[12] According to Tumulty, "Not until the morning of the caucuses did the campaign reach its goal of 97,000 Iowans pledged to support Obama that it thought it would need to win."[13] On January 3, 2008, Obama won the Iowa caucuses by eight percentage points over John Edwards who finished second while Hillary Clinton finished third. Obama counted Iowa as his biggest victory. In a speech that night, Obama reflected, "On this January night, at this defining moment in history, you have done what the cynics said we couldn't do . . . And our time for change has come."[14] The following day two of the Democratic contenders, Joe Biden and Christopher Dodd, withdrew from the presidential race.

Obama appeared to have seized the momentum coming out of Iowa and going into New Hampshire one week later, but Clinton won a surprising victory over Obama in New Hampshire. On the night of the New Hampshire primary, Barack Obama delivered a rousing speech in Nashua, New Hampshire. After congratulating Clinton on her victory, Obama then began to reiterate his message of change and talk about a new American majority. He answered his critics, who accused him of offering the American people false hope:

> But in the unlikely story that is America, there has never been anything false about hope. For when we have faced down impossible odds; when we've been told that we're not ready, or that we shouldn't try, or that we can't, generations of Americans have responded with a simple creed that sums up the spirit of a people

. . . we will begin the next great chapter in America's story with three words that will ring from coast to coast; from sea to shining sea—Yes. We. Can.[15]

Will.i.am, founding member of the musical group The Black Eyed Peas, said that the speech touched him and he was inspired to write and perform Obama's speech in a song titled "Yes We Can Song" on the Internet with many of his fellow musicians—musicians of different races and ethnicities. This song, an instant hit on the Internet, was a game changer for Obama. Obama's message of hope was registering particularly with young people. Ironically, as the political pundits wondered whether America was ready to vote for an African American as president, the youth of America were saying, "Yes, we are." Young people, 18- to 30-year-olds, liked Obama's inspirational message of hope. They liked someone who was trying to appeal to something other than fear. The millennial generation, on the whole, likes to think that it is beyond the racial divisions that have marked this country in the past. So, the fact that Obama was a minority was appealing to many of the majority, particularly the young. The song came to embody the spirit and essence of this new majority coalition Obama was building. By early February, the song already had over five million views on the Internet.

Bill Richardson, the only Hispanic in the Democratic primary, withdrew from the race two days after the New Hampshire primary. Clinton went on to win the Nevada caucuses eleven days later. Dennis Kucinich withdrew from the race after Nevada. In a span of sixteen days, four candidates had dropped out of the Democratic race. Only Obama, Clinton, Edwards, and Gravel remained.

The Hillary and Bill Stonewall

Up to this point, all of the contests had taken place in states with a relatively small African American population. Toward the end of January, all eyes turned to the South Carolina primary, where roughly 50 percent of the Democratic electorate was black. The Democratic primary turned ugly in South Carolina (see Chapter 5). The atmosphere was rife with tension. A debate was held at Myrtle Beach, South Carolina, hosted by the Congressional Black Caucus and the Cable News Network (CNN). The three top contenders were the only participants. Obama and Clinton engaged in one heated exchange about Ronald Reagan being a transformative political leader with Obama telling

TABLE 6.2 SOUTH CAROLINA OFFICIAL RESULTS

	Hillary Clinton	John Edwards	Barack Obama
Totals	140,990	93,801	294,898
Percentage	27%	18%	55%

Source: South Carolina State Election Commission: Democratic Presidential Preference Primary—01/26/08.

Clinton at one point "OK. Well, I can't tell who I'm running against sometimes."[16] Obama would go on to win the South Carolina primary by more than a two to one margin over Clinton (see Table 6.2). Shortly thereafter, John Edwards suspended his candidacy.

Super Tuesday

After the South Carolina primary, Obama received a huge boost from two members of America's most famous political family, the Kennedys. On Sunday, January 27, Caroline Kennedy, the daughter of President John F. Kennedy, wrote an op-ed piece in the *New York Times* whereby she endorsed Barack Obama for president. This was quite unique given that Hillary Clinton was the junior senator from New York, Caroline Kennedy's own state, and that Clinton was the first woman candidate to have a realistic chance of winning her party's nomination and becoming president. In her op-ed piece, Kennedy drew comparisons between her father and Obama. She said that many people had told her that Obama was generating the kind of excitement in the electorate not seen since John F. Kennedy, and that his message of inspiration and hope reminded them of Kennedy.[17] Obama also received the endorsement of Senator Ted Kennedy, the lone surviving brother of John F. Kennedy; this was a huge endorsement for Obama. Both Clinton and Obama headed into Super Tuesday relatively neck and neck in the delegate count.

Super Tuesday was held on February 5, 2008, with primaries in twenty-three states and territories. Clinton and Obama came out of Super Tuesday essentially tied (though Obama lost California) with Obama winning 847 delegates to Clinton's 834. For the remainder of February, ten states, one territory, and the District of Columbia held primaries or caucuses and Obama won all of them—an amazing ten consecutive victories after Super Tuesday. By the end of February, Obama led Clinton in the pledged delegate count

1,192 to Clinton's 1,035. Four contests were held on March 4 with Clinton winning more delegates. However, Obama erased that lead by winning Wyoming and Mississippi.

The Reverend Wright Controversy

In March 2008, clips of Rev. Jeremiah Wright, Obama's former pastor, resurfaced on YouTube and the cable news networks began playing them around the clock. Rev. Wright was pastor of Trinity United Church of Christ on the South Side of Chicago. Trinity is a large African American church (with a membership that had grown to 4,000) known for its community organizing to provide social programs for the disadvantaged. When Obama had first moved to Chicago to engage in community organizing in 1985, he worked in low-income neighborhoods on the far South Side of the city through an organization called the Developing Communities Project (DCP), a faith-based program that involved about twenty-five churches. In 1987, Obama was given the name of Rev. Jeremiah Wright when he was trying to make introductions to pastors who he thought might be interested in organizing. Wright's church was known for being popular among young black professionals. Obama wrote of his first encounter with Wright in his book, *Dreams from My Father*:

> He had grown up in Philadelphia, the son of a Baptist minister. He had resisted his father's vocation at first, joining the Marines out of college, dabbling with liquor, Islam, and black nationalism in the sixties. But the call of his faith had apparently remained, a steady tug on his heart, and eventually he entered Howard, then the University of Chicago, where he spent six years studying for a Ph.D. in the history of religion. He learned Hebrew and Greek, read the literature of Tillich and Niebuhr and the black liberation theologians. The anger and humor of the streets, the book learning and occasional twenty-five cent word, all this he had brought with him to Trinity . . . it became clear in this very first meeting that, despite the reverend's frequent disclaimers, it was this capacious talent of his—this ability to hold together, if not reconcile, the conflicting strains of black experience—upon which Trinity's success had ultimately been built.[18]

To understand Obama's relationship with Rev. Wright, one needs to understand Obama's ties to Chicago. According to David Mendell, in his 2007 book, Obama first met Michelle Robinson after his first year at Harvard Law in 1988, when he was a summer intern in the Chicago office of a law firm now called Sidney Austin. Robinson was assigned to be Obama's mentor. Barack and Michelle continued to date throughout his remaining years at Harvard. Michelle was from the South Shore neighborhood of Chicago's sprawling South Side African American community. Obama, who referred to his own childhood as an orphan, found Michelle's upbringing to be the stability he longed for.

The Obamas chose to live in Chicago's Hyde Park neighborhood along the lakefront on the city's South Side, a racially integrated neighborhood, college educated with mixed-race couples. After a four-year courtship the couple were married in 1992 by Rev. Wright at Trinity United Church of Christ; later they joined the church. The first hint of controversy arose when Obama announced his candidacy for president of the United States in Springfield, Illinois, on February 10, 2007. Rev. Wright was originally scheduled to deliver the invocation but he was removed from the program after Obama called him the night before and rescinded the invitation.[19] According to *New York Times* journalist Jodi Kantor, some black leaders questioned "Obama's decision to distance his campaign from Rev. Jeremiah Wright because of the campaign's apparent fear of criticism over Wright's teachings, which some say are overly Afrocentric to the point of excluding whites."[20] However, the Obama campaign stated that Rev. Wright's invitation was withdrawn "because it did not want the church to face negative attention."[21] Wright, however, did attend the announcement and even prayed with Obama beforehand.

Tapes of some of Rev. Wright's sermons emerged on YouTube in March 2008. One in particular was played repeatedly on cable news television. In it, Wright said, "God damn America for treating our citizens as less than human. God damn America for as long as she acts like she is God and she is supreme."[22] Obama had a close relationship with Rev. Wright. He had served as a mentor for Obama. In fact, Obama named the title of his second book, *The Audacity of Hope* (2006), after one of Rev. Wright's sermons. Many of the political pundits wondered how Obama could run for president of the United States of America, yet for twenty years remain a member of a church whose pastor, during the course of some of his sermons, so forcefully condemned America. Obama responded that he hadn't attended service when Wright had delivered those incendiary sermons. The pressure on Obama to do something was mounting as Wright's inflammatory comments threatened to derail Obama's bid for the presidency. News accounts surfaced that talk show host Oprah Winfrey had once been a member of Wright's church from 1984 to 1986 but had left because of his incendiary comments. Religion scholar Jason Byassee argues that black churches and their role in American society has been that "African Americans have generated distinctly black forms of Christianity since they arrived on these shores."[23] For example, in the 1930s, Nation of Islam leader Elijah Muhammad relocated his headquarters from Detroit to Chicago and began preaching black nationalism—the concept that blacks had to radically separate from all whites. Trinity United Church of Christ has played an important role in Chicago by providing blacks with a Christian alternative to the black nationalist groups that had headquartered in the city during the modern civil rights movement. In a discussion of the interpretive models of black churches found in the scholarly literature, religion historian Julia Speller argues Trinity United Church of Christ fits a more recently developed model, *The Dialectical Model*, which is mirrored in sociologist W. E. B. Du Bois' concept of "double consciousness."[24] Du Bois explained this dichotomy:

> The history of the American Negro is the history of this strife— this longing to attain self-conscious manhood, to merge his double self into a better and truer self. In this merging he wishes neither of the older selves to be lost. He does not wish to Africanize America, for America has too much to teach the world and Africa; he does not wish to bleach his Negro blood in a flood of white Americanism, for he believes that Negro blood has yet a message for the world. He simply wishes to make it possible for a man to be both a Negro and an American without being cursed and spit upon by his fellows, without losing the opportunity of self-development.[25]

Barack Obama had not foreseen that one day he would have to defend his continued association with Wright. Obama decided to address the issue of race front and center. Ironically, in a campaign that Obama was running to deemphasize race, and to transcend race, his former African American pastor forced him to talk about race. On March 18, 2008, Obama delivered a speech in Constitution Center in Philadelphia, across the street from where the founding fathers of this nation gathered to write the U.S. Constitution in the spring of 1787.

In the speech, Obama spoke of how slavery as an institution was sanctioned by the Constitution but how successive generations have protested to make America's ideals ring true for all Americans. He condemned the incendiary comments that Wright had made but he stated that he could not disown the man who made them. Obama proclaimed,

> The profound mistake of Reverend Wright's sermons is not that he spoke about racism in our society. It's that he spoke as if our society was static, as if no progress has been made, as if this country—a country that has made it possible for one of its own members to run for the highest office in the land and build a coalition of white and black, Latino and Asian, rich and poor, young and old—is still irrevocably bound to a tragic past.[26]

Moreover, he spoke of the wonderful work that Wright had done in helping those who were less fortunate in his community. Lastly, Obama returned to the theme of unity across racial lines in America. It was a speech that Obama had to make. Rev. Wright, however, would not go away. He appeared at the National Press Club in Washington, D.C., on Monday, April 28. Among other things, he stated this about Obama: "Politicians say what they say and do what they do based on electability, based on sound bites, based on polls."[27] Obama had had enough. Wright's continued outbursts were now threatening to derail Obama's campaign before the upcoming primaries in Indiana and North Carolina.

On Tuesday, April 29, Obama called a press conference and denounced his association with Wright.[28] In an article written for blackamericaweb.com, journalist Tonyaa Weathersbee reflected on the controversy and America's ability to move past race: "Because if America was truly getting past race, Americans wouldn't expect for a black person to not ever have attended a black church in which pastors never vent about the black condition or the racism that many blacks deal with all the time."[29] Obama had to set the record straight and deemphasize Wright's influence on his thinking. However, in an article that appeared in *Chicago* magazine, journalist James Merriner stated that "according to *Obama* . . . by David Mendell, Obama sometimes used Wright as a sounding board for his political aspirations . . ."[30] The question remains, was Obama's decision to leave Trinity motivated by politics or conscience?

Father's Day Speech

Obama gave a Father's Day speech on the South Side of Chicago at the Apostolic Church of God on June 15, 2008. The speech emphasized personal responsibility and the need for African American men, in particular, to take responsibility in the lives of children they have fathered. The speech tackled a sensitive topic and was one that only Obama could have delivered. Obama, who was raised by a single mom, spoke of the burden placed on him by not having a father around growing up. This topic has struck a sensitive chord in the African American community for many years. It is a topic that Daniel Patrick Moynihan, as an official in the Department of Labor, identified in a 1965 report titled, *The Negro Family: The Case for National Action*. In the report, Moynihan pointed to a disturbing new trend in the black community which included the rise in single-parent families and fatherlessness, among other things, collectively referred to by Moynihan as a "tangle of pathology" in the black ghetto. The report was attacked by civil rights leaders, civil servants, and academics. However, Christopher Jencks, Professor of Social Policy at the John F. Kennedy School of Government at Harvard University, stated that "the most important reason it was attacked was that it seemed to be saying that the problems of black America were attributable, at least in part, to choices that black Americans themselves made about what kind of families they were going to live in, and not to discrimination and racism and job opportunities and all that sort of thing. I think that's a misreading of the report because the report actually suggests pretty strongly that if job opportunities were improved, family structure would improve."[31] Critics who agreed with Moynihan dropped their criticisms and the report faded.

In his speech, Obama proclaimed,

> But if we are honest with ourselves, we'll admit that what too many fathers also are is missing—missing from too many lives and too many homes. They have abandoned their responsibilities, acting like boys instead of men. And the foundations of our families are weaker because of it. You and I know how true this is in the African-American community. We know that more than half of all black children live in single-parent households, a number that has doubled—doubled—since we were children . . . But we also need families to raise our children. We need fathers to realize that responsibility does not end at conception. We need them to realize that what makes you a man is not the ability to have a child—it's the courage to raise one.[32]

This was a theme Obama had hinted at as early as his keynote address at the Democratic National Convention in 2004. Some political observers saw this as a "Sister Souljah" moment for Obama, a reference to President Bill Clinton chastising rapper Sister Souljah for exhorting violence. Many said Clinton had done this to score points with white America—an allegation that also was being leveled against Obama. Veteran civil rights leader Rev. Jesse Jackson was one to take offense. The father of an illegitimate child himself, he retorted into an open microphone that he "would like to cut Obama's nuts off for talking down to black people."[33] In a July 14, 2008, speech that Obama gave to the NAACP at its 99th Annual Convention in Cincinnati, Ohio, Obama talked about how, as Americans, we have to demand more responsibility not only from government and from Wall Street, but also from ourselves. Obama acknowledged that some had said he was too tough on people when talking about personal responsibility, but Obama stated that he wasn't going to stop talking about it. Obama's black African father had abandoned him at an early age and he was raised by a single mother and grandparents, which may be one reason why he takes this issue so personally.[34]

Michelle Obama and the Media

Michelle Obama presented somewhat of an enigma to the press. The American press never before had to cover an African American woman as a prospective First Lady. Michelle Obama was bright, having graduated from Princeton University and Harvard Law School, and successful in her career. Her senior thesis at Princeton was titled, "Princeton-Educated Blacks and the Black Community." According to Jeffrey Ressner of Politico.com, it "shows a document written by a young woman grappling with a society in which a black Princeton alumnus might only be allowed to remain on the periphery."[35] Though an interesting topic for an African American student at a predominantly white Ivy League school, her thesis became immensely popular in the blogosphere. As a black female who was confident as to whom she was and assertive, she quickly was labeled as an "angry black woman." Nothing unusual there; pop culture and television often stereotype black women as such. This was not what America wanted in its perception of a "First Lady." Michelle Obama would have to tone down her sarcasm and appear to be a little more demure.

On February 18, 2008, when speaking about her husband and the campaign at a rally, she stated, "For the first time in my adult life, I am proud of my country because it feels like hope is finally making a comeback."[36] Although she reworded her comments later that day, the damage had been done. She was criticized by the media for those remarks. The following day, John McCain's wife Cindy commented, "I am proud of my country. I don't know if you heard those words earlier . . . but I am very proud of my country."[37] Now, according to her critics, not only is Michelle Obama an "angry black woman" but she is an unpatriotic one as well.

The cover of the July 2008 issue of *The New Yorker* magazine, a liberal leaning publication, portrayed Barack Obama, the Democratic presidential candidate, dressed as a Muslim with sandals, and a turban, and his wife Michelle dressed, not in traditional female Muslim attire, but in camouflage fatigues, combat boots, and an AK-47 assault rifle strapped over her shoulder and wearing an Afro. The two of them are standing in the Oval Office with a picture of Osama bin Laden hanging above the mantle and an American flag burning in the fireplace. The Obama campaign criticized the cover as "tasteless" and "offensive." Obama, whose middle name is Hussein and whose father was a Muslim, had been accused by some of being a Muslim. His wife Michelle clearly was depicted as a radical black nationalist in tune with the image that her critics were projecting. The magazine contended it was only trying "to hold up a mirror to prejudice, the hateful, and the absurd."[38] If that was their stated goal, they misjudged the cover's effect. The cover played into the hands of racists and bigots who looked for any chance, the slightest of indications, to show the black couple as outside the mainstream of American life and values. *The New Yorker* contended that the cover "is a satirical lampoon of the caricature Senator Obama's right-wing critics have tried to create . . ."[39] This country has a history of political satire going back to the first presidential election. However, *The New Yorker* chose not to lampoon John McCain, Cindy McCain, or Sarah Palin as possibly neo-Nazi white supremacists or Ku Klux Klanspeople donning white robes and pointed hoods as a large cross burns in the front yard.

Obama Wins the Democratic Nomination

The Reverend Wright controversy had threatened to derail Obama's campaign. Despite Obama's lead in the delegate count, Clinton knew that the negative media attention surrounding Wright's remarks had hurt Obama's support among white working-class voters—voters that the Democrats would need to win in the general election in November. Moreover, Clinton was now making the case that the undecided superdelegates should side with her because she would be the stronger candidate in November. To make matters worse, John McCain had secured the Republican nomination on March 4, 2008. The national chairman of the Democratic Party, Howard Dean, was quoted in the *Daily Mail* as saying "either Mrs. Clinton or Sen. Obama must drop out of the race after the final primaries on June 3 so the party can unite in time for the August convention and win the November election."[40] Some Democrats felt that Clinton staying in the race, even when she had little chance of winning the nomination, would only hurt Obama's chances in the November election. Others defended Clinton's right to stay in the race until the end and felt that she still had a realistic chance to win and that it was good for the party.[41] On April 22, Clinton scored a decisive victory in Pennsylvania. However, two weeks later, on May 6, 2008, Obama scored a huge victory in North Carolina, a state he was expected to win, and Clinton only won Indiana by one point, a state her campaign thought she would win big. Obama now had a 164 pledged delegate lead with only 217 pledged delegates left.

Journalist Tim Russert of NBC News stated, "We now know who the Democratic nominee's going to be, and no one's going to dispute it."[42] Primaries in West Virginia on May 13 and Kentucky on May 20 gave Clinton big victories. However, Obama won big in Oregon on May 20, which allowed him to clinch a majority (2,025) of the pledged delegates. That night, Obama delivered his victory speech in Des Moines, Iowa, the state where he had scored an upset in the first contest of the primary season and where he had begun his improbable journey. The Democratic Party held its last primaries on June 3 in Montana and South Dakota. What had been a long and arduous nomination season had finally come to a close. Clinton did not concede the election that night, however. On the following Saturday, June 7, Clinton endorsed Obama and gave him her full support.

Speculation immediately began as to whether Obama would choose Hillary Clinton as his running mate to round out the Democratic ticket. Many female Clinton supporters had vowed that they would not support the Democratic ticket unless Clinton was chosen as Obama's vice presidential running mate. Many Democrats saw an Obama-Clinton ticket as the "Dream Team." Senator Evan Bayh of Indiana, Senator Joe Biden of Delaware, Governor Tim Kaine of Virginia, and Senator Hillary Rodham Clinton were among the top contenders.

On Thursday, August 21, 2008, Obama announced that he had made his selection but would not make the announcement until Saturday, August 23,

2008. Obama made the announcement by text message to supporters and on his official campaign website barackobama.com. After a two-month search that was conducted almost entirely in secret, Obama chose Senator Joe Biden. Biden was chair of the Senate Foreign Relations Committee. Although he initially authorized the war in Iraq, he subsequently became a strong critic of Bush's war policies. According to a *New York Times* article, "Mr. Biden is Roman Catholic, giving him appeal to that important voting bloc, though he favors abortion rights. He was born in a working-class family in Scranton, Pa., a swing state where he remains well-known."[43] Biden offered strengths where Obama was perceived to be weak; in particular in the areas of foreign policy and national security. He served as chairman or ranking member of the Senate Judiciary Committee for seventeen years, and chairman or ranking member of the Senate Foreign Relations Committee since 1997. Joe Biden at age 65 and with his long tenure of thirty-six years in the Senate balanced the relatively youthful and short tenure in the Senate of Barack Obama. Moreover, Biden appeared as someone who would be ready to assume the presidency, if that occasion happened.

Overseas Trip

In July 2008, Barack Obama embarked on an overseas trip to the Middle East and Europe. He planned the trip as a way to bolster his foreign policy experience. Obama was quoted in the *New York Times* as saying, "This trip will be an important opportunity for me to assess the situation in countries that are critical to American national security and to consult with some of our closest friends and allies about the common challenges we face."[44] The trip had much more at stake for Obama as a presidential candidate in the upcoming 2008 general election. He needed to show the American voters that he was "ready" to be president. To accomplish that, Obama needed to appear presidential with the foreign heads of state without acting as the president.

In an unusual move, all three major network anchors traveled with Obama's press corps to cover his tour throughout the Middle East and Europe. Obama's stance on foreign policy signaled a change in U.S. foreign policy from the Bush administration, and many foreign leaders welcomed his willingness to respect opposing points of view.[45] The highlight of his trip was a speech he delivered in Berlin, Germany, to an estimated crowd of 200,000. Obama had initially planned to speak at the Brandenburg Gate where Ronald Reagan spoke and Kennedy visited, but both were U.S. presidents and not a candidate for president. Obama settled on speaking at the Victory Column in Berlin. Throughout his trip to Germany, the German press constantly made comparisons to Obama and John F. Kennedy, who when he visited in 1963 made his famous "Ich bin ein Berliner" speech. Crowds lined the route of Obama's motorcade from the government building to his hotel. His speech was titled, "This is the Moment to Stand as One." In commenting on his speech, op-ed columnist Frank Rich wrote in the *New York Times* that "What was most striking about the Obama speech in Berlin was not anything he said so much as the alternative reality it fostered: many American children have never before seen huge crowds turn out abroad to wave American flags instead of burn them."[46] Obama completed his tour by visiting France and Britain. He largely accomplished his goal: He was well received by foreign dignitaries and citizens and there were no major gaffes.

The Democratic Convention

Custom dictates that the party of the incumbent president holds its convention after that of the opposition. The Democrats had chosen Denver, Colorado, as their national convention site for 2008. It was a battleground state and the Democrats were hopeful that they could capture it, along with Nevada and New Mexico. As national conventions go, they are usually little more than a show of unity by the party for the American public. The presidential candidate has been chosen during the primaries and caucuses and the nomination process at the convention is usually just a formality. However, the Democrats had to settle some unfinished business about the seating of delegates from Florida and Michigan after both states were stripped of their delegates because they improperly moved forward their primaries to January 2008 in violation of the party rules. At the convention, at the request of the presidential nominee, both state delegations were restored their full voting rights.

Obama's wife and sister spoke on the first night of the convention. There was a special tribute to Senator Ted Kennedy who made a surprise appearance. On day two, Senator Hillary Clinton was the headline speaker. Joe Biden, the vice presidential candidate, was featured on the third day. During the customary roll call vote by the delegates on the convention floor to determine the nominee, in addition to Barack Obama, the presumptive nominee, Hillary Clinton's name was also placed in nomination. Clinton interrupted the official roll call to move that Obama be selected by acclamation. Senator Joe Biden accepted the vice presidential nomination on that same night and gave a speech for the first time as the nominee. After Biden spoke, Obama made a surprise visit to the convention hall that night.

The last night of the convention moved from the Pepsi Center outside to INVESCO Field at Mile High Stadium. The historic nature of that night was not to be forgotten. Obama accepted the Democratic nomination in front of 84,000 people on August 28, 2008, forty-five years to the day since Reverend Martin Luther King, Jr., delivered his "I Have a Dream Speech" in Washington, D.C.. Obama was the first African American ever selected by a major political party in this country as its presidential nominee. It was the realization of a dream. Obama's speech was magnificent. He spoke of America's promise and his vision for uniting America. He began his speech by saying, "It is that promise that has always set this country apart—that through hard work and sacrifice, each of us can pursue our individual dreams but still come together as one American family, to ensure that the next generation can pursue their dreams as well."[47] He ended his speech going back to that promise.

> And it is that promise that 45 years ago today brought Americans from every corner of this land to stand together on a mall in Washington, before Lincoln's Memorial, and hear a young preacher from Georgia speak of his dream . . . [W]hat the people heard . . . people of every creed and color, from every walk of life—is that in America, our destiny is inextricably linked. That, together, our dreams can be one . . . Let us keep that promise.[48]

It was a well-staged political convention and a strong showing of together-ness on the part of the Democrats. The two presidential candidates were tied at 45 percent in the last Gallup poll daily tracking results that were conducted before the convention began.[49] Overall, the Democrat Convention was well received by the public, "And 64 percent rated Obama's acceptance speech as excellent or good."[50] As a result, Obama appeared to have received an initial bounce from the convention and a 49 percent to 41 percent lead over Republican John McCain.

However, on Friday, August 29, less than twelve hours after Obama accepted the Democratic nomination, the Republican presidential candidate John McCain announced his vice presidential selection, Governor Sarah Palin of Alaska. This surprise move appears to have done two things: First, it didn't allow any time at all for Obama's bounce to grow, and secondly, it shifted the media focus from an extraordinarily unified Democratic Convention to McCain and his new vice presidential pick. Consequently, a CNN/Opinion Research Corporation poll that came out Sunday night showed the Obama-Biden ticket leading the McCain-Palin ticket by only one point, 49 percent to 48 percent.[51] Palin had been elected Alaska's first female governor in 2006. She served on the Wasilla city council from 1992 to 1996 and she was mayor of Wasilla, Alaska, from 1996 to 2002. At age 44, Palin was more than a generation younger than her Democratic counterpart, Joe Biden. She had a strong anti-abortion record and was viewed very favorably by social conservatives. Matthew Staver, dean of Liberty University School of Law, was quoted as saying, "This will absolutely energize McCain's campaign and energize conservatives."[52] Palin immediately made an appeal to women voters. After McCain introduced her, she stated that she "followed in the footsteps of Geraldine Ferraro, who was the Democratic vice presidential running mate in 1984."[53] She even spoke favorably of Hillary Clinton who drew eighteen million votes in her unsuccessful bid against Obama. Palin added, "But it turns out the women of America aren't finished yet and we can shatter that glass ceiling once and for all."[54]

Questions immediately began to surface about McCain's selection. Some of the political pundits speculated that McCain's motive was not only to shore up his conservative base but also to attract the many disaffected Clinton voters who vowed to support McCain if Clinton was not offered the vice presidential slot. Curiously, McCain's selection of Palin seemed to undermine McCain's recent attacks on Obama that he was too inexperienced to be president. Moreover, there was speculation in the media that she was not McCain's first choice, but that Senator Joe Lieberman, an Independent from Connecticut, and former Republican governor Tom Ridge of Pennsylvania were the two favorites. However, both men favor abortion rights, which was unacceptable to the Christian conservatives.

Questions also arose as to whether Palin had been properly vetted. According to a *New York Times* article, "A Republican with ties to the campaign said the team assigned to vet Ms. Palin in Alaska had not arrived there until Thursday, a day before Mr. McCain stunned the political world with his vice-presidential choice."[55] Unlike the Democrats who conducted a two-month investigation before selecting Biden, it appeared that Palin may have been hastily selected as a gamble. McCain, known as a maverick for much of his political career, seemed to raise questions about his decision-making abilities by choosing someone so inexperienced in national politics or issues of foreign policy and national security.

The Palin Effect

John McCain's choice of Sarah Palin had an immediate effect on the public opinion polls. The Republican National Convention was held from September 1 through September 4, 2008, but shortened to three days because of Hurricane Gustav. Sarah Palin gave her vice presidential acceptance speech on Wednesday night. She was enthusiastically received by the audience by "espousing social conservative values and presenting herself as a small-town mother taking on the cosmopolitan media."[56] Moreover, almost all the national polls gave McCain a big bump after the Republican National Convention and he actually led in two national polls. A USA Today/Gallup poll that surveyed 1,022 likely voters Friday through Sunday (immediately following the Republican Convention) showed McCain ahead of Obama by ten points, 55 percent to 45 percent, with a margin of error of +/–3 points. A Zogby Internet survey of 2,312 likely voters taken Friday and Saturday showed McCain leading Obama 49.7 percent to 47.1 percent with a margin of error of +/–2.1 points.[57] The campaign momentum coming out of the Republican Convention seemed to be shifting to McCain, and according to journalist Ewen MacAskill, it was largely due to the "Palin effect." MacAskill noted, "White women voters are deserting the Democratic presidential candidate Barack Obama because of the sudden emergence on the Republican ticket of Sarah Palin, according to the polls yesterday."[58]

General Election

In a historic nomination campaign that captured the attention of the world, the Democrats had an African American and a woman competing for the nomination of a major political party. The Republicans were making history of their own. Sarah Palin became the first woman nominated to be on a Republican presidential ticket and the first Alaskan to appear on a national ticket. With incumbent vice president Dick Cheney having decided not to run for president, the 2008 general election was the first since 1952 that neither the incumbent president nor the incumbent vice president had chosen to run for president and the first since 1928 that neither had sought his party's nomination.

Presidential Debates and Forums

The Commission on Presidential Debates proposed a total of three ninety-minute presidential debates: two would be informal and seated; the third would be in a town hall format that allowed the candidates to move around. No third party candidates or independent candidates were extended an invitation to join in any of the debates.[59] McCain, who had a reputation of doing best in town hall meetings, had originally proposed ten town hall meetings with Obama, something Obama rejected. Additionally, one vice presidential debate was scheduled.

Although not considered an official debate, on August 16, 2008, Pastor Rick Warren held a civil forum for the two major party presidential candidates at Saddleback Church in Lake Forest, California. Warren, a social conservative evangelical minister, is anti-abortion, against same-sex marriage, and against stem cell research. However, he has called on churches worldwide to fight poverty and disease. Each candidate was interviewed in front of a group of evangelical Christians. This unofficial debate is noteworthy because it highlights the importance of religion in the 2008 presidential election. Secondly, it showed that Obama, unlike his Democratic predecessors, was not ceding the religious vote to the Republican candidate. Republicans have painted the Democrats in general as lacking in Christian values. Warren interviewed the two candidates back to back and each was asked the same questions. Obama went first and appeared rigid and professorial. McCain seemed more relaxed with his answers. Obama knew his performance at Saddleback was unimpressive. Stated Evan Thomas, "Obama studied for the three official presidential debates, scheduled for roughly once a week from late September to mid-October, as if he were taking the bar exam."[60] But Obama's real challenge, asserted Thomas, was not the depth of his knowledge of policy detail. "He would need to show something more ineffable but profound—a true command presence. As his aides never ceased to remind him, he would have to look 'presidential.'"[61]

The first presidential debate was scheduled for Friday, September 26, 2008, at the University of Mississippi in Oxford. This is the site where James Meredith, an African American student, was denied admission into the all white university in 1962 because of his race. The campus erupted into violence before Washington sent in federal troops. It was a pivotal flashpoint in the civil rights movement. Now, forty-six years later, the first African American candidate of a major political party was invited to this university to participate in the first presidential debate of the season. Not unlike the drama that unfolded at "Ole Miss" in 1962, the presidential debate was filled with theatrics. On Monday, September 15, Wall Street was in meltdown with another giant financial firm filing for bankruptcy. On Wednesday, September 24, 2008, John McCain announced publicly that he was suspending his campaign, and asked Barack Obama to postpone the debate scheduled the next day, and to join him for crisis talks with President Bush on the economy and the proposed $700 billion bailout package.[62] Obama replied, "This is exactly the time when the American people need to hear from the person who, in approximately 40 days, will be responsible for dealing with this mess."[63] McCain even asked the debate commission to cancel the debate. The debate commission insisted that the debate was still on. Obama subsequently decided that he would go to the University of Mississippi and not disappoint the debate organizers there whether McCain showed up or not.

The next day, the president convened a summit on the bailout proposal which included Barack Obama and John McCain. Both men subsequently boarded planes and flew to the University of Mississippi for their first debate that night. There were two more presidential debates, one at Belmont University in Nashville, Tennessee, on October 7, 2008, and the last one at Hofstra University in Hempstead, New York, on October 15, 2008. Debates had not been Obama's strong suit. However, the Democrats held so many debates during the nomination process, it had given Obama the opportunity to practice and become more focused. McCain's behavior during the economic crisis gave the appearance that he was erratic and unsteady. First, he suspended his campaign when the economic crisis on Wall Street and the financial markets disaster occurred in mid-September, vowing only to debate Obama after Congress passed the stimulus bill. He then changed his mind and decided to attend the first debate after all. The first debate was on foreign policy and national security, strengths of John McCain. However, because of the financial crisis, some of the questions centered on the economy. Conversely, Obama appeared confident, cool and collected in the first debate. McCain would not look at Obama and did not appear relaxed. Public opinion polling gave Obama the edge in the debate, 46 percent to 34 percent with 20 percent unsure according to a *USA Today*/Gallup poll of debate watchers, which was conducted on just a single day (Saturday).[64]

The second debate, which was in the town hall meeting format, was supposed to be the format for which John McCain was known to excel. However, he appeared awkward and stiff from the start, frequently walking incoherently around the stage, while Obama remained calmly seated on his stool. When the second debate ended, both of the candidates were joined by their wives. The television cameras continued to roll as the two couples mingled with the audience. After only a few minutes, McCain and his wife abruptly exited, while Obama and his wife stayed and walked around the entire stage and talked to most members of the audience, even standing for pictures with audience members. McCain's campaign staff gave the reason for his sudden departure that he had a plane to catch. Nonetheless, it gave the appearance that McCain was anxious to leave while Obama was willing to stay and make his case to any and all who would listen. On the afternoon of the second debate, the Dow Jones Industrial Average dropped five hundred points. So, adding to McCain's debate woes, the economy had plunged into a deep recession. A *USA Today*/Gallup reaction poll taken the night after the debate found that a random sample of debate watchers felt that Barack Obama (56 percent) did a better job than John McCain (23 percent) in the second debate.[65]

The third presidential debate was formatted into a number of segments, similar to the first debate, where the candidates were seated. However, in the third debate, "Joe the plumber," a blue-collar, working-class McCain supporter who had interacted with Obama at one of Obama's rallies over the issue of Obama's tax plan, took center stage. McCain wanted to use Joe the plumber to highlight how Obama wanted to raise taxes to spread the wealth. It allowed both candidates to highlight their differences on their tax plans.[66] A public opinion poll of debate watchers, taken by *USA Today*/Gallup, conducted October 16 (the day after the third debate), showed that respondents felt that Obama did a better job, 56 percent to McCain's 30 percent.[67] In fact, Obama had a higher approval rating than McCain in all three debates (see Table 6.3). While winning the debates can have very little effect on actually winning the presidency, these debates were important to Obama for other

TABLE 6.3 2008 PRESIDENTIAL DEBATE PERFORMANCE POLLS

	Obama	*McCain*
Debate 1	46	34
Debate 2	56	23
Debate 3	56	30

Source: Gallup Organization: *USA Today*/Gallup polls conducted after each debate.

reasons. As an African American running as a major party candidate for the first time, there was much uncertainty surrounding Obama. He was relatively unknown to many Americans. The debates allowed Obama to be seen by those who did not know him. And what they saw was Obama being intelligent, youthful, cool and calm, and *presidential*.

Ultimately, it appeared that McCain's lackluster debate performances, or his erratic behavior in response to the financial crisis, mattered less to the voters than the economy. As the economy worsened in mid-September, so did McCain's level of support among the American voters. Voters became less concerned with national security and foreign policy—McCain's strengths—than they were about their personal finances, employment security, and retirement pensions. Eight years of fellow Republican George Bush being president, whose public opinion approval ratings were in the 20s and low 30s throughout the general election, became a huge albatross around John McCain's neck.[68] Although Bush publicly endorsed McCain, he failed to make one campaign appearance on his behalf. Furthermore, Obama repeatedly reminded voters that McCain had voted with Bush roughly 90 percent of the time, and Obama's slogan of "Change We Can Believe In" was an appealing alternative to McCain's experience argument to voters.

Furthermore, McCain made a series of blunders as the bad economic news continued to dominate the media. In an interview, McCain was asked how many houses he owned. He began to try to answer, then told the reporter that his staff would have to get back to him on that. The Obama camp picked up on this, and the fact that McCain owns seven houses, and portrayed McCain as being out of touch with the average American.[69] Moreover, on Black Monday, September 15, 2008, the day of the Wall Street meltdown, McCain stated at a rally, "the fundamentals of our economy are sound" as he acknowledged the turmoil in the financial markets.[70]

Palin Becomes a Liability

Republican vice presidential candidate Sarah Palin was a huge hit at the Republican National Convention. She energized the Republican base, she gained the support of white females who had supported Clinton, and she began drawing huge crowds at her rallies. McCain's polling numbers increased due to the excitement of Palin being on the Republican ticket. However, after a series of high profile interviews, questions started to surface as to her qualifications to be one "heartbeat" away from the presidency.[71] One interview more than any other was particularly troublesome: the interview conducted by Katie Couric, anchor of the CBS Evening News. Palin became unglued in the interview and tried to revert back to her talking points, which made most of her answers seem incoherent. At one point, Palin asserted that she felt Alaska's proximity to Russia enhanced her foreign policy experience. The interview became a defining moment in the campaign. It was an indication to voters that John McCain had made a poor choice for his running mate. After that interview, Palin was "barely allowed to open her mouth to the press."[72] Palin never fully recovered from the Couric interview; shortly thereafter "Saturday Night Live" began doing skits reprising snippets of the interview. The weekly skits continued to remind voters of her lack of knowledge on key domestic and international issues, which made her unqualified to be president.

In the lone vice presidential debate on October 3, at Washington University in St. Louis, Palin attempted to redeem herself. The debate was moderated by Gwen Ifill, an African American commentator for the PBS News Hour. Right before the debate, news reports surfaced that Ifill was writing a pro-Obama book timed for release on Inauguration Day.[73] Some journalists argued that this would bias her nonpartisan role as moderator toward the Obama-Biden camp. There were other journalists who saw Ifill as a fair journalist but remarked that appearances could cause difficulties. As a result of this, Palin, who was becoming increasingly independent on the campaign trail, at times during the debate disregarded the questions Ifill asked her, referred to the media as the "media elite" and repeated talking points as opposed to directly answering questions. By all accounts, however, most people felt that she redeemed herself with voters.

Race and the General Election

One strategy of the Obama campaign had been to run a deracialized campaign from the beginning. In the Democratic primary, race had always provided a subtext but it was below the surface, usually never front and center. That began to change for the general election. In reacting to a series of negative advertisements from the McCain camp, Obama remarked at a rally in Springfield, Missouri, in late July 2008, "You know, he's not patriotic enough. He's got a funny name. You know, he doesn't look like all those other presidents on those dollar bills, you know. He's risky. That's essentially the argument they're making."[74] In a rejoinder to Obama's comments, Rick Davis, McCain's campaign manager, exclaimed, "Barack Obama has played the race card, and he played it from the bottom of the deck . . ."[75] The issue was a delicate one for both candidates. Howard Wolfson, a former chief strategist for Hillary Clinton, remarked, "I think the McCain camp watched our primary on the Democratic side very carefully and they know that any accusation of racial divisiveness can be very, very harmful for a candidate's prospects . . . They heard something that Senator Obama said and they felt they had to respond quickly to make sure that nobody got the impression that they were engaged in those kinds of racial politics."[76]

In a strange twist of irony, McCain had been the victim of a Republican smear campaign in the 2000 South Carolina primary where rumors were circulating that McCain's daughter, Bridget—whom he and his wife Cindy adopted from Bangladesh—was his own, illegitimate black child.[77] Curiously, right before the Democratic primary in Pennsylvania, Bill Clinton had protested that Barack Obama had played the "race card" against him. The Obama camp knew that race was a sensitive issue and that their white opponents would have to tread lightly not to be accused of being racists or playing the race card; they used this to their advantage in the primary and general election. In an article titled "Race Man" that appeared in *The New Republic*, journalist Sean Wilentz argues how Team Obama played the race card against Hillary Clinton and then blamed her for doing just that.[78]

Obama's argument that the McCain camp was using code words continued with the airing of an advertisement criticizing Obama's overseas trip to the Middle East and Europe in August of 2008. The advertisement flashes shots of international celebrities Britney Spears and Paris Hilton, and the narrator states, "He's the biggest celebrity in the world. But is he ready to lead? With gas prices soaring, Barack Obama says no to offshore drilling and says he'll raise taxes on electricity. Higher taxes, more foreign oil—that's the real Obama." All of this is said while images of crowds screaming "Obama!" are shown.[79] According to journalist Sam Stein of *The Huffington Post*, David Gergen, former White House operative under both Republican and Democratic administrations, took exception to the advertisement asserting that "There has been a very intentional effort to paint Obama as somebody outside the mainstream, other, 'he's not one of us.'"[80] Gergen went on to say that McCain was smart in not directly saying it, but it was the subtext of the campaign.

Race and the Palin Effect

As Sarah Palin hit the campaign trail, she was drawing extremely large crowds. However, the rhetoric at these rallies was becoming increasingly caustic. She began railing about William Ayers, the former Weather Underground bomber who knew Obama through Chicago politics and had served with him on corporate boards. Palin extorted, "I'm afraid that this is someone who sees America as imperfect enough to work with a former domestic terrorist who targeted his own people."[81] But in a rally in Clearwater, Florida, someone in the crowd used a racial epithet in referring to an African American cameraman for NBC, and someone else yelled "Kill him!" either referring to Obama or Ayers. YouTube began airing clips of Palin rallies which showed footage of McCain rallies where Obama was referred to as a "terrorist," an "Arab," a "traitor," and "socialist," among other things. Representative Ed Towns, a black Democrat from New York, said in response to some of the campaign rhetoric at the Palin rallies, "Racism is alive and well in this country."[82] Representative Gregory Meeks, also a black Democrat from New York, remarked, "They are trying to throw out these codes."[83] The rhetoric seemed to reach a head when veteran civil rights leader and U.S. Congressman John Lewis of Atlanta came out with a public warning for McCain.

> As one who was a victim of violence and hate during the height of the Civil Rights Movement, I am deeply disturbed by the negative tone of the McCain-Palin campaign. Sen. McCain and Gov. Palin are sowing the seeds of hatred and division, and there is no need for this hostility in our political discourse. During another period, in the not too distant past, there was a governor of the state of Alabama named George Wallace who also became a presidential candidate. George Wallace never threw a bomb. He never fired a gun, but he created the climate and the conditions that encouraged vicious attacks against innocent Americans who were simply trying to exercise their constitutional rights . . .[84]

McCain was dumbfounded when he heard Lewis' remarks, and his advisers felt Lewis had just called McCain a racist—and he needed to respond. McCain opted to put out a statement calling on Obama to repudiate Lewis' comments. The Obama camp released a statement that read "Obama does not believe that John McCain or his policy criticism is in any way comparable to George Wallace or his segregationist policies. But Lewis was right to condemn some of the hateful rhetoric . . ."[85]

McCain, who had most of the time campaigned separately from Palin, seemed to be taken aback by Lewis' comments. McCain, who had devoted a chapter to John Lewis in one of his books, *Why Courage Matters*, began telling supporters at rallies, "that if you want a fight, we will fight, but we will be respectful."[86] McCain attacked Obama on many fronts. First, he accused Obama of being a celebrity and intimated that his speeches were simply "celebrity power." When that did not work, he accused Obama of being "a leftist, one who 'pals around with terrorists'."[87]

Latino Voters, Independents, and Clinton Female Supporters

Two large groups the Obama camp was having difficulty attracting during the primary were Latino voters and white female voters. During the general election campaign, they attempted to gain these votes. However, John McCain appeared to be poised to capture the Hispanic vote during the general election. Bush did very well with Hispanics in 2004 capturing 44 percent of the vote. McCain had sponsored legislation for comprehensive immigration overhaul in Congress, and was well received by Latinos in Arizona which borders three battleground Southwest states: New Mexico, Colorado, and Nevada. It appears that the McCain campaign miscalculated what issues to key in on to appeal to Latinos. According to *New York Times* journalist Larry Rohter, "immigration does not rank as high on the list of Hispanic concerns as the economy, education, and heath care."[88] Furthermore, McCain was hurt by the tough stand his own party took on the immigration debate even though McCain advocated a comprehensive approach. Moreover, the McCain camp felt that by focusing on socially conservative issues like abortion and same-sex marriage they would win over the Latino vote. Not so, said Christine M. Sierra, a professor of political science at the University of New Mexico. According to Sierra, "survey after survey tells us that even among socially conservative Hispanics, it's the other issues that matter most."[89]

During the Democratic primary, the Latino vote went heavily for Hillary Clinton. Many political observers felt this was because under Bill Clinton, Hispanics prospered in this country. The tensions between blacks and Latinos in this country caused many political observers to see the majority of the Latino vote going to McCain as opposed to Obama in the general election. However, those apprehensions never materialized. Although the Hispanic vote was divided among Obama and McCain, a Hispanic mother in a family-owned chili business in Espanola, New Mexico, summed up the more common attitude: "We need change, so the fact that Obama is not an Anglo appeals to me. He understands what discrimination is about, and if he gets in there and does a good job, that will make it easier for the rest of us, whether black, Hispanic or Indian, to get past that problem."[90]

In an article that appeared in the *New York Times* on October 2, 2008, a CBS/*New York Times* poll showed Obama leading McCain 49 percent to 40 percent, a nine-percentage-point lead. It was the first time that Obama held a statistically significant lead over McCain in 2008 in polls conducted by CBS News or joint polls by CBS News or the *Times*. The poll was taken five weeks before the election. Obama would not relinquish this lead in most polls through election day. It appears that the severe economic downturn more than anything else caused McCain's plummet in the polls and ultimately damaged his ability to win the election. Many of the Clinton female supporters began moving back to Obama after the Democratic National Convention with the percentage saying they would vote for Obama in November moving from 70 percent pre-convention to 81 percent post-convention.[91] Moreover, Independents began moving into the Obama camp as Palin's readiness to be president came to be questioned.

Campaign Financing and the General Election

The Federal Election Commission (FEC) ruled in April 2007 that presidential candidates may accept private contributions for potential general election campaigns and still remain eligible for public financing if they win their party's nomination. The ruling came at the request of Barack Obama, who had stated he would like the option of running a general election campaign that was publicly financed.[92] Obama subsequently chose not to accept public funding and was labeled as breaking his pledge, or a flip-flopper. Obama had pledged earlier to discuss with McCain the possibility of having an equitable system if the two candidates were to accept public funds. An article that appeared in *Fairness and Accuracy in Reporting* on July 3, 2008, stated,

> Obama justified his decision in a video posted on his website, expressing concern about a system which "as it exists today is broken" and "opponents" who have become masters at gaming this "broken system." In particular, he referred to his belief that during the presidential race, John McCain will benefit from 527s— independent organizations that run negative ad campaigns, such as

the Swift Boat Veterans for Truth, who launched a smear campaign against Democratic presidential nominee John Kerry in 2004.[93]

It appears that Obama never promised to forgo public financing unless certain conditions were worked out between the two campaigns; that never happened. However, this decision had a huge impact on the general election campaign. John McCain ultimately chose to accept public financing which limited him to $84.1 million. Conversely, Barack Obama, who opted not to accept public funding, had broken records in raising campaign contributions over the Internet during the Democratic primary. He saw that accepting public financing would actually limit the amount of money he could spend to mount a fifty-state campaign.

Obama is the first presidential nominee not to accept public financing since it was established by the FEC in 1976. McCain was coauthor of the McCain-Feingold Campaign Reform Act, also known as the Bipartisan Campaign Reform Act of 1972 (BCRA). If he had not been so closely identified with limiting the role of private money in political campaigns, he may also have declined public funding and the spending limits it imposed. Obama would benefit greatly during the course of the general election by being able to outspend McCain by almost two to one. Anthony Corrado, a government professor and campaign finance expert, stated that about Obama's campaign: "He's run a far more expansive and expensive campaign than any presidential campaign in history. He's done more advertising . . . built a bigger national organization, and spent more on voter registration and turnout than any candidate before."[94]

GOP Campaign Chest vs. Democrats'

During the Democratic primaries and caucuses, much of the discussion centered on the record amounts of money being generated by the Clinton and Obama campaigns. However, for the general election, campaign fund-raising had an interesting twist. When Obama clinched the Democratic nomination in June, he announced that his ban on lobbyist and Political Action Committee (PAC) contributions would extend to the Democratic National Committee. Obama had been such a prolific fundraiser during the nomination process, he believed that any losses incurred by the ban would be made up by his large number of small donors. But Obama's success in the primaries was attributable to a combination of small and large donors.

According to Marian Currinder, a senior fellow at the Government Affairs Institute at Georgetown University, and an expert in campaign finance, "Obama's primary campaign relied on at least 35 bundlers who raised more than $500,000 each."[95] Moreover, Obama saw his general election campaign boosted by his ability to call on his 1.5 million small donors from the primary/caucus campaign.

Since Obama had chosen not to accept public financing, to McCain's consternation, and McCain had chosen to opt into the public financing limitation, it appeared that Obama would have a huge advantage going into the general election campaign in the fall. McCain got a boost after both parties held their national conventions, and the Republican National Committee (RNC) raised more money than the Democratic National Committee (DNC). Currinder stated,

> The RNC and the DNC can make unlimited independent expenditures on behalf of their candidates; each national committee can also spend $19 million in coordination with its party's candidates. Independent expenditures are funds spent on behalf of a candidate but not coordinated with the candidate's campaign. Coordinated expenditures are funds a party spends for services such as polling and media time on behalf of a candidate who has requested it.[96]

McCain had an excess of $27 million on hand when the general election began that he could not directly use, so he transferred $18 million to the RNC and $9 million to state party committees.[97] One way candidates can help their campaigns, whether they accept public funding or not, is by raising money for the national and state party committees using joint-funding committees, which are allowed to use the candidates' names to raise money for their parties—money that the parties can then spend to support their campaigns. Both McCain and Obama used major donors to increase funding in these joint-funding committees.

By September 2008, the DNC had $17.7 million in cash on hand and the RNC had $76.5 million. So, McCain and the RNC started the general election with $187.6 million to spend, and Obama and the DNC only had $95.1 million to spend.[98] But Obama quickly made up that deficit. In September alone, Obama raised $153 million, half of which came in donations of $200 or less. The final weeks of the campaign witnessed an all out "blitzkrieg" of campaign spending. On October 29, 2008, just several days before the election, Obama purchased thirty minutes of primetime air space for an infomercial shown on three broadcast television networks (Fox, NBC, and CBS).

Obama outspent McCain by a four to one margin between September 1 and November 4, according to FEC records.[99] He raised close to $500 million in the fall contest alone and spent a total of $740.6 million for the entire campaign, eclipsing the combined total of $646.7 million spent by Bush and Kerry four years earlier. "The amount of spending by both candidates allowed them and their running mates to make personal appearances throughout the country, in contrast to previous elections," asserts Pomper, "when the contenders concentrated their attention on a very few 'battleground' states."[100]

Obama's huge war chest gave him an advantage over McCain in several ways. One way was in television advertising. Right after the primary season ended, Obama began running a biographical commercial campaign in eighteen states, including traditional Republican strongholds. Secondly, Obama spent a lot of time and money in states that Republicans had taken for granted in the past and could bypass to spend more campaign dollars in battleground states. Obama's strategy pressured McCain to campaign in states that Republicans had not had to defend for years, forcing the McCain campaign to make calculated choices on where to spend money and how much. Because of Obama's huge war chest, by the end of June 2008, he had a director and staff members in all fifty states—which allowed him to execute his fifty-state strategy.[101] Total spending by both presidential candidates surpassed the $1 billion mark, reaching roughly $1.7 billion.

7

Innovations in Technology
and Media

There was an emergence of rap and Hip Hop songs from a generation of people that really had very little, in their perception, to write, sing, and rap about that was positive in our communities.[1]

Rep. Mel Watt (D-NC)

Barack Obama's bold and innovative strategy to win the White House in 2008 began with the use of technology and new media. Obama assembled a grassroots movement from the bottom up that changed the face of democracy in America. Obama has been able to break the grip of big money politics controlling presidential elections. He has helped to open up the democratic process and to facilitate the political mobilization of millions of Americans. In doing so, he has created a new paradigm for running a presidential campaign for the twenty-first century. One of the main tools for this success was the Internet. Obama created more than simply a grassroots campaign, he created a movement. His foot soldiers were the hundreds of thousands of virtual network citizens who were drawn to Obama's national community of purpose. Howard Dean saw the potential of the Internet to raise money in the 2004 election. Barack Obama used the Internet not only to raise money but to organize as well. "They were Apollo 11, and we were the Wright Brothers," said Joe Trippi, the manager of Howard Dean's campaign.[2]

Reliance on Technology in New Ways

Obama relied on technology in many new and innovative ways. The online community was supporting Obama before he even entered the presidential fray. A MySpace page created by Obama supporters not connected to any official campaign quickly signed up 160,000 supporters. This influenced Obama's decision to run.[3] Obama was an excellent fit for a technologically based campaign. According to *Chicago Tribune* journalists Christi Parsons and John McCormick, "What is sometimes missed in Obama's story is that his message of change was ideally suited to the new medium of the Internet, with its appeal to young people and independents."[4] Moreover, since many Obama supporters were digital "natives," they were able to easily navigate the online scene and round up supporters.[5] For example, they helped make Obama speech clips and a "Yes, We Can" music video that was extremely popular on YouTube. Obama's goal was to create a community to do more than make campaign contributions. This community engaged in a high level of political participation, which included writing emails and letters to superdelegates, attending house parties and other events, and making phone calls and going door to door. Journalist Frank Davies of the *Media News* quotes David All, a Republican strategist specializing in new media: "Barack Obama is successful because he is Barack Obama, and his message is spot-on with the Democrats. But he is leveraging that with the most effective, comprehensive online strategy of any campaign. He's using the tools that help you find and mobilize new voters."[6]

The Obama campaign committed to the Internet early. In 2007, it spent $2 million on software and hardware. From the beginning, the campaign relied on the Web-management tools of Central Desktop to organize its field operation. So, when Obama announced his campaign in February 2007, his website was ready to go, a sign of his commitment to the new medium.[7]

Many of the presidential candidates saw the capability of modern technology in new ways as well. Obama's campaign decided early on that the Web needed to play a central role in helping to organize large numbers of supporters if they would have any chance of countering Hillary Clinton's influence within the Democratic Party's inner circle. Catherine Holahan, writing for *BusinessWeek*, quoted Joe Rospars, director of new media for the Obama campaign, who stated, "If we were going to do this and be successful it had to be from the bottom up."[8] Obama used mass text message updates throughout the campaign and reminders of upcoming primaries, as well as other information designed to keep his backers connected.[9] But it was the Clinton campaign that used online networking and more traditional camp- aigning, including its army of cell phone users to make two million calls in the weekend before the California primary. Clinton won California by nine per- centage points.[10] According to Holahan, "Obama is himself actively engaged in the social networks. Before Super Tuesday he solicited opinions on the business social network site LinkedIn about how the next President could help small businesses and entrepreneurs survive."[11] Obama had multiple tech savvy teams to head up his online operations: One technology team handled infrastructure; another managed his new media operations, design of his website and tools that were provided to its users; and yet another team photo- graphed his speeches and interactions on the campaign trail and posted those to YouTube and Obama's blog, which was written by campaign staff.[12]

The Internet favors outsiders, allowing them to quickly mobilize supporters and money. Supporters of Ron Paul pioneered "money bombs." Ron Paul, a Republican congressman from Texas who made an unsuccessful bid for the Republican nomination for president, collected $6 million on the Internet on December 16, 2007, the most money ever raised over the Internet in a single day.[13] The Obama campaign was starting from scratch with limited resources and name recognition.[14] He was an outsider and a long shot. Added to that, the Democratic primary opponent was Hillary Clinton, the best brand name in Democratic politics.

Obama was able to increase political participation. Blacks constituted 13 percent of the total voting population, which was up 2 percent from 2004. Voter participation among the young (18–29) was the highest since 1972, the first presidential election since 18- to 21-year-olds gained the right to vote in 1971. One of the biggest changes in 2008 was an increase in voter registration, early voting, and attendance at Obama's rallies.[15] These were all a reflection of the extraordinary interest that was generated by Obama's campaign. During the Democratic nomination period, Obama had many more locally organized house parties than the other two Democrats, Hillary Clinton and John Edwards. One example from mid-January 2008: 189 house events planned for Obama campaigners in San Francisco, but only twenty-nine house events planned for Edwards and nine for Clinton.[16] He excited a group of Americans in particular, who had largely been "turned off" by and "tuned out" from politics to become active participants—those 18- to 29-year-olds.

Technology and particularly the Internet played an important role in the 2008 presidential election. Americans are increasingly getting their political news and information from the Internet. Obama's Internet savviness gave him a grassroots network. This is changing the nature of politics because candidates no longer have total control over their message. According to a Pew Internet and American Life Project study released in June 2008, "46 percent of all adults are using the Internet, e-mail or phone text messaging for political purposes. Forty percent said they look up campaign information online, up from 31 percent in the 2004 election."[17] Democrats appear to be outpacing Republicans in their use of the Internet for political purposes according to the same study, from "social networking to watching online video to contributing money online or signing up for campaign-related e-mail."[18] What do these numbers mean for the digital divide, if anything? In other words, if 46 percent of all adults are using the Internet, who are the 54 percent of all adults who are not, and why not? So, as the Internet wrests the presidential election process from the big money "Fat Cats" and opens it up to average Americans, thus making it more democratic, are we now limiting this new form of political activism to those who are "wired" for the Digital Age, and opening up the democratic process on one level while closing it on another?

Rejection of the Traditional Top-Down Model of Campaigning

One key strategy of the Obama campaign was to reject the traditional top-down, command-and-control, broadcast-TV model of campaigning.[19] One key tactic of this strategy was that volunteers were not micromanaged; they were able to call their own shots, from organizing rallies to recruiting and training a cadre of Obama supporters to work their precincts on election day. According to Tim Dickinson, in an article he wrote for *Rolling Stone* magazine, "the Obama campaign has quietly worked to integrate the online technologies that fueled the rise of Howard Dean . . . as well as social networking and video tools that didn't even exist in 2004 . . . with the kind of neighbor-to-neighbor movement building that Obama learned as a young organizer on the streets of Chicago."[20] The objective was not to simply put people to work, but to empower them to make decisions at the local level, without relying on the campaign for guidance. As Temo Figueroa, national field director for Obama's campaign, put it, "We decided we didn't want to train volunteers, we wanted to train organizers . . . folks who can fend for themselves."[21]

Obama developed this philosophy as a young community organizer in Chicago (see his memoir, *Dreams from My Father*). Obama stated during the primary season, "One of my fundamental beliefs from my days as a community organizer is that real change comes from the bottom up. And there's no more powerful tool for grassroots organizing than the Internet."[22] Obama learned this neighbor-to-neighbor movement building as a community organizer in Chicago.[23]

Obama Recruits Facebook Founder for the Campaign

Key to the Obama campaign's new media strategy was the hiring of Chris Hughes, one of three Harvard University roommates who invented Facebook in 2004. Hughes (who remains on leave from Facebook) became the campaign director of online organizing and created a social networking site similar to Facebook and MySpace called my.barackobama.com. It has "taken the use of the Internet to another level by allowing masses of volunteers to self-organize . . . and communicate through their own social networking site."[24] MyBo (as campaign staffers call it) supporters "can join local groups, create events, sign up for updates and set up personal fund-raising pages," all organized through the website.[25] The point was never to get a large number of people signed up for it, but to enable those who did sign up to organize into manageable groups.[26]

On MyBo, any member could click on a list of phone numbers to call in order to create a campaign database. The member making the most calls was awarded with a meeting with Obama.[27] Hundreds of thousands of calls were made by volunteers in the winter of 2007 and the spring of 2008, without the callers ever leaving their homes.[28] The data gleaned from voters could then be uploaded to campaign staff.[29] This army of volunteer callers was used to identify supporters and get out the vote.[30] This is one of the reasons why Obama produced such strong turnouts in Democratic "backwaters." Organizers were able to organize early voting open houses which would be publicized on MyBo, where "instead of hoping that your neighbors vote . . . you're going to take them to the polls."[31] According to Tim Dickinson, "This is the same grass-roots effort that has trounced the Clinton campaign—a classic top-down operation run by high paid consultants—in 10 straight contests by an average of more than 30 points. It has evolved into the mother of all get-out-the-vote campaigns . . ."[32] Moreover, this type of grassroots organizing made a big difference in states like Texas which had a combination of a primary and caucuses. Team Obama had volunteers using the Internet to organize themselves months before the campaign staff arrived. In Texas, on March 4, 2008, Clinton won the popular vote, but Obama came away with a lead of five delegates, due to a caucus win. Caucuses are a test of organizational strength.[33]

Chris Hughes remarked that "People in the country are excited about change in general, and when you combine that with organizing tools that allow them to do stuff without someone looking over their shoulder, they can get a lot done."[34] The level of organization and structure was incredible. "Using the social-networking tools of MyBo, the volunteers were able to create city- and statewide networks with names like IdahObama, groups that could be tapped later by the professional staff to organize down to the precinct level. In Maryland, the campaign was able to mobilize 3,000 volunteers in only three weeks, thanks to the months of groundwork by groups like Baltimore for Barack Obama."[35] Voters were not told to just get online and blog, but to get online and connect with people from their zip code.[36] David Axelrod, chief campaign strategist, remarked that "Part of this new era of politics has been learning how to surrender command-and-control aspects of the campaign. If you really want grass-roots participation, then you have to give folks at the grass roots some autonomy to do this in their own way."[37]

On MyBo, which is a modified version of what can be found on a commercial social networking site, supporters can post a photo, a brief description of why they support Obama, issues that are important to them, and limited biographical information.[38] Hughes, according to journalist Brian Stelter, "brought a growth strategy, borrowed from Facebook's founding principles: keep it real and keep it local."[39] Mr. Hughes wanted to duplicate what he had done with Facebook with Obama's social network and create the same environment where supporters would connect with each other at neighborhood meetings. This was made possible because of the Internet.[40] Candidates have always communicated with supporters, but MyBo allowed supporters to communicate with each other. MyBo grew exponentially, and by summer of 2008, it had 900,000 members.[41] The site became a conduit for supporters of Obama to independently raise money for the candidate.

One example was the creation of the "Obama Minute" by some fans of Obama with the goal of raising $1 million in a minute. The minute was 1:00 p.m. on Monday, April 21, 2008, the day before the Democratic presidential primary in Pennsylvania. The effort was created by Scott Cohen, an independent filmmaker and photographer in New York, who had no connection with the campaign but found Obama inspirational. The fundraiser with a twist was yet another way in which the campaign harnessed the Web and allowed supporters to do the same. "An 'Obama Minute' is a great example of our grassroots supporters utilizing My.BarackObama.com as a tool to help raise money for our campaign," said Tommy Vietor, a campaign spokesman. The event raised $250,000.[42]

Though Obama's campaign had its own networking site, Facebook still maintained an integral role in organizing supporters. In January 2007, a student government coordinator at the University of Missouri launched a Facebook group, "One Million Strong for Barack." One year later, the group had signed up half a million Obama supporters.[43] Mark Penn, then the chief strategist for Hillary Clinton, back in November 2007, mockingly remarked that Barack Obama's supporters "look like Facebook."[44] Harnessing Facebook was an integral part of the Obama strategy.

By July 2008, Facebook was the social network of choice for 70 million Americans. More than 1.25 million users added the U.S. politics application. Cheryl Doyle is an example of how this election has involved so many who may not have gotten involved in years past because of the big campaign contributions. A self-employed attorney, she pledged $25. Journalist Kimberly Johnson quoted her as saying: "I can't afford to go to those big dinners: I'm just a working mom."[45] Thousands of online donors were transformed into street-level activists. Said Donna Brazile, Al Gore's campaign manager in 2000, "He gave them seats at the table and allowed them to become players."[46]

Friends on Facebook received automatic news feeds from the Obama campaign sent to their profiles, which were in turn seen by the recipients' friends.[47] The primary means of political conversation has always been people talking to each other. Social networking makes these conversations easier and more widespread.[48] Obama's use of social networking has tapped into the youth vote, a vote traditionally apathetic when it comes to politics.[49] A survey conducted by the Pew Internet and American Life Project in January 2008 found that 27 percent of those younger than 30 had received campaign news through social networking sites.[50]

Camp Obama

In the summer of 2007, the Obama campaign held summer camp. But this was not your typical summer camp. For one, the site was a downtown Chicago office building. It was a camp for adults, mostly young adults and college students. It was designed for them to hone their political skills and learn the basics of organizing for the campaign ahead. According to Hans Riemer, national youth vote director for the Obama campaign,

> Barack Obama is inspiring a new generation of people to come in, and a lot of people have not been involved in the political process before . . . We are training them, teaching them how to be effective, showing them what their role is in our strategy to win the election . . . We're taking people from raw enthusiasm to capable organizers.[51]

All campaigns use volunteers to get the candidate's message out and to do grunt work. But the Obama campaign saw a huge number of young people interested in the election and they capitalized on it. They took a demographic of voters who generally do not show up on election day and they gave them the tools to successfully organize and mobilize.

The Obama campaign had the benefit of avoiding the mistakes that former Vermont governor Howard Dean made when his campaign in late 2003 helped to mobilize 1,200 volunteers in Iowa ahead of the state's January 2004 caucuses. But because of an inexperienced and ill-trained team, the results were disappointing and Dean finished in third place behind John Kerry and John Edwards. The training sessions lasted a total of four days, with about fifty volunteers in each weekly session. The sessions had no registration fee but volunteers were responsible for their own transportation and lodging. Camp Obama director Jocelyn Woodards said her job was to "capture the enthusiasm of the political novices who are so eager to volunteer . . . and teach them the nuts and bolts of presidential campaigning."[52] Noted Woodards, "We go through everything from canvassing, phone banking, volunteer recruitment, our campaign message, how to develop an organization locally."[53]

Team Obama Stood Above the Rest in Internet Applications

Other candidates for president in 2008 were successful in using the Internet for social networking and fundraising, but none was able to really compete with Obama on the Internet. In an attempt to compete with MyBo, McCain created "McCainSpace," which was a part of John McCain's primary website, just as MyBo was a part of BarackObama.com. But McCainSpace was nearly impossible to navigate and was virtually abandoned.[54] Even with her paid staff of seven hundred, Clinton did not have the manpower to compete against

Obama's grassroots organizers in caucus states.[55] With the development of an online army, Obama was able to summon enough volunteers to more than negate the advantage Clinton had in traditional campaign structure.[56] While Edwards and Clinton were barnstorming in Iowa and New Hampshire, the Obama campaign sent out an email asking its supporters to sign up for a day of door-knocking and precinct-walking across the country. On a Saturday in June 2007 (months before the first caucus and primary vote would be cast), more than 10,000 supporters hit the pavement in all fifty states to persuade their neighbors to back Obama.[57]

YouTube Becomes a Vital Source for the Campaign

By 2008, video-sharing website YouTube had become a platform for politics. Obama's message of hope and unity was very inspirational, and his campaign attracted many more artists to create unsolicited music and music videos than any other candidate in American political history. Many of them were able to showcase their artistic talents with songs and skits in support of Obama. For example, the musician Will.i.am used film of Obama's speech "Yes, We Can" after Obama lost the New Hampshire primary, to make his "Yes, We Can" music video. It turned into the most watched political entry on the site, being viewed fifteen million times. The campaign's upload of the actual "Yes, We Can" speech by Barack Obama had less than two million views.[58]

One of the most popular YouTube videos showcased actress and model Amber Lee Ettinger, or "Obama Girl." Obama Girl's performance in the "I've Got a Crush on Obama" video and its variations was viewed more than sixty million times.[59] It helped increase Obama's public profile early on in the campaign. Many of the websites were created by private parties to target specific audiences and their particular biases. For example, TheGreatSchlep. com was created by Mik Moore for Jewish voters (Comedy Central comedian Sarah Silverman urges Jewish grandchildren to flock to Florida and convince their grandparents to vote for Obama); "Viva Obama" was created by Miguel Orozco to get Latinos involved in organizing for Obama. Obama's videos drew more than twenty-four million plays a day in March 2008.

According to an article by Virginia Heffernan in the *New York Times*, "During the presidential election, YouTube turned from a hectic mosaic of weird video clips to a first-stop source for political everything."[60] Every gotcha moment, spoof, pundit's musing, TV clip, campaign speech, formal ad and handmade polemic cropped up there. YouTube did not exist during the presidential election of 2004; it was not founded until 2005. The 2008 presidential election "was the site's first shot at wielding influence in national politics."[61] In 2006, YouTube's political team came up with the idea of YouChoose, a section of the site devoted to showing videos of the candidates that began in February 2007.[62] YouTube as a company made themselves available by meeting with almost every candidate at the start of the campaign season. They encouraged each candidate to start his or her own channel that would allow viewers to contribute directly to campaigns via Google checkout. Seven of the sixteen people who ran for the presidency announced their candidacies on YouTube.[63]

YouTube signed on as a partner for two CNN-YouTube presidential debates, at which some YouTube users had their questions for the candidates of both parties broadcast and answered on CNN. Following MTV's lead, YouTube first presented itself as a way for candidates to connect to the "youth" vote.[64] Obama made a greater effort at exploiting YouTube than did his competitor. McCain's channel ended with 330 videos, Obama's ended with 1,821 videos.[65] As a sign of a new age of politics in the twenty-first century, Heffernan noted, "all the foot soldiers for a candidate need skills with digital technology—as editing and uploading video is now more important to a campaign than direct mail."[66]

Both the Obama campaign and the McCain campaign took advantage of YouTube for free advertising.

> This was a boon for the campaigns, which could post an ad on YouTube for free, rather than paying high rates to broadcast it on TV. At times, both campaigns called press conferences to announce a new ad, hoping that reporters would provide free coverage of the ad's message, even though the ad was rarely shown in paid media slots. This tactic, known as a "vapor" or "ghost" ad was used more often in 2008 . . . Posting the ad on YouTube enhanced the legitimacy of the ad claimed by the campaigns. Once the ad was posted to YouTube, the campaign could give the ad widespread exposure by emailing its online address to millions of supporters, who in turn could send them to their network of friends.[67]

The Obama campaign also developed an iPhone application that would rearrange an individual's cell phonebook so that the numbers appeared in the same order of the campaign's targeting efforts, and numbers in highly targeted states would appear first.[68] The Obama campaign's commitment to the cell phone was evident with the Get-Out-The-Vote (GOTV) phone events that the campaign conducted. The campaign would take the whole floor of a building and there were no landline phones. When you arrived, you were given a list of numbers to call, but you used your own cell phone. Something this simple saved the campaign the expense of having to install banks of phones.[69]

Black Radio and Television

Rush Limbaugh is the "king" of conservative talk radio in America. He has even been called the voice of the Republican Party. One of the interesting forms of old media to emerge as a pivotal player in the 2008 presidential election is black radio. As a news forum, it provided a counterbalance to right-wing conservative talk radio. In fact, Obama conducted frequent interviews with black radio personalities during the election season, appearing on programs like "The Tom Joyner Morning Show," the "Michael Baisden Show," and "The Steve Harvey Morning Show," and with former Democratic presidential candidate Rev. Al Sharpton, who has a radio program that is now syndicated across the country.[70] Black radio reaches a wide audience across America providing news and entertainment for millions of Americans who feel largely ignored by traditional mainstream media outlets. Actor and comedian Jamie Foxx has a show on satellite radio called "the Foxxhole."

Support for Obama extended beyond black radio and into other black media outlets as well. *Ebony* magazine regularly did features on Obama and his family. Black Entertainment Television network's annual awards program, with recording artists like Alicia Keyes and Sean Combs, turned it into an impromptu rally for Obama.[71] Many African American viewers listened and became extremely protective of Obama. Tavis Smiley, an African American PBS and public radio host, resigned as a regular commentator on "The Tom Joyner Morning Show" after listeners sent in angry emails and phone calls in response to Smiley's questioning of Obama's commitment to black issues.[72] But Obama did come under some criticism from some members of the major trade group for black newspaper owners, the National Newspaper Publishers Association, when Obama declined to appear at the group's events.[73] Moreover, there was some criticism that the Obama campaign was not spending much money in African American media markets on advertisements although Obama had become the first presidential candidate to become the primary sponsor of a car in a NASCAR race.[74]

Role of the Internet in Fundraising

The Internet played a pivotal role in fundraising for the 2008 presidential election, for money is essential for allowing candidates to carry their message to the American electorate. Obama was incredibly successful in fundraising during the presidential election campaign. For the first quarter of 2007, Obama raised $25 million from 104,000 donors, more than half on the Internet. He declined public financing for the primaries and the general election to take advantage of the huge network he had built online. Michael Luo, writing for the *New York Times*, reported that the "Obama officials said their final tally of individual contributors surpassed 3.95 million . . ."[75] In January 2008, the first month of the nomination contest, Obama raised $32 million, $27 million of which came from online supporters, many in micro-payments of less than $50, according to Julie Germany, director of the Institute for Politics, Democracy and the Internet. Another change from politics as usual, noted Germany, was, "until recent elections, the general public has 'perceived' that people who donate to campaigns are political 'fat cats' looking for political favors . . . But with [2004 Democratic candidate Howard] Dean, [Republican candidate Ron] Paul and Obama, they've recreated the political game. It's about reaching out to every man and woman that can donate. That's a sign of the democratization of political contributions and political campaigns."[76]

Obama raised nearly $750 million for his campaign, a record amount that exceeds what all the candidates combined raised in private donations in the 2004 presidential election.[77] The relative ease of making Internet donations allowed the number of small donors to explode to a sizable force. And Obama gave them ownership in the campaign and the democratic process. Furthermore, notes Kimberly Johnson, when Internet donations are made, websites like Facebook and MySpace "simply direct people to the donation page on a candidate's Website. Campaigns, in turn, can track which sites those visitors are coming from."[78]

Negative Effects of the New Media and the Internet

The "new media" and the Internet were not always so positive for Obama. There were chain emails circulating from the outset about Obama's life as a Muslim. Even though the emails were untrue because Obama is a Christian, many believed them.[79] Emails are cheaper to circulate, easier to initiate, and can reach people faster than traditional mailing. The Internet gave life to the most damaging story to surface about Obama—the Reverend Jeremiah Wright controversy. Originally broadcast on cable television, the availability of clips on YouTube coupled with the right-wing cable news stations' 24-hour news cycle threatened to derail Obama's candidacy. To address the rumors and half-truths circulating about Obama, his campaign created a website on June 12, 2008—FightTheSmears.com—to counter the false accusations. The campaign was forced to devote resources to this newly created website. The site gave responses to issues brought up about the candidate, such as:

- Claims he is not a natural-born citizen of the United States.
- Portrayals of his relationship with Bill Ayers.
- Claims that he is a Muslim and not a Christian.
- Assertions that he does not put his hand over his heart during the Pledge of Allegiance.[80]

The website was created to allow supporters acting as a truth squad to untangle accusations.[81]

Obama found innovative ways to use the "new media" during his campaign but he also utilized the "traditional media" as well. One example of how his huge fundraising capability gave him an advantage over his opponent in a traditional medium came in the twilight of the general election campaign. On October 29, 2008, Obama aired a thirty-minute infomercial "American Stories, American Solutions" during prime time viewing at 8:00 p.m. eastern standard time on NBC, CBS, Fox, Univision, MSNBC, BET, and TVONE. Game 5 of the 2008 World Series was scheduled for that night as well. After a discussion of several campaign issues, the infomercial moved to an Obama speech live from Florida. ABC News was the only major network not to air the advertisement. The ad, which cost $4 million, was viewed by 30.1 million viewers.[82] With all the emphasis on Obama and how he was light years ahead of John McCain with the use of "new media," this was a stark reminder that Obama was beating McCain by outspending him on television as well.

The Landscape of Political Campaigns Has Been Indelibly Altered

Obama's use of technology has changed the political landscape and created a new paradigm for how you mobilize supporters, give them the tools to organize and then step out of the way and let them take control. Key to this strategy is the ability to release control to others. According to Adam Nagourney, Obama "has rewritten the rules on how to reach voters, raise money and withstand . . . political attacks, including many carried by blogs that did not exist four years ago."[83] One thing this election has done is probably put an end to public financing for all time. Terry Nelson, the political director of the Bush campaign in 2004, stated, "We are in the midst of a fundamental transformation of how campaigns are run, and it's not over yet."[84] One key tactic of Obama's strategy was not to simply rely on the mainstream media to get his word out. He allowed the Internet to become a vehicle for "new media."

> One of the distinguishing characteristics of the 2008 election is the amazing proliferation of videos. Obama's team put them out there on the Web sites, and then the community took over. They decided whether to watch a film, and whether to paste it onto their blogs or MySpace pages and spread it around the globe. Using Photoshop and other tools, they created their own versions of the videos—reworking images, changing text, combining elements of different videos into so-called mashups. Some of the altered films were elaborate parodies, some were simple sight gags—like one that compared Obama to Star Trek's Mr. Spock and McCain to Batman's nemesis, the Penguin.[85]

Mark McKinnon, senior adviser to both of President George W. Bush's campaigns, said, "I think we'll be analyzing this election for years as a seminal, transformative race."[86] The change, which was integral to Obama's overall strategy, was the result of Obama's ability to reach voters and supporters who do not rely primarily on information from newspapers or television. Furthermore, this new electorate appears to be more skeptical of what is said by campaigns and used the Web to do its own fact checking. "You do focus groups and people say, 'I saw that ad and I went to this Web site to check it,'" said David Plouffe, the Obama campaign manager. "They are policing the campaigns."[87] According to Patrick Ruffini, a Republican strategist who was the Webmaster for President Bush's 2004 campaign, a campaign's culture largely determines its digital strategy. The McCain campaign "could hire the best people, build the best technology, and adopt the best tactics on the Internet. But it would have to be in sync with the candidate and the campaign."[88] Obama's campaign embodied change. It was the slogan of the campaign, "Change We Can Believe In," and Obama was committed to changing the status quo of politics.

The Hip Hop Genre Backs Obama

Many artists and musicians were attracted to the Obama campaign. Ironically, Obama was selective about which artists were out publicly supporting him. The Obama campaign had wanted to reach out to young African American male voters but they wanted to do this in a way they perceived would not antagonize white voters. So, when the rapper Jay-Z offered to perform in concert for Obama in October, the campaign was reluctant. *Newsweek* journalist Evan Thomas recalled that "Black leaders from the community in Detroit and Miami pleaded with Obama headquarters . . . saying in effect, 'You keep saying to us, "Go produce sporadic African-American young voters." Give us the tools. Jay-Z is a tool and you have to give him to us.'" The campaign agreed but asked Jay-Z not to riff on Republican candidates. Jay-Z agreed, and in a song that contained lyrics that were derogatory to Bush, "Blue Magic," the rapper skipped the line about Bush but the crowd, familiar with the lyrics, sang it out anyway.[89]

In July 2008, the Obama campaign criticized a song by rapper Ludacris, "Politics As Usual." Peru-born political activist and rapper Immortal Technique pointed out in an Al Jazeera (an independent news network headquartered in the Middle East) interview how the media makes Barack Obama go through what he referred to as "Toby Moments" (Toby was the slave name given to Kunta Kinte in the novel *Roots* by Alex Haley), where they force Obama to publicly denounce his supporters. It is almost as though the Obama campaign wanted it both ways: They wanted the support of Hip Hop because its energy and enthusiasm, and financial assistance, would generate support for the Obama campaign and translate into votes; however, the Obama campaign also wanted to control the message of Hip Hop artists. And Hip Hop did its part in supporting Obama.

The Hip Hop Caucus (yes, there is such a thing) launched an eighteen-city swing-state-targeted tour featuring numerous artists including Jay-Z, Jeezy, and Keyshia Cole. YouTube videos highlighting the tour soon appeared. In a notable moment of the campaign, on November 3, Jay-Z stood on a North Philadelphia stage—flanked by Sean Combs, Mary J. Blige, Beyoncé, and Philadelphia mayor Michael Nutter—and told a crowd of 10,000: "Rosa Parks sat so Martin Luther King could walk. Martin Luther King walked so Obama could run. Obama's running so all the children can fly."[90] Ironically, though Obama had reservations about using rappers to reach out to young African American men, rappers clearly embraced him and helped mobilize supporters for his campaign and election.

The Candidates' Efforts to Get Out the Vote

Obama had been holding GOTV cell phone parties throughout the campaign. According to Evan Thomas, "The Obama Campaign ran the biggest, best-financed get-out-the-vote campaign in the history of American politics. Staffers for Obama in the New Media department coordinated with the field department and created a program that would allow a flusher—a term for a volunteer who goes out to round up nonvoters on Election Day—to know exactly who had, and had not, voted in real time."[91]

> The New Media staffers called it Project Houdini, because of the way names disappear off the list instantly once people are identified as they wait in line at their local polling station. Project Houdini has the potential to change the way Get Out the Vote campaign efforts will be conducted in the future.[92]

Predictably, both of the candidates spent a lot of time the last weeks and days of the campaign in swing states or battleground states. Obama was spending time and resources in Florida, Indiana, Missouri, North Carolina, Nevada, and Ohio, all states won by Bush in 2004.[93] The Obama campaign estimated that it had 1.5 million volunteers helping it to get out the vote in battleground states.[94] By Obama campaigning vigorously in states that traditionally had gone Republican, he forced McCain to spend time and resources in these states, which diverted valuable resources away from other states.

McCain's campaign also had its own high-tech voter turnout and social networking tools. The Republican National Committee ran a database called Voter Vault, which was similar to the Obama campaign's database on voters. The McCain campaign also offered supporters their own set of social net-working tools. However, according to Wired.com journalist Sarah Lai Stirland, some volunteers were saying they really do not use the sites. Harout Samra, chairman of the Florida College Republicans, notes that McCain launched his services—McCainSpace and McCain Nation—relatively late in the campaign, and Samra and his fellow organizers had already gotten used to relying on Facebook and Storm, the College Republicans' social networking tool.[95] Some of McCain's supporters even acknowledged Obama's superior online organizing. Said the twenty-year-old Central Florida chairman of Students for McCain, "I do have a lot of respect for whoever cooked up their operation, because it's an impressive machine that they have built among young people . . . We don't have anything nearly as advanced as the Obama campaign."[96] As sophisticated and technologically advanced as Obama's get-out-the-vote operation was, McCain's was not nearly as advanced.

McCain clinched the Republican nomination on March 4, 2008. The general election campaign did not begin in earnest until September 5, 2008, after the Republican National Convention was over. McCain wasted valuable organizational time that he could have used to raise money, organize an army of volunteers, and adequately vet potential vice presidential running mates prior to the fall campaign against Obama. He was outspent and out-organized by Obama who was still competing in a primary when McCain had long since won the Republican nomination.

The potential change in the electorate as a result of efforts by the Democrats to register and mobilize new African American, Hispanic, Asian, and young voters bodes well for the Democratic Party.[97] This could signal a change in long-term party coalitions with the possibility that this election is the beginning of a party realignment. Ninety-four percent of the Millennials (individuals born between the years of 1980 and 1995) said that the party they voted for in 2008 is the party they will vote for in future elections (though this was said before the election).[98]

The Obama campaign's innovative use of "new media" as well as old media was nothing short of spectacular. Had his campaign not been so skilled in its many applications of the new technology, which allowed Obama to raise the necessary money to be competitive in all fifty states, he probably would not have won the presidential election. However, it must be noted that much of the grassroots movement developed apart from Obama. Much of the Internet activity done by the foot soldiers of the campaign was done independent of the Obama campaign. Much of the support (financial and otherwise) generated on Facebook, YouTube, blogs, forums, and the like, should be attributed to the ingenuity and commitment of the supporters involved. The foundational principle that one should glean from Obama's 2008 presidential campaign is decentralization. One of the real lessons to come out of the campaign is that more can be accomplished when a campaign is turned over to its supporters rather than the traditional model of micromanagement.

The Obama campaign's use of the Internet targeted 18- to 29-year-olds. They are educated and technologically savvy. Obama connected well with this age group that had largely "tuned out" and been "turned off" by politics. Too often, many of them had seen in the past their voices drowned out by powerful special interests. Obama saw this cohort as crucial to the new coalition he was building. To that end, Obama embraced them and tapped into the issues that concerned them: opposition to the Iraq War, expansion of health care, and tax cuts for the middle class. He also tapped into their new way of communication and turned the traditional top-down model of running a successful campaign for president on its head. And because of this, Obama was seen as the candidate who appealed more to the youth vote. More can be accomplished when a campaign is given over to its supporters: this is the essence of democracy. It is the masses of Obama supporters who truly made this campaign a unique one.

Obama was more successful than the other candidates in his use of the Internet because cyberspace, with its progressive political leanings, longed for the political paradigm touted by Obama. He should be lauded for the willingness to let go of the reins guiding his campaign. By ceding control to a passionate group of followers, he was able to accomplish far more than was ever possible in the traditional model of micromanagement. He provided the message, "Change We Can Believe In," then allowed individuals to creatively spread that manifesto in a way that only "true believers" could.

8

Change Comes to America

I met Barack Obama in the fall of 1990. I was a first-year law student at Harvard. Barack was the incoming president of the Harvard Law Review and I remember Barack giving a presentation to first-year law students. That was the first time that I met him. Already there was a very strong sense that he was not just another bright and intelligent law student who was going to do well because there were plenty of those at Harvard Law School. There was a sense that there was something extraordinary about Barack Obama. And there was already an assumption, even at that point in his life, that he was going to be a major political figure and even then you would hear people say that Barack Obama was going to be the first black president of the United States.[1]

Rep. Artur Davis (D-AL)

The presidential campaign of 2008 was truly momentous. On November 4, 2008, this nation would decide if it could finally get past race and vote for the first African American as president of the United States. For the previous twenty months, this country had witnessed an exhilarating election season. Barack Obama was the first African American to receive the nomination of a major political party. Hillary Clinton was the first woman to run as a serious contender for the nomination of a major political party. And Sarah Palin was the first woman nominated to be vice president by the Republican Party. Rarely had a presidential election generated so much excitement not just at home, but also around the world.

Most of the major polls showed Barack Obama with a lead going into election day on November 4, 2008. The majority of states allowed early voting and absentee balloting. Public opinion polling showed Obama coming out of the Democratic National Convention in late August with a lead over John McCain. However, the day after the convention ended, John McCain surprised everyone by picking little known Alaska governor Sarah Palin as his vice presidential choice. The Republicans, whose base (the Christian conservatives) was not excited about its candidate, all of a sudden were reenergized with the selection of Palin. The Republican National Convention attracted a large television audience. Her selection caused a ten-point boost in a Gallup poll and seemed to dissipate any bump in the polls candidates usually receive after their convention. However, with the Wall Street crash of September 15, 2008, coupled with the nation's financial crisis, which voters tended to blame on Republican president George Bush, by September 19, Obama had regained the lead in the public opinion polls.

Public opinion polling meant little particularly to the African American community. After all, this was America with its troubled racist past. Many blacks refused to believe that America would vote for an African American as president of the United States. They remained optimistic, but cautious. After all, Obama was provided Secret Service protection earlier in the campaign than any other candidate for president ever. Democrats, in general, remained wary of an Obama victory. They had seen their hopes dashed in the controversial 2000 election and with the ultimate Supreme Court decision in *Bush v. Gore* (2000) that ruled in favor of George W. Bush. Furthermore, in 2004, they watched as John Kerry lost to George W. Bush in a close election that came down to the battleground state of Ohio.

Barack Obama had become the future of the Democratic Party after his electrifying keynote address at the 2004 Democratic National Convention. That was the same year that he was elected to his first term as a U.S. senator from Illinois. Just three years into his first term, he would declare his candidacy for president of the United States. Many felt that he was too young, and too inexperienced to run for president. Some of the elders of the civil rights movement told him to wait his turn. Now was not the time. In a strange twist of irony, he would later remark on the campaign trail how a young minister and leader of the civil rights movement forty-five years ago would often speak of the "fierce urgency of now" when told by others that he needed to wait.

Race provided a powerful subtext throughout the entire campaign season. Since Obama was the only African American in the Democratic field of candidates, the other candidates appeared awkward when trying to step around the issue of race. Joe Biden's clumsy description of Obama as the "first mainstream African American who is articulate and bright and clean and a nice-looking guy" had the implication that these were unusual characteristics for a black man. Hillary Clinton would later find herself on the defensive when she remarked that the Voting Rights Act of 1965 was passed because President Lyndon Johnson made it happen, which seemed to ignore the numerous acts of civil disobedience by the civil rights demonstrators in the South leading up to Bloody Sunday in Selma, Alabama, where protesters were beaten when they staged a symbolic march in protest of being denied the right to vote. So, the larger question loomed: Would America finally shed its racist past and elect an African American to the White House (a building that was built by slaves) for the first time ever?

Content of One's Character

Could America live up to Dr. Martin King's dream and judge Barack Obama by the content of his character and not the color of his skin? Obama inspired a nation at a time when it was as divided and polarized as ever. He offered us a politics of inclusion and unity as opposed to the vitriolic rhetoric of division and hatred that all too readily spewed from the mouths of politicians. Much of that hope was rooted in Obama's reference to one of his heroes, "an appeal to the better angels of our nature," which was a call of unity and the shared hopes and dreams of all Americans that Abraham Lincoln sounded in his first inaugural address. Obama's hope was also rooted in a younger generation, the Millennials, who seemed to care less about the color of a person's skin than his ability to solve many of the nations's pressing problems. This is largely due to the racial progress this country has made in the last half-century. The beating and murder of Emmett Till, the Montgomery Bus Boycott, the March on Washington, and Bloody Sunday are all events of the civil rights movement that they read about with awe in high school and college courses, but did not actually witness. Signs saying "Whites Only" and "Colored Only" are merely relics of American history and no longer the law of the land.

The younger generation was one of the real stories of the 2008 election. This 18- to 29-year-old cohort, the same group that had been written off by the social scientists as not interested in politics, proved the experts wrong. Not only did the younger generation "tune in," but they "turned on," and "turned out" a vast army of foot soldiers ready to do battle with cell phones, wireless Internet connections, BlackBerrys, and iPods, and they set out to change the way we run political campaigns in this country. Obama ran a campaign as a post-racial candidate. He ran as a candidate who happened to be black, not as a black candidate. And his message of unity and hope excited a nation that had forgotten how to dream and to look toward tomorrow as a promise of better things to come.

Obama's supporters were intergenerational and interracial, and multi-generational and multiracial. His campaign rallies looked like America, young, old, black, white, brown, yellow, and red. People were taking their children to Obama rallies because they felt that history was being made and they wanted them to be a part of it. Many parents across America said that they were supporting Obama because their children would not have it any other way. Many older African Americans felt that it was not Obama's time, Hillary Clinton was their candidate. After all, wouldn't America vote for a white female before it would vote for an African American male? Ironically, as the baby boomers feared that Obama's race might cause him to lose, the younger generations embraced Obama because he *was* African American. America learned a lesson from its youth in this presidential election: that change is good, change is a constant, and change is to be embraced. Obama's candidacy was the embodiment of change.

The Debate Season

It was a long and fascinating election. The Democratic primary season lasted until the last contests in June of 2008. Under normal circumstances, this would have been detrimental to a political party in terms of the resources and finances the eventual winner would have expended. In a strange way, however, the long nomination contest tended to work to the advantage of Barack Obama. It helped to season him, allow him to refine his message, and become a more focused candidate. One of the most important things the primary season did for Obama was it enabled him to become a more poised and polished debater. The Democrats held an unprecedented number of debates during their primary season. Between April 2007 and April 2008, the Democrats conducted twenty-six presidential debates. The last six were held between Barack Obama and Hillary Clinton. This would later turn out to be a significant advantage for Obama against McCain; McCain secured his party's nomination so early that he never had the chance to go one on one with a Republican challenger.

It became obvious from the beginning of the Democratic debates that this was not one of Obama's strong suits. In the early debates, Obama appeared too deferential and repeatedly made mistakes. He seemed unfocused and not as comfortable in this setting as when delivering an inspirational speech. He got "bloodied-up" but took the hits. More importantly, however, primary season prepared him for his debates with his Republican opponent, John McCain. There were only three official presidential debates scheduled during the general election. No third party or Independent candidates were extended an invitation to attend any of these debates, so each debate would see Obama and McCain going head to head.[2] Questions persisted about Obama's foreign policy experience and leadership ability. Obama knew the debates would be crucial; he would need to show the American people that he had the temperament and disposition along with the knowledge to be commander in chief. Obama gave a solid performance in all three debates. He showed voters that he was up to the challenge and, overall, gave them the reassurance that he was ready to step into the presidency and hit the ground running from day one.

Secondly, the Democratic primaries allowed the "issue" of Rev. Jeremiah Wright to be aired openly and often. The Clinton campaign pounced on statements made by Obama's former pastor over the course of twenty years where Wright made incendiary comments about America and its treatment of some its citizens. The cable news stations played the clips repeatedly and they were all over YouTube and the Internet. In response, Obama was forced to address the issue and he gave that powerful speech on race in Philadelphia. He used the occasion to his advantage and turned his response to Rev. Wright's divisive statements on race into a message of racial reconciliation in America. When Wright continued to speak out against Obama with outrageous remarks, Obama finally disowned his former pastor. The good fortune for Obama was that by the time the general election rolled around, Rev. Wright was no longer news and the story had lost its impact.

Obama suspended his campaign two weeks before election day on November, 4, 2008, to visit his gravely ill 85-year-old grandmother in Hawaii.[3] Obama had said in his first book, *Dreams from My Father*, that his grandmother had been the one who had provided stability in his life as his mother shuffled Obama from one place to another. At one point in his life, Obama was returned to Hawaii to live with his grandmother and grandfather (while his mother and sister had remained in Indonesia) to attend a prestigious private school, Punahou. Obama remarked in his book how his grandmother, whom he affectionately called "Toot" (after Tutu, the Hawaiian word for grandmother), had poured everything she had into him and had often gone without to make sure that he didn't. When Obama claimed the status of "presumptive nominee" for the Democratic Party on June 3, 2008, in St. Paul, Minnesota, he dedicated the speech to Toot. The day before the election, Obama announced that his grandmother had died of cancer late Sunday night. However, before she passed away, she had cast an absentee ballot for her grandson for president of the United States of America.

Tuesday, November 4, 2008, was election day. After a 22-month campaign season (seventeen months were spent determining the nominee for the two major parties), the election would come down to turnout, or Get Out The Vote (GOTV) in campaign speak. Actually, around 31 percent of the electorate had already voted early or by absentee ballot. Both campaigns had encouraged early voting so that they would have fewer people to track on election day.[4] The big question that still remained was whether turnout would be as large as the political pundits were predicting. There were still many questions at the start of election day. Would racism keep the South from voting for an African American? Would the young show up and vote? Would white women and Latinos who supported Hillary Clinton vote for Obama? Would the conservative base turn out and vote for McCain? What about Independents? Would they decide the election?

Obama voted early and took his daughters with him to the voting booth. Many other parents saw this as a historic election and they wanted their children to take part as well. Grade schools and high schools around the country held mock elections for the president this year. In fact, there was a National Student/Parent Mock Election held for students of all ages—from kindergarten through college—to vote for their candidates of choice on October 30.[5] The idea was to allow young citizens to let their voices be heard.

One of the initial concerns was the possibility of too many voters and problems with ballots or voting machines. Due to the high voter registration levels around the country, there was concern as to whether election officials would be able to handle a tremendous volume.[6] The media were reporting heavy turnout and long lines in some precincts around the country as the polls opened. Throughout the day, there were voting machine glitches across the country, but in most instances, the election officials were able to resolve the problems and accommodate people who were eligible to vote.

Old Style Get Out the Vote

There is a time-honored tradition in politics that enhances get-out-the-vote efforts. It is called "walking around passing out money." It is a tradition as old as politics itself, and like negative campaigning, it is disreputable, but effective. There were allegations made during the nomination campaign that the Clintons were walking around passing out money to black ministers but these allegations were not substantiated. Evan Thomas notes that "The money is usually given out to local pols, grassroots community leaders and preachers, particularly in poorer areas inhabited by racial and ethnic minorities. As money changes hands, a certain amount of winking is typically involved; not all of the funds go to, say, hiring drivers or passing out leaflets, and the recipients are not shy about asking."[7] Obama, who refused to engage in this practice during the primary, was confronted with this opportunity on election day. Obama was told that it was part of the culture in some locations around the country. Although legal, the Obama campaign ultimately refused to provide any walking around money, but some was provided by local operatives.[8]

Election Results

Polls began to close around the country at 7:00 p.m. eastern standard time. Shortly thereafter, the news media, based on exit polling, began announcing their state-by-state projected winners. Pennsylvania, Illinois, Maine, Maryland, Michigan, and New York all went into the Obama column. After Ohio was called for Obama at approximately 9:20 p.m. eastern standard time, McCain's path to victory appeared increasingly impossible.[9] No Republican had ever won the presidency without winning Ohio. CNN and Fox News projected that Obama would win Virginia, which put him only fifty electoral votes short of victory. Six West Coast states were still voting, as well as Hawaii. California alone had fifty-five Electoral College votes, more than enough to put Obama over the top. At 11:00 p.m. eastern standard time, when the polls closed on the West Coast, all the networks simultaneously called the election for Barack Obama.

Katie Couric of CBS News broke in at the top of the hour, "No matter who you voted for, you'd have to agree, this is an incredible milestone in the history of this country."[10] After Brian Williams of NBC News called the election for Obama, he asked Tom Brokaw, NBC News analyst, for his reaction. Brokaw stated, "This is a very emotional moment for everyone in this country and for the world, for that matter. This is not just a moment in American history; this is a profoundly important passage out of the deep shadows of our racist past that began with that first slave off-loaded on a ship. Race has been a curse for America for a long time. We have been working our way through it."[11] Obama was declared the winner in Washington, California, Oregon, and Hawaii; McCain won Idaho. The Electoral College total now stood at 297 for Obama and 146 for McCain. Obama had surpassed the 270 threshold needed to win the election. Where the two candidates spent election night and planned to hold their victory parties said volumes about the two campaigns: Obama held his election night event in Chicago at Hutchinson Field in Grant Park, an open-air venue used for concerts and sporting events; McCain held his election night event at the Arizona Biltmore, a luxury hotel in Phoenix where he and his wife were married.

One half-hour after the election was called for Obama, McCain gave an eloquent and dignified concession speech. He acknowledged the milestone this country had achieved with the election of the first African American president. At 12:00 a.m. eastern standard time, President-Elect Barack Obama appeared in Grant Park, Chicago, Illinois, to give his victory speech to a jubilant crowd of 250,000 people. Celebrations erupted around the world from Washington, D.C., to San Francisco, California, to Obama, Japan, to Nairobi, Kenya. Change had finally come to America.

Turnout in the 2008 General Election

Turnout for the election was expected to be high. Voter registration numbers were up and a record number of voters cast a vote due to tremendous efforts on the part of both campaigns to get out the vote. The final results showed 131.2 million Americans voted in the 2008 presidential election, compared to 122.3 million in 2004 (an increase of nine million votes). The turnout rate increased 1.5 percent from 2004 to 61.6 percent.[12] According to George Pomper, turnout varied among the states. He noted that it "increased by double digits in seven Southern states, as well as Arizona, Colorado, Hawaii, Indiana, and Nevada, largely because of registration drives by the Obama campaign focused on African Americans and Latinos."[13] More Democrats voted than Republicans, according to exit polls, by a 39 percent to 32 percent margin, which represented a change from 2004 when turnout for the two parties was 36 percent for the Democrats and 37 percent for the Republicans.[14] One can only speculate as to why Republican turnout declined for this election; however, Curtis Gans, director of American University's Center for the Study of the American Electorate, asserted, "Some of the culturally conservative Republicans did not see McCain as one of their own, while moderates were appalled by the selection of Governor Palin and McCain's hawkish view on foreign policy. A portion of the GOP registrants also likely perceived . . . a Democratic landslide and became discouraged."[15]

Region

According to Pomper, Democrats changed their strategy to win a majority of the electoral votes and, thus, win the White House. Rather than repeat the minimalist strategy of Gore in 2000 and of Kerry in 2004, Obama opened up the contest to more states and more areas (often Republican) within these states.[16] As a result of this strategy, notes Pomper, "Obama won a majority of the states, 28, and the District of Columbia. Holding all of the 20 states won by Kerry in 2004, Obama added nine states carried by Bush in 2004, as well as one electoral vote from Nebraska."[17] Obama won the entire Northeast, the entire West Coast, and Hawaii. Moreover, Obama swept the Midwest, including three states won by Bush in 2004, won three of the Confederate states of the South (one Deep South and two Upper South), and won three of eight Rocky Mountain states.[18] Obama was particularly impressive in that he won almost all of the battleground states including Florida, Indiana, North Carolina, Ohio, Virginia, and the two western states of Nevada and Colorado.

Diversity

The electorate in the 2008 presidential race was the most racially and ethnically diverse in American history according to a Pew Hispanic Center study.[19] Whites were still the largest voting bloc, comprising slightly over three-fourths (76.3 percent) of the total electorate. Blacks made up 12.1 percent, Hispanics 7.4 percent, and Asians 2.5 percent. The white percentage voting was the lowest ever, but still higher than the 65.8 percent of the total nation's population.[20] Voter participation levels increased for blacks, Hispanics, and Asians, closing the gap between their level of voting and whites'. For black eligible voters, the turnout rate increased 4.9 percentage points, from 60.3 percent in 2004 to 65.2 percent in 2008, which almost reaches parity with the turnout rate of white eligible voters (66.1 percent). This is significant because as a result of the Voting Rights Act of 1965, black voter registration in the eleven states of the Old Confederacy has nearly reached parity with white voters.

Voter participation levels also increased for Hispanics, with voter turnout increasing 2.7 percentage points, from 47.2 percent in 2004 to 49.9 percent in 2008. Asian Americans increased their voter participation levels as well, from 44.6 percent in 2004 to 47.0 percent in 2008.[21] According to the Pew Study, much of the surge in black voter participation in 2008 was due to increased participation among black women and younger voters. Eligible black female voters increased their turnout rate 5.1 percentage points, from 63.7 percent in 2004 to 68.8 percent in 2008. Among all racial, ethnic, and gender groups, black women had the highest voter turnout rate on November 4, 2008. Blacks ages 18 to 29 increased their voter turnout rate from 49.5 percent in 2004 to 58.2 percent in 2008. Furthermore, the voter turnout rate among young black eligible voters was higher than that for young eligible voters of any other racial and ethnic group in 2008.[22] Additionally, the Pew Study emphasized that the rise in diversity in the electorate was largely a result of the population growth, particularly among Hispanics. From 2004 to 2008, the number of Hispanic eligible voters rose from 16.1 million in 2004 to 19.5 million in 2008, 21.4 percent, as compared to just a 4.6 percent increase in the number of eligible voters in the general population. One telling statistic was that with population growth and increased voter participation among blacks, Latinos, and Asians, voters of all three groups increased their percentage of all eligible voters. Moreover, the percentage of eligible voters who were white dropped from 75.2 percent in 2004 to 73.4 percent in 2008.[23]

The Pew Hispanic Center election study found a regional pattern in the state-by-state increases in voter turnout. According to their findings, the largest turnout increases were in Southern states with large black eligible populations: Mississippi, Georgia, North Carolina, Louisiana, and Washington, D.C.[24] The changing demographics will have electoral consequences for years to come. As noted in the Pew Hispanic Center report, the fastest growing group of eligible voters is Hispanics. And due to immigration and population increases, they are the nation's largest and fastest growing minority group, and were a part of Obama's majority coalition.

The Electoral College

The president is not elected by direct popular vote, but by a group of individuals known as electors. Each state is given a number of electors equal to its number of congressional representatives and senators. The District of Columbia is given three electors for a total of 538. To win the presidency, a candidate needs to garner a simple majority of the electoral votes (270). The presidential election is not a national election, and therefore, it is up to each state to determine how its electoral votes will be allotted. Most states use a winner-take-all system, in that all the state's electors go to the winner of the popular vote in that state. Two states (Maine and Nebraska) divide their electoral votes by congressional district.[25] On November 4, 2008, America was not voting directly for the presidential candidates, but was voting for each state's (and the District of Columbia's) slate of electors. The results of the popular vote gave Barack Obama 69,498,216 votes (53 percent) and John McCain 59,948,240 (46 percent). That translated into 365 electoral votes for Obama (68 percent) and 173 electoral votes for John McCain (32 percent).[26] It was a decisive victory for Obama and his popular vote percentage was the best showing for any president since George H. W. Bush in 1988.

A Transformative Election for America

This election is transformative for America. Peggy Wallace Kennedy, 58, the daughter of the late Governor George Wallace of Alabama who once vowed to maintain segregation forever, voted for Barack Obama for president. Bob Moses, who as a member of the Student Nonviolent Coordinating Committee (SNCC) headed the Mississippi Freedom Summer Project in 1964 when three civil rights workers were murdered, said, "The country is trying to reach for the best part of itself."[27] The Rev. James Zwerg, who almost lost his life in the "Freedom Rides" during the civil rights movement, noted, "Obama's victory means the country has gone full circle."[28] John Lewis, who as a member of SNCC led the civil rights marchers as they attempted to cross the Edmund Pettus Bridge in what became known as "Bloody Sunday," is now a member of the U.S. Congress. On election night, after victory was declared for Obama, he said he never thought he would live to see the day that America elected an African American as president of the United States.[29]

Barack Obama did not run a flawless campaign, but he did run a highly disciplined and smart campaign. Obama has keen political instincts and is politically savvy. He chose to run for president when others advised him it was too soon. He chose to announce his candidacy when others told him it was too early. His campaign was bold and innovative from the beginning. But the lessons learned from this campaign are that he used old media (radio, television, newspapers) in addition to new media (Facebook, MySpace, YouTube, Blackberry, Twitter) to get his message out. He also used old money (bundlers and big money campaign donors) along with new money (thousands of small contributions of $10, $15, and $25). He integrated old style campaign organizing (canvassing door to door) with new style organizing (cell phone GOTV parties). His campaign has changed the way presidential campaigns will be carried out forever. He attracted a cadre of young foot soldiers and gave them inspiration and a reason they could believe in—and then he turned them loose. He gave America a message of hope and unity and taught us all once again that words do matter. He built a coalition of Americans that truly looks like America from all ages, backgrounds, races, and ethnicities.

The election of Barack Obama as the 44th president of the United States provides redemption for America. Numerous African Americans have told the story of how proud they were to be an American; they have a renewed faith in their country, and a sense of pride and patriotism. Other minorities are equally proud that an African American was elected as president. Many in the white community are relieved that race did not decide this election. It has renewed their faith, also, that America can live up to the lofty ideals extolled in the Declaration of Independence and codified in the Constitution—of equality, liberty, and opportunity for all. Obama's election brought needed redemption for America.

Out of forty-four presidents that have taken the oath of office, Obama is the first African American. The youngest cohort that voted in this election seemed to be eager to elect Obama based on his message and embrace his diverse background and heritage. Change was his campaign slogan. Not only did Obama offer a message of change but he embodied change. He offered a change in the direction for this country from the previous eight years, he offered a change as to how he would run his campaign, and he personified change with an African father from Kenya and a white mother from Kansas and his birth in the 50th state, Hawaii. The personal growth of the candidate is an equally compelling story to come out of this election. He stumbled in his early debates, and his initial speeches, although powerful, were often professorial. He learned to embrace his audiences and they in turn embraced him. He found his voice on the campaign trail. Furthermore, he grew in his ability to act and be presidential. At the end of the campaign, John McCain may have had just too many obstacles to overcome: an unpopular president of his party, an economic recession, an inexperienced vice presidential choice, and campaign finance limitations. But in the final analysis, it was Barack Obama who made the better case as to why *he* should be elected president of the United States.

On election night in Chicago's Grant Park, when President-Elect Barack Obama took the stage after his incredible victory, he proclaimed, "If there is anyone out there who still doubts that America is a place where all things are possible; who still wonders if the dream of our fathers is alive in our time; who still questions the power of our democracy—tonight is your answer."[30] Obama fully recognizes what barriers he has broken and what possibilities now exist for all Americans. The symbolism of his victory alone is enormous. Civil rights icon and current chairman of the National Association for the Advancement of Colored People Julian Bond stated, "This election means Black parents will no longer have to lie when they tell their children they can do anything."[31] Obama faced fear mongering and racism through-out his campaign but he persevered and triumphed. Hill Harper, a classmate of Obama's at Harvard Law School, said with the election of Obama as president that "Obama has sparked a transformation in the psyche, self-esteem and aspiration of young Black males. His positive impact will be seen for generations to come."[32] Obama represents not just a new style of black leadership, but a new style of charismatic leadership. Throughout the campaign, he always told supporters that this election was about them. He turned the traditional top-down management style of campaigning on its head with his grassroots, bottom-up approach. He is a transformational individual. He has changed the way political campaigns will be managed, organized, and run forever.

The significance of Barack Obama's election is that the doors of opportunity are now open to all Americans: Women, Asian Americans, Latinos, African Americans, and Whites. His ability to motivate and empower his supporters to set their own goals and achieve them during the campaign was remark-able and has broad applicability beyond the political arena. His campaign was a profound example of leadership. His leadership style and management style are already being adopted by titans of corporate America, as well as other institutions of American society. Finally, his election offers enormous possi-bilities for the democratic process in this country. Obama inspired a large cohort of young American voters who were uninterested in politics to get organized and involved. Moreover, many more Americans became involved in the election because they now believe that the United States is truly their democracy.

Notes

1: Introduction

1   Carolyn Kilpatrick, interview by author, Louisville, Kentucky, December 19, 2008.

2   Article 1, Section 2, United States Constitution.

3   Kenneth Janda, Jeffrey Berry, and Jerry Goldman, *The Challenge of Democracy*, 10th ed. (Boston, MA: Wadsworth, 2009), 494.

4   John Hope Franklin and Alfred A. Moss, Jr., *From Slavery to Freedom: A History of Negro Americans*, 6th ed. (New York: Knopf, 1988), 220.

5   Franklin and Moss, *From Slavery to Freedom*, 220.

6   Franklin and Moss, *From Slavery to Freedom*, 230.

7   Franklin and Moss, *From Slavery to Freedom*, 226.

8   Franklin and Moss, *From Slavery to Freedom*, 230.

9   Franklin and Moss, *From Slavery to Freedom*, 230.

10   Franklin and Moss, *From Slavery to Freedom*, 230.

11   Hanes Walton and Robert C. Smith, *American Politics and the African American Quest for Universal Freedom*, 5th ed. (New York: Longman Publishing, 2010), 31.

12   Franklin and Moss, *From Slavery to Freedom*, 236.

13   Franklin and Moss, *From Slavery to Freedom*, 236.

14   Franklin and Moss, *From Slavery to Freedom*, 237.

15   Derrick Bell, *Race, Racism, and American Law*, 6th ed. (New York: Aspen Publishers, 2008), 482–484.

16   Bell, *Race, Racism, and American Law*, 486–488.

17   George Davis and Fred Donaldson, *Blacks in the United States: A Geographic Perspective* (Boston, MA: Houghton Mifflin Company, 1975), 31.

18   Franklin and Moss, *From Slavery to Freedom*, 280.

19   Davis and Donaldson, *Blacks in the United States*, 31.

20   Jack C. Plano and Milton Greenberg, *The American Political Dictionary* (Fort Worth, TX: Holt, Rinehart, and Winston, Inc., 1993), 347.

21   Franklin and Moss, *From Slavery to Freedom*, 412.

22   Plano and Greenberg, *The American Political Dictionary*, 347.

23 Janda, Berry, and Goldman, *The Challenge of Democracy*, 502–503.

24 Lucius Barker, Mack Jones, and Katherine Tate, *African Americans and the American Political System*, 4th ed. (Englewood Cliffs, NJ: Prentice-Hall, Inc., 1999), 234–235.

25 C. Vann Woodward, *The Strange Career of Jim Crow*, 3rd ed. (New York: Oxford University Press, 1966), 122–147.

26 William Clay, Just Permanent Interests: *Black Americans in Congress, 1870–1991* (New York: Amistad Press, 1992), ix.

27 Walton and Smith, *American Politics and the African American Quest*, 186.

28 Quoted in Paula McClain, Niambi Carter, and Michael Brady, "Gender and Black Presidential Politics: From Chisholm to Moseley Braun," *Journal of Women, Politics, and Policy* 27, nos. 1–2 (2005), 56.

29 McClain, Carter, and Brady, "Gender and Black Presidential Politics," 56.

30 Charles W. Carey, Jr., *African-American Political Leaders: A–Z of African Americans* (New York: Fact on File, 2004), 46.

31 Carey, *African-American Political Leaders*, 142.

32 Katherine Tate, "Black Political Participation in the 1984 and 1988 Presidential Elections," *American Political Science Review* 84 (1991): 1159–1176.

33 Quoted in Francis X. Clines, "The Powell Decision," *New York Times*, November 9, 1995, http://query.nytimes.com/gst/fullpage.html?res=9A06E5 DB1439F93AA35752C1A963958260 (June 29, 2009).

34 Carey, *African-American Political Leaders*, 219.

35 McClain, Carter, and Brady, "Gender and Black Presidential Politics," 60.

36 McClain, Carter, and Brady, "Gender and Black Presidential Politics," 59, 60.

37 McClain, Carter, and Brady, "Gender and Black Presidential Politics," 60.

38 Anne Raso, "His Early Life," *Today's Black Woman Presents: Barack Obama*, Collector's Edition #87, vol. 15, no. 5 (2008): 10–17.

39 David Mendell, *Obama: From Promise to Power* (New York: HarperCollins Publishers, 2007), 59.

40 Mendell, *Obama*, 62.

41 Mendell, *Obama*, 63.

42 Mendell, *Obama*, 63.

43 Mendell, *Obama*, 63.

44 Mendell, *Obama*, 64.

45 Barack Obama, *Dreams from My Father* (New York: Three Rivers Press, 2004), 289.

46 James L. Merriner, "The Friends of O," *Chicago* 57, no. 6 (June 2008), 78.

47 Merriner, "The Friends of O," 97.

48 Merriner, "The Friends of O," 97.

49 Quoted in Merriner, "The Friends of O," 97.

50 Richard Wolffe and Daren Briscoe, "Across the Divide," *Newsweek*, July 16, 2007, http://www.newsweek.com/id/33156/output/print (July 19, 2009).

51 Quoted in Merriner, "The Friends of O," 98.

52 Wolffe and Briscoe, "Across the Divide."

53 David Mendell, "Obama Routs Democratic Foes; Ryan Tops Crowded GOP Field," *Chicago Tribune*, Campaign 2004: Illinois Primary, March 17, 2004, http://www.chicagotribune.com/features/custom/fashion/chi-04031 70332mar17,0,4716349.story (July 21, 2009).

54 CNN.com, "AmericaVotes2004: Election Results," Cable News Network, LP, http://www.cnn.com/ELECTION/2004/pages/results/states/IL/S/01/index.htm l (July 19, 2009).

55 Robert Starks, "How He Did It: An Analysis of the Obama Tsunami," *N'Digo Profiles*, December 2008, 34.

56 Merriner, "The Friends of O," 98.

57 Merriner, "The Friends of O," 98.

58 Quoted in Mark Blumenthal, "Ambinder: Race Over?," *Pollster.com*, January 7, 2009, http://www.pollster.com/blogs/ambinder_race_over.php (July 20, 2009).

59 Quoted in Peter Katel, "Race and Politics," in *Issues in Race and Ethnicity*, Congressional Quarterly Researcher, 4th ed., 1–24 (Washington, DC: CQ Press, 2009), 3.

60 Quoted in Jackson Putnam, *Jess: The Political Career of Jesse Marvin Unruh* (Lanham, MD: University Press of America, 2005), 523.

61 Steve Schifferes, "Internet Key to Obama Victories," *BBC News*, Technology Section, June 12, 2008, http://news.bbc.co.uk/2/hi/technology/7412045.stm (July 20, 2009).

62 Schifferes, "Internet Key to Obama Victories."

63 Starks, "How He Did It," 34.

64 Jann Wenner, "A New Hope," *Rolling Stone*, Commemorative Edition 55 (March 20, 2008): 53–55.

65 Barack Obama, "Keynote Address," delivered at the 2004 Democratic National Convention, Fleet Center, Boston, MA, July 27, 2004.

66 Obama, "Keynote Address."

67 Obama, "Keynote Address."

68 Amy Sullivan, "A Star Is Born," *Time*, Special Commemorative Edition (2008), 64.

69 Quoted in Sullivan, "A Star Is Born," 64.

2: Descriptive and Substantive Representation

1   Steve Cohen, interview by author, Louisville, KY, December 19, 2008.

2   H. F. Pitkin, *The Concept of Representation* (Berkeley: University of California Press, 1967).

3   Jeffrey Elliot and Sheikh R. Ali, *The Presidential-Congressional Political Dictionary* (Santa Barbara, CA: ABC-Clio Information Services, 1984), 182.

4   Hanes Walton and Robert C. Smith, *American Politics and the African American Quest for Universal Freedom*, 5th ed. (New York: Longman Publishing, 2010), 31.

5   V. O. Key, *Southern Politics* (New York: Alfred Knopf, 1949), 6.

6   Derrick Bell, *Race, Racism and American Law*, 6th ed. (New York: Aspen Publishers, 2008), 42.

7   Eric Anderson, *Race and Politics in North Carolina:1872–1901* (Baton Rouge: Louisiana State University Press, 1981), 310.

8   Robert Dahl, *A Preface to Democratic Theory* (Chicago, IL: University of Chicago Press, 1956), 95.

9   Dahl, *A Preface to Democratic Theory*, 95.

10 Joseph Schumpeter, *Capitalism, Socialism, and Democracy* (New York: Harper and Row, 1942).

11 Thomas L. Brunell, *Redistricting and Representation: Why Competitive Elections are Bad for America* (New York: Routledge, 2008), 21–22; Schumpeter, *Capitalism, Socialism, and Democracy*.

12 Pitkin, *The Concept of Representation*, 61.

13 Carol M. Swain, *Black Faces, Black Interests: The Representation of African Americans in Congress* (Cambridge, MA: Harvard University Press, 1993), 5.

14 Jack C. Plano and Milton Greenburg, *The American Political Dictionary* (Fort Worth, TX: Holt, Rinehart, and Winston, Inc., 1993), 23.

15 Michael C. Dawson, *Behind the Mule: Race and Class in African-American Politics* (Princeton, NJ: Princeton University Press, 2004), 76.

16 Bell, *Race, Racism, and American Law*, 517–518.

17 Pitkin, *The Concept of Representation*, 90.

18 Timothy Bledsoe, "A Research Note on the Impact of District/At-Large Elections on Black Political Efficacy," *Urban Affairs Quarterly* 22 (1986): 166–174; Lawrence Bobo and Franklin D. Gilliam, Jr., "Race, Sociopolitical Participation, and Black Empowerment," *American Political Science Review* 84, no. 2 (June 1990): 377–393; James Vanderleeuw, Baodong Lui, and Erica Williams, "The 2006 New Orleans Mayoral Election: The Political Ramifications of a Large-Scale Natural Disaster," *PS: Political Science and Politics* 41 (October 2008): 1–7.

19 Brunell, *Redistricting and Representation*, 16; Edmund Burke, *Reflections on the Revolution in France* [1790] (Essex, England: Pearson Longman, 2006).

20   Chris T. Owens, "Black Substantive Representation in State Legislatures from 1971–1994," *Social Science Quarterly* 86, no. 4 (2005): 779–791.

21   Kenny J. Whitby, *The Color of Representation: Congressional Behavior and Black Interests* (Ann Arbor: University of Michigan Press, 2000); Charles S. Bullock and Susan A. MacManus, "Policy Responsiveness to the Black Electorate: Programmatic Versus Symbolic Representation," *American Politics Quarterly* 9 (1981): 357–368; Charles Cameron, David Epstein, and Sharyn O'Halloran, "Do Majority-Minority Districts Maximize Substantive Black Representation in Congress?," *American Political Science Review* 90 (1996): 794–812.

22   Dawson, *Behind the Mule*, 144

23   Dawson, *Behind the Mule*, 144.

24   Bell, *Race, Racism, and American Law*, 517–518.

25   Katherine Tate, "The Political Representation of Blacks in Congress: Does Race Matter?," *Legislative Studies Quarterly* 26, no. 4 (November 2001): 623–638.

26   Swain, *Black Faces, Black Interests*.

27   David Lublin, *The Paradox of Representation: Racial Gerrymandering and Minority Interests in Congress* (Princeton, NJ: Princeton University Press, 1997); Whitby, *The Color of Representation*; David T. Canon, *Race, Redistricting, and Representation: The Unintended Consequences of Black Majority Districts* (Chicago, IL: Univeristy of Chicago Press, 1999); Katherine Tate, *Black Faces in the Mirror: African Americans and Their Representatives in the U.S. Congress* (Princeton, NJ: Princeton University Press, 2003).

28   Walton and Smith, *American Politics and the African American Quest*, 185.

29   Walton and Smith, *American Politics and the African American Quest*, 185.

30   Walton and Smith, *American Politics and the African American Quest*, 185.

31   Quoted in Walton and Smith, *American Politics and the African American Quest*, 186.

32   Walton and Smith, *American Politics and the African American Quest*, 186.

33   Walton and Smith, *American Politics and the African American Quest*, 210.

34   Walton and Smith, *American Politics and the African American Quest*, 164–165.

35   Walton and Smith, *American Politics and the African American Quest*, 164–165.

36   Walton and Smith, *American Politics and the African American Quest*, 165.

37   E. Cose, "The 'Bradley Effect,'" *Newsweek*, October 30, 2006, http://www.msnbc.msn.com/id/15366427/site/newsweek/ (April 12, 2007).

38   David Bositis, interview by author, Louisville, KY, October 23, 2008.

39   Thomas Schaller, *Whistling Past Dixie: How Democrats Can Win Without the South* (New York: Simon and Schuster, 2006), 88.

40   Walton and Smith, *American Politics and the African American Quest*, 167.

41   Walton and Smith, *American Politics and the African American Quest*, 167.

42 Rachel Swarns, "Quiet Political Shifts as More Blacks Are Elected," *New York Times*, October 14, 2008, http://www.nytimes.com/2008/10/14/us/politics/14race.html (July 1, 2009).

43 Quoted in Swarns, "Quiet Political Shifts as More Blacks Are Elected."

44 Swarns, "Quiet Political Shifts as More Blacks Are Elected."

45 Quoted in Swarns, "Quiet Political Shifts as More Blacks Are Elected."

46 James Clyburn, interview by author, Louisville, KY, December 1, 2008.

47 Bernard Grofman and Chandler Davidson (eds.), *Controversies in Minority Voting: The Voting Rights Act in Perspective* (Washington, DC: Brookings Institution, 1992).

48 Quoted in Bernard Grofman, "Expert Witness Testimony and the Evolution of Voting Rights Case Law," in *Controversies in Minority Voting*, eds. Bernard Grofman and Chandler Davidson, 197–229 (Washington, DC: Brookings Institution, 1992), 206.

49 Quoted in Grofman, "Expert Witness Testimony and the Evolution of Voting Rights Case Law," 207.

50 Quoted in Grofman, "Expert Witness Testimony and the Evolution of Voting Rights Case Law," 207.

51 Grofman, "Expert Witness Testimony and the Evolution of Voting Rights Case Law," 207.

52 Grofman, "Expert Witness Testimony and the Evolution of Voting Rights Case Law," 207–208.

53 Carolyn Kilpatrick, interview by author, Louisville, KY, December 19, 2008.

54 Matt Bai, "Is Obama the End of Black Politics?," *New York Times Magazine*, August 6, 2008, http://www.nytimes.com/2008/08/10/magazine/10politics-t.html (July 21, 2009).

55 Bai, "Is Obama the End of Black Politics?," 3.

56 Bai, "Is Obama the End of Black Politics?," 4.

57 Bai, "Is Obama the End of Black Politics?," 4.

58 Gwen Ifill, *The Breakthrough: Politics and Race in the Age of Obama* (New York: Doubleday, 2009), 113.

59 Ifill, *The Breakthrough*, 113.

60 Ifill, *The Breakthrough*.

61 Ifill, *The Breakthrough*, 26.

62 Quoted in Ifill, *The Breakthrough*, 27.

63 Artur Davis, interview by author, Louisville, KY, November 18, 2008.

64 Bai, "Is Obama the End of Black Politics?," 5.

65 Quoted in Bai, "Is Obama the End of Black Politics?," 5.

66 Walton and Smith, *American Politics and the African American Quest*, 184.

67 Derrick Bell, *Faces at the Bottom of the Well: The Permanence of Racism* (New York: Basic Books, 1992), 23.

68 Lawrence Mishel, Jared Bernstein, and Heidi Shierholz, *The State of Working America 2008/2009*. Economic Policy Institute, State of Working America Series, 2006–2009, http://www.stateofworkingamerica.org (July 21, 2009).
69 Kilpatrick, interview by author, December 19, 2008.
70 Patricia Ardon, *Post-War Reconstruction in Central America: Lessons from El Salvador, Guatemala, and Nicaragua* (Oxford: Oxfam GB, 1999), 9.
71 Article 1, Section 8, United States Constitution.
72 Richard E. Neustadt, *Presidential Power* (New York: Wiley, 1980), 10.
73 Kenneth Janda, Jeffrey Berry, and Jerry Goldman, *The Challenge of Democracy*, 10th ed. (Boston, MA: Wadsworth, 2009), 375.
74 Janda, Berry, and Goldman, *The Challenge of Democracy*, 375.
75 Samuel Kernell, *Going Public: New Strategies of Presidential Leadership*, 3rd ed. (Washington, DC: CQ Press, 1997), 2.
76 Janda, Berry, and Goldman, *The Challenge of Democracy*, 375.
77 Rachel Swarns, "Could It Really Be Him? Yeah, Probably," *New York Times*, March 26, 2009, http://www.nytimes.com/2009/03/26/fashion/26washington.html (July 21, 2009).
78 Swarns, "Could It Really Be Him?"
79 Swarns, "Could It Really Be Him?"
80 Swarns, "Could It Really Be Him?"
81 Swarns, "Could It Really Be Him?"
82 Janda, Berry, and Goldman, *The Challenge of Democracy*, 375.
83 Janda, Berry, and Goldman, *The Challenge of Democracy*, 375.
84 Byron D. Orey and Boris E. Ricks, *A Systematic Analysis of the Deracialization Concept* (University of Nebraska: Faculty Publications, 2007), 325.
85 Orey and Ricks, *A Systematic Analysis*, 326.
86 Orey and Ricks, *A Systematic Analysis*, 326.
87 Orey and Ricks, *A Systematic Analysis*, 326.
88 Quoted in Orey and Ricks, *A Systematic Analysis*, 327.
89 Orey and Ricks, *A Systematic Analysis*, 327.
90 Quoted in Orey and Ricks, *A Systematic Analysis*, 327.
91 Quoted in Orey and Ricks, *A Systematic Analysis*, 328.
92 Orey and Ricks, *A Systematic Analysis*, 328.
93 Orey and Ricks, *A Systematic Analysis*, 328.
94 William Lacy Clay, interview by author, Louisville, KY, December 9, 2008.
95 James Clyburn, interview by author, Louisville, KY, December 1, 2008.
96 John Harrigan and Ronald Vogel, "The City as a Place of Opportunity," in *Political Change in the Metropolis*, 146–159 (New York: HarperCollins, 2000).
97 Vanderleeuw, Lui, and Williams, "The 2006 New Orleans Mayoral Election," 795–801.

98   Erica Williams, Untitled Master's Thesis, University of Louisville, 2009; Ricky
     L. Jones, *What's Wrong with Obamamania? Black America, Black Leadership, and
     the Death of Political Imagination* (New York: State University of New York Press,
     2008).
99   Williams, Untitled Master's Thesis, University of Louisville, 2009.

3: Obama's Winning Coalition

1   G. K. Butterfield, interview by author, Louisville, KY, November 19, 2008.
2   Ronald Brownstein, "Obama Buoyed by Coalition of the Ascendant," in *Annual
     Editions: American Government 09/10*, 39th ed., ed. B. Stinebrickner (New York:
     McGraw-Hill, 2010), 141–143.
3   Quoted in Brownstein, "Obama Buoyed by Coalition of the Ascendant,"
     141–143.
4   Quoted in Alan Greenblatt, "Changing U.S. Electorate," in *Issues in Race and
     Ethnicity*, Congressional Quarterly Researcher, 4th ed., 25–47 (Washington,
     DC: CQ Press, 2009), 26.
5   Gerald Pomper, "The Presidential Election: Change Comes to America," in *The
     Elections of 2008*, ed. Michael Nelson, 45–73 (Washington, DC: CQ Press,
     2010), 55.
6   Pomper, "The Presidential Election," 55.
7   Pomper, "The Presidential Election," 55.
8   Pomper, "The Presidential Election," 55.
9   Pomper, "The Presidential Election," 55.
10   Pomper, "The Presidential Election," 55.
11   Brownstein, "Obama Buoyed by Coalition of the Ascendant," 142.
12   Brownstein, "Obama Buoyed by Coalition of the Ascendant," 142.
13   Brownstein, "Obama Buoyed by Coalition of the Ascendant," 143.
14   John Judis and Ruy Teixeira, *The Emerging Democratic Majority* (New York:
     Scribner, 2002).
15   John Judis, "America the Liberal," in *Annual Editions: American Government
     09/10*, 39th ed., ed. B. Stinebrickner, 109–111 (New York: McGraw-Hill,
     2010), 109.
16   Judis, "America the Liberal," 109.
17   Quoted in Judis and Teixeira, *The Emerging Democratic Majority*, 12–13.
18   Quoted in Judis and Teixeira, *The Emerging Democratic Majority*, 13.
19   Judis and Teixeira, *The Emerging Democratic Majority*, 13–14 (see footnote).
20   Judis and Teixeira, *The Emerging Democratic Majority*, 14.
21   Hanes Walton and Robert C. Smith, *American Politics and the African American
     Quest for Universal Freedom*, 5th ed. (New York: Longman Publishing, 2010),
     96.

22 Judis and Teixeira, *The Emerging Democratic Majority*, 14.

23 Michael Nelson, "How the GOP Conquered the South," *The Chronicle of Higher Education*, *The Chronicle Review*, October 21, 2005, http://chronicle.com/free/v52/i09/09b01401.htm (July 21, 2009).

24 Nelson, "How the GOP Conquered the South."

25 Peter Katel, "Race and Politics," in *Issues in Race and Ethnicity*, Congressional Quarterly Researcher, 4th ed., 1–24 (Washington, DC: CQ Press, 2009), 11.

26 Quoted in Katel, "Race and Politics," 11.

27 Katel, "Race and Politics," 12.

28 Greenblatt, "Changing U.S. Electorate," 37–38.

29 Greenblatt, "Changing U.S. Electorate," 38.

30 Quoted in Greenblatt, "Changing U.S. Electorate," 38.

31 Greenblatt, "Changing U.S. Electorate," 37.

32 Katel, "Race and Politics," 13.

33 Greenblatt, "Changing U.S. Electorate," 39.

34 Walton and Smith, *American Politics and the African American Quest*, 134.

35 Quoted in Katel, "Race and Politics," 15.

36 Katel, "Race and Politics," 16

37 Katel, "Race and Politics," 16.

38 Greenblatt, "Changing U.S. Electorate," 41.

39 Walton and Smith, *American Politics and the African American Quest*, 134–135.

40 Walton and Smith, *American Politics and the African American Quest*, 135.

41 Walton and Smith, *American Politics and the African American Quest*, 135.

42 Walton and Smith, *American Politics and the African American Quest*, 135–136.

43 Walton and Smith, *American Politics and the African American Quest*, 136.

44 Walton and Smith, *American Politics and the African American Quest*, 138.

45 Walton and Smith, *American Politics and the African American Quest*, 138.

46 Walton and Smith, *American Politics and the African American Quest*, 138.

47 Quoted in Jerry Large, "A New Era Begins: The Significance of the Barack Obama Victory for America and the World," *BlackPast.org*, Perspectives on African American History, 2007–2008, http://www.blackpast.org/?q=perspectives/new-era-begins-significance-barack-obama-victory-america-and-world (July 21, 2009).

48 Quoted in Adam Nossiter, "For South, a Waning Hold on National Politics," *New York Times*, November 10, 2008, http://www.nytimes.com/2008/11/11/us/politics/11south.html?_r=1&scp=1&sq=for%20south%20a%20waning%20hold%20on%20national%20politics&st=cse (November 11, 2008).

49 Thomas Schaller, *Whistling Past Dixie: How Democrats Can Win Without the South* (New York: Simon and Schuster, 2006), 2.

50 Schaller, *Whistling Past Dixie*, 2.

51 Quoted in Nossiter, "For South, a Waning Hold on National Politics."

52   Nossiter, "For South, a Waning Hold on National Politics."

53   Quoted in Nossiter, "For South, a Waning Hold on National Politics."

54   Nossiter, "For South, a Waning Hold on National Politics."

55   Quoted in Robin Toner, "Obama Camp Thinks Democrats Can Rise in South," *New York Times*, June 30, 2008, http://www.nytimes.com/2008/06/30/us/politics/30south.html?scp=2&sq=Obama%20camp%20thinks%20democrats&st=Search (June 30, 2008).

56   Quoted in Toner, "Obama Camp Thinks Democrats Can Rise in South."

57   Toner, "Obama Camp Thinks Democrats Can Rise in South."

58   Quoted in Toner, "Obama Camp Thinks Democrats Can Rise in South."

59   Chuck Todd and Sheldon Gawiser, *How Barack Obama Won* (New York: Vintage Books, 2009), 61.

60   Sara Lai Stirland, "Obama's Secret Weapons: Internet, Databases and Psychology," *Wired*, Elections, October 29, 2008, http://www.wired.com/threatlevel/2008/10/obamas-secret-w/ (July 21, 2009).

61   Todd and Gawiser, *How Barack Obama Won*, 61.

62   Todd and Gawiser, *How Barack Obama Won*, 60.

63   Todd and Gawiser, *How Barack Obama Won*, 58–61.

64   Todd and Gawiser, *How Barack Obama Won*, 80.

65   Todd and Gawiser, *How Barack Obama Won*, 80.

66   Todd and Gawiser, *How Barack Obama Won*, 92.

67   Pomper, "The Presidential Election," 55.

4: Demographic Groups that Supported Obama

1   Nancy Bruner, interview by author, Jeffersonville, IN, October 23, 2008.

2   Quoted in Alan Greenblatt, "Changing U.S. Electorate," in *Issues in Race and Ethnicity*, Congressional Quarterly Researcher, 4th ed., 25–47 (Washington, DC: CQ Press, 2009), 26.

3   Chuck Todd and Sheldon Gawiser, *How Barack Obama Won* (New York: Vintage Books, 2009), 29.

4   Todd and Gawiser, *How Barack Obama Won*, 29.

5   Jeffrey M. Elliot and Sheikh R. Ali, *The Presidential-Congressional Political Dictionary* (Santa Barbara, CA: ABC-Clio Information Services, 1984).

6   Quoted in Greenblatt, "Changing U.S. Electorate," 26.

7   Greenblatt, "Changing U.S. Electorate," 31.

8   Greenblatt, "Changing U.S. Electorate," 31.

9   Quoted in Greenblatt, "Changing U.S. Electorate," 32.

10   Quoted in Greenblatt, "Changing U.S. Electorate," 32.

11   Todd and Gawiser, *How Barack Obama Won*, 29.

12   Gerald Pomper, "The Presidential Election: Change Comes to America," in *The*

Elections of 2008, ed. M. Nelson, 45–73 (Washington, DC: CQ Press, 2010), 55.

13 Pomper, "The Presidential Election," 55.

14 Michael Nelson, "The Setting: Diversifying the Presidential Talent Pool," in *The Elections of 2008*, ed. M. Nelson, 1–21 (Washington DC: CQ Press, 2010), 14.

15 Barack Obama, "Keynote Address," delivered at the 2004 Democratic National Convention, Fleet Center, Boston, MA, July 27, 2004.

16 Obama, "Keynote Address."

17 Bruner, interview by author, October 23, 2008.

18 Quoted in Evan Thomas, *A Long Time Coming* (New York: Public Affairs, 2009), 2–7.

19 Molefi Asante, "Barack Obama and the Dilemma of Power: An Africological Observation," *Journal of Black Studies* 38, no. 1 (September 2007): 105–115.

20 Robert Starks, "How He Did It: An Analysis of the Obama Tsunami," *N'Digo Profiles*, December 2008, 34.

21 Marjorie Hershey, "The Media: Coloring the News," in *The Elections of 2008*, ed. M. Nelson, 122–144 (Washington, DC: CQ Press, 2010), 130.

22 Hershey, "The Media: Coloring the News," 130.

23 Hershey, "The Media: Coloring the News," 131.

24 Ronald Brownstein, "Obama Buoyed by Coalition of the Ascendant," in *Annual Editions: American Government 09/10*, 39th ed., ed. B. Stinebrickner (New York: McGraw-Hill, 2010), 143.

25 Brownstein, "Obama Buoyed by Coalition of the Ascendant," 143.

26 Brownstein, "Obama Buoyed by Coalition of the Ascendant," 143.

27 Nelson, "The Setting," 14.

28 Nelson, "The Setting," 14.

29 Nelson, "The Setting," 15.

30 Nelson, "The Setting," 15.

31 James L. Merriner, "The Friends of O," *Chicago* 57, no. 6 (June 2008), 98.

32 Amanda Ripley, "A Mother's Story," *Time*, Special Commemorative Edition (April 21, 2008), 46.

33 Ifill, *The Breakthrough*, 35.

34 Ifill, *The Breakthrough*, 35.

35 Ifill, *The Breakthrough*, 35.

36 Quoted in Ifill, *The Breakthrough*, 36.

37 David Bositis, interview by author, Louisville, KY, October 23, 2008.

38 John Yarmuth, interview by author, Louisville, KY, February 4, 2009.

39 Nelson, "The Setting," 15.

40 Nelson, "The Setting," 15.

41 Nelson, "The Setting," 15.

42 Nelson, "The Setting," 15.

43 Julius Chambers, interview by author, Louisville, KY, March 4, 2009.

44 G. K. Butterfield, interview by author, Louisville, KY, November 19, 2008.

45 William Lacy Clay, interview by author, Louisville, KY, December 9, 2008.

46 Greenblatt, "Changing U.S. Electorate," 29.

47 Robert Bernstein and Tom Edwards, "An Older and More Diverse Nation by Midcentury," *U.S. Census Bureau News*, Department of Commerce, Bureau of the Census, August 14, 2008, http://www.census.gov/Press-Release/www/releases/archives/population/012496.html (July 17, 2009).

48 Yarmuth, interview by author, February 4, 2009.

49 Quoted in Greenblatt, "Changing U.S. Electorate," 37.

50 Quoted in Greenblatt, "Changing U.S. Electorate," 36.

51 Greenblatt, "Changing U.S. Electorate," 36.

52 Greenblatt, "Changing U.S. Electorate," 36.

53 Greenblatt, "Changing U.S. Electorate," 36.

54 Mark Hugo Lopez, "How Hispanics Voted in the 2008 Election," *Pew Hispanic Center*, November 7, 2008, http://pewresearch.org/pubs/1024/exit-poll-analysis-hispanics (July 21, 2009).

55 Larry Rohter, "McCain is Faltering Among Hispanic Voters," *New York Times*, October 23, 2008, http://www.nytimes.com/2008/10/23/world/americas/23iht-23latino.171197720.html (July 23, 2009).

56 Rohter, "McCain is Faltering Among Hispanic Voters."

57 Greenblatt, "Changing U.S. Electorate," 26.

58 Greenblatt, "Changing U.S. Electorate," 26–27.

59 Quoted in Greenblatt, "Changing U.S. Electorate," 27.

60 Quoted in Greenblatt, "Changing U.S. Electorate," 27.

61 Jennifer Parker, "Democratic Women Torn Between Clinton and Obama," *ABC News*, February 4, 2008, http://abcnews.go.com/print?id=4235711 (July 17, 2009).

62 Parker, "Democratic Women Torn."

63 Parker, "Democratic Women Torn."

64 Katharine Seelye, "Clinton-Obama Quandary for Many Black Women," *New York Times*, October 14, 2007, http://www.nytimes.com/2007/10/14/us/politics/14carolina.html (July 22, 2009).

65 Quoted in Parker, "Democratic Women Torn."

5: The Clinton Factor: Hillary and Bill

1 James Clyburn, interview by author, Louisville, KY, December 1, 2008.

2 Quoted in Mara Liasson and Scott Simon, "Hillary Clinton Enters Race for President," *NPR*, January 20, 2007, http://www.npr.org/templates/story/story.php?storyId=6929745 (July 22, 2009).

3 Quoted in Adam Nagourney, "The Pattern May Change If . . . ," *New York Times*, Week in Review, December 10, 2006, http://www.nytimes.com/2006/12/10/weekinreview/10nagourney.html (July 22, 2009).

4 Joshua Green, "The Front-Runner's Fall," *The Atlantic*, September 2008, http://www.theatlantic.com/doc/print/200809/hillary-clinton-campaign (May 22, 2009).

5 Green, "The Front-Runner's Fall."

6 Karen Tumulty, "The Five Mistakes Clinton Made," *Time*, Politics, May 8, 2008, http://www.time.com/time/politics/article/0,8599,1738331,00.html (July 22, 2009).

7 Chuck Todd and Sheldon Gawiser, *How Barack Obama Won* (New York: Vintage Books, 2009), 11.

8 Todd and Gawiser, *How Barack Obama Won*, 11.

9 Green, "The Front-Runner's Fall."

10 Patrick Healy, "On Eve of Primary, Clinton Campaign Shows Stress," *New York Times*, Politics, January 8, 2008, http://www.nytimes.com/2008/01/08/us/politics/08clinton.html (July 22, 2009).

11 Kathleen Dolan, "Do Women Candidates Play to Gender Stereotypes? Do Men Candidates Play to Women? Candidate Sex and Issues Priorities on Campaign Websites," *Political Research Quarterly* 58, no. 1 (March 2005), 31.

12 Dolan, "Do Women Candidates Play to Gender Stereotypes?," 31.

13 Dewey Clayton and Angela Stallings, "Black Women in Congress: Striking the Balance," *Journal of Black Studies* 30, no. 4 (2000): 574–603.

14 Chingching Chang and Jacqueline Hitchon, "Mass Media Impact on Voter Response to Women Candidates: Theoretical Development," *Communication Theory* 7, no. 1 (March 1997): 29–52.

15 Media Matters, "Tucker on Sen. Clinton: '[T]here's just something about her that feels castrating, overbearing, and scary,'" *Media Matters in America*, March 20, 2007, http://mediamatters.org/mmtv/200703200013 (July 22, 2009).

16 Susan Carroll, *Women as Candidates in American Politics*, 2nd ed. (Bloomington: Indiana University Press, 1994); Chang and Hitchon, "Mass Media Impact on Voter Response."

17 Carroll, *Women as Candidates in American Politics*.

18 Patricia Lee Sykes, "Gender in the 2008 Presidential Election: Two Types of Time Collide," *PS: Political Science & Politics* 42, no. 4 (October 2008): 762.

19 Sykes, "Gender in the 2008 Presidential Election," 762.

20 Sykes, "Gender in the 2008 Presidential Election," 762.

21 Sykes, "Gender in the 2008 Presidential Election," 762.

22 Clayton and Stallings, "Black Women in Congress," 584.

23 Sykes, "Gender in the 2008 Presidential Election," 763.

24 Danny Shea, "Anna Wintour Takes Hillary Clinton to Task." *The Huffington Post*, January 18, 2008, http://www.huffingtonpost.com/2008/01/18/anna-wintour-takes-hillar_n_82132.html?view=screen (July 22, 2009).

25 Robert Reyes, "Sharon Stone: Hillary Clinton Too Sexy To Run For President," *American Chronicle*, March 27, 2006.

26 Kathleen Hall Jamieson, "Transcript," *Bill Moyers Journal*, December 7, 2007, http://www.pbs.org/moyers/journal/12072007/transcript1.html (July 22, 2009).

27 David Weissler, "Obama Raises $32.5 Million for White House Race," *Reuters*, July 1, 2007, http://www.reuters.com/article/politicsNews/idUSN0135051620070701 (July 22, 2009).

28 BBC News, "Obama Fundraising Rivals Clinton," *BBC News*, April 4, 2007, http://news.bbc.co.uk/2/hi/americas/6527081.stm (July 18, 2009).

29 James L. Merriner, "The Friends of O," *Chicago* 57, no. 6 (June 2008), 76–78.

30 Quoted in Tim Reid, "Hillary Clinton Gaffe over Martin Luther King May Cost Votes in South Carolina," *Times Online*, January 12, 2008, http://www.timesonline.co.uk/tol/news/world/us_and_americas/us_elections/article3173652.ece (July 22, 2009).

31 James Clyburn, interview by author, Louisville, KY, December 1, 2008.

32 Reid, "Hillary Clinton Gaffe over Martin Luther King May Cost Votes."

33 Ryan Lizza, "Bill vs. Barack," *The New Yorker*, Campaign Journal, May 5, 2008, http://www.newyorker.com/talk/2008/05/05/080505ta_talk_lizza (July 22, 2009).

34 Todd and Gawiser, *How Barack Obama Won*, 13.

35 Lizza, "Bill vs. Barack," 2.

36 Todd and Gawiser, *How Barack Obama Won*, 13.

37 Candy Crowley, "Clinton Campaign Advisers: Bill Clinton 'Needs to Stop,'" *CNN Political Ticker*, January 8, 2008, http://politicalticker.blogs.cnn.com/category/presidential-candidates/hillary-clinton/0politicalticker.blogs.cnn.com/category/ bill-clinton/page/6/ (July 22, 2009).

38 Vaughn Ververs, "Analysis: Bill Clinton's Lost Legacy," *CBS News*, January 26, 2008, http://www.cbsnews.com/stories/2008/01/26/politics/main3755521.shtml (July 22, 2009).

39 Todd and Gawiser, *How Barack Obama Won*, 13.

40 Todd and Gawiser, *How Barack Obama Won*, 13.

41 Quoted in Tumulty, "The Five Mistakes Clinton Made."

42 Kenneth Janda, Jeffrey Berry, and Jerry Goldman, *The Challenge of Democracy*, 10th ed. (Boston, MA: Wadsworth, 2009), 265.

43 Tumulty, "The Five Mistakes Clinton Made."

44 Howard Kurtz, "For Clinton, A Matter of Fair Media," *Washington Post*, December 19, 2007, C01, http://www.washingtonpost.com/wp-dyn/content/article/2007/12/18/AR2007121802184.html (July 22, 2009).

45 Kurtz, "For Clinton, A Matter of Fair Media."

46 Ben Smith, "Bill on Going Negative: Media Bias Made Her Do It," *Politico.com*, January 4, 2008, http://www.politico.com/blogs/bensmith/0108/Bills_reason_ to_ go_negative_media_bias.html (accessed July 22, 2009)

47 Sykes, "Gender in the 2008 Presidential Election," 762.

48 Paul S. Herrnson and Jennifer Lucas, "The Fairer Sex? Gender and Negative Campaigning in U.S. Elections," *American Politics Research* 34, no. 1 (2006): 69–94, 70.

49 Lizza, "Bill vs. Barack," 2.

50 Wilfred McClay, "The Weakness of Our Political Parties," *Society* 45, no. 5 (September 2008): 403–405.

51 Gina Misiroglu, *The Handy Politics Answer Book* (Canton, MI: Visible Ink Press, 2003).

52 Lizza, "Bill vs. Barack," 2.

53 Lizza, "Bill vs. Barack," 2.

54 Dennis Roddy, "Race on the Trail: Large Numbers of Voters Say Color of Skin Played a Role in Choice," *Pittsburgh Post-Gazette*, May 18, 2008, http://www. post-gazette.com/pg/08139/882900-176.stm (May 28, 2009)

55 Rick Pearson, "Clinton: No Last Call at Maker's Mark," *The Swamp*, May 17, 2008, http://www.swamppolitics.com/news/politics/blog/2008/05/hillary_ clinton_no_last_call_a.html (July 22, 2009).

56 Peter Baker and Jim Rutenberg, "The Long Road to a Clinton Exit," *New York Times*, June 8, 2008, http://www.nytimes.com/2008/06/08/us/politics/08recon. html (May 28, 2009).

6: The Campaign for the White House

1 John Yarmuth, interview by author, Louisville, KY, February 4, 2009.

2 Ben Smith, "Obama Campaign Learns from Others' Missteps," *Politico. com*, August 27, 2008, http://www.cbsnews.com/stories/2008/08/27/politics/ politico/main4386932.shtml (July 22, 2009).

3 Karen Tumulty, "How Obama Did It," *Time*, Politics, June 5, 2008, http:// www.time.com/time/politics/article/0,8599,1811857-2,00.html (July 22, 2009).

4 Quoted in Amy Sullivan, "A Star is Born," *Time*, Special Commemorative Edition (2008): 64–65.

5 Evan Thomas, *A Long Time Coming* (New York: Public Affairs, 2009), 16.

6 David Broder, "Obama Gets Them Fired Up," *Real Clear Politics*, December 23, 2007, http://www.realclearpolitics.com/articles/2007/12/obama_gets_them_ fired_up.html (July 22, 2009).

7 John McCormick, "Obama Marks '02 War Speech; Contender Highlights His

Early Opposition in Effort to Distinguish Him from His Rivals," *Chicago Tribune*, October 3, 2007, 7.

8 Katharine Seelye, "Oprah May Campaign for Obama," *The Caucus*, November 21, 2007, http://thecaucus.blogs.nytimes.com/2007/11/21/oprah-may-campaign-for-obama/ (July 22, 2009).

9 Jay Newton-Small, "Will Clinton's Obama Attacks Backfire?," *Time*, December 4, 2007, http://www.time.com/time/printout/0,8816,1690519,00.html (July 24, 2009).

10 Thomas, *A Long Time Coming*, 24.

11 Tumulty, "How Obama Did It."

12 Quoted in Tumulty, "How Obama Did It."

13 Tumulty, "How Obama Did It."

14 Quoted in Mark Reiter, "The Real Baracketology," *Washington Post*, April 3, 2009, http://www.washingtonpost.com/wp-dyn/content/article/2009/04/03/AR2009040303276.html (July 22, 2009).

15 Barack Obama, "Remarks of Senator Barack Obama: New Hampshire Primary," delivered in Nashua, NH, January 8, 2008, http://www.barackobama.com/2008/01/08/remarks_of_senator_barack_obam_82.php (July 22, 2009).

16 Quoted in Mark Preston and Robert Yoon, "Analysis: Sparks Fly in Most Contentious Debate to Date," *CNNPolitics.com*, January 22, 2008, http://www.cnn.com/ 2008/POLITICS/01/22/sc.debate.anlysis/index.html (July 22, 2009).

17 Caroline Kennedy, "A President Like My Father," *New York Times*, Opinion, January 27, 2008, http://www.nytimes.com/2008/01 27/opinion/27kennedy.html (July 22, 2009).

18 Barack Obama, *Dreams from My Father: A Story of Race and Inheritance* (New York: Three Rivers Press, 2004).

19 Jodi Kantor, "Disinvitation by Obama Is Criticized," *New York Times*, March 6, 2007, http://www.nytimes.com/2007/03/06/us/politics/06obama.html (July 22, 2009).

20 Kantor, "Disinvitation by Obama Is Criticized."

21 Kantor, "Disinvitation by Obama Is Criticized."

22 Quoted in Brian Ross and Rehab El-Buri, "Obama's Pastor: God Damn America, U.S. to Blame for 9/11," *ABCNews*, March 13, 2008, http://abcnews.go.com/Blotter/DemocraticDebate/story?id=4443788&page=1 (July 22, 2009).

23 Jason Byassee, "Africentric Church: A Visit to Chicago's UCC," *The Christian Century*, May 29, 2007, http://www.christiancentury.org/article.lasso?id=3392 (July 22, 2009).

24 Cited in Eric C. Lincoln and Lawrence H. Mamiya, *The Black Church in the African American Experience* (Durham, NC: Duke University Press, 1990), 12–15.

25 W. E. B. Du Bois, "Strivings of the Negro People," *Atlantic Monthly* 80 (1897): 194–198.

26 Quoted in Jason Linkins, "Obama: Reverend Wright Made a 'Profound Mistake,'" *The Huffington Post*, March 18, 2008, http://www.huffingtonpost. com/2008/03/18/obama-reverend-wright-mad_n_92117.html (July 22, 2009)

27 Quoted in Dana Milbank, "Still More Lamentations from Jeremiah," *Washington Post*, April 29, 2008, http://www.washingtonpost.com/wp-dyn/ content/article/2008/04/28/AR2008042802269.html (July 22, 2009).

28 Vaughn Ververs, "Obama's Risky Denunciation of Rev. Wright," *CBSNews,* April 29, 2008, http://www.cbsnews.com/stories/2008/04/29/politics/main 4056166.shtml (July 22, 2009).

29 Tonyaa Weathersbee, "Barack Obama's Decision to Leave Trinity Has Pros and Cons—But Ultimately, It Won't Matter," *Blackamericaweb.com*, June 4, 2008, http://www.blackamericaweb.com/site.aspx/sayitloud/weathersbee604 (June 6, 2008).

30 James L. Merriner, "The Friends of O," *Chicago* 57, no. 6 (June 2008): 74–99.

31 Quoted in New River Media, "Interview with: Christopher Jencks," *PBS Interviews*, no date, http://www.pbs.org/fmc/interviews/jencks.htm (July 22, 2009).

32 Barack Obama, "Obama's Father's Day Speech," *CNNPolitics*, delivered in Chicago, IL, June 15, 2008, http://www.cnn.com/2008/POLITICS/06/27/ obama.fathers.ay/index.html (July 22, 2009).

33 Quoted in Don Lemon, "Jackson Apologizes for 'Crude' Obama Remarks," *CNNPolitics*, July 9, 2008, http://www.cnn.com/2008/POLITICS/07/09/jesse. jackson.comment/ (July 22, 2009).

34 Lynn Sweet, "Obama's NAACP Speech," delivered at the 99th Annual Convention of the NAACP in Cincinnati, Ohio, July 14, 2008, http://blogs.suntimes. com/sweet/2008/07/obamas_naacp_speech_cincinnati.html (July 22, 2009).

35 Jeffrey Ressner, "Michelle Obama Thesis Was on Racial Divide," *Politico.com*, February 22, 2008, http://dyn.politico.com/printstory.cfm?uuid=42FC5818- 3048-5C12-005E33B3C0F4E64B (July 20, 2009).

36 Quoted in Mosheh Oinounou and Bonney Kapp, "Michelle Obama Takes Heat for Saying She's Proud of My Country for the First Time," *FoxNews.com*, February 19, 2008, http://www.foxnews.com/printer_friendly_story/0,3566, 331288,00.html (July 20, 2009).

37 Quoted in Oinounou and Kapp, "Michelle Obama Takes Heat for Saying She's Proud."

38 Katie Fretland, "Obama Campaign Slams New Yorker Cover," *The Swamp*, July 14, 2008, http://www.swamppolitics.com/news/politics/blog/2008/07/printer- barack_obama_new_yorker_cover.html (July 20, 2009).

39 Fretland, "Obama Campaign Slams New Yorker Cover."

40   Daily Mail, "Obama's Presidential Bid Stutters as His Former Pastor Repeats the Claim: America Brought 9/11 on Itself," *Daily Mail*, April 29, 2008, http:// www. dailymail.co.uk/news/article-562716/Obamas-presidential-bid-stutters-pastor-repeats-claim-America-brought-9-11-itself.html;jsessionid=0217283AC 4E0147057553A129C7DB4F0 (June 2, 2009).

41   Adam Nagourney and Carl Hulse, "Clinton Success Changes Dynamic in Delegate Hunt," *New York Times*, March 6, 2008, http://query.nytimes.com/ gst/fullpage.html?res=9E05E0DA163BF935A35750C0A96E9C8B63 (July 23, 2009).

42   Quoted in Jim Rutenberg, "Pundits Declare the Race Over," *New York Times*, May 8, 2008, http://www.nytimes.com/2008/05/08/us/politics/07cnd-pundits. html (July 23, 2008).

43   Adam Nagourney and Jeff Zeleny, "Obama Chooses Biden as Running Mate," *New York Times*, August 24, 2008, http://www.nytimes.com/2008/08/24/us/ politics/24biden.html?_r=1 (June 8, 2009).

44   Quoted in Jeff Zeleny, "Burnishing Credentials, Obama Will Visit the Middle East and Europe," *New York Times*, June 29, 2008, http://www.nytimes.com/ 2008/06/29/us/politics/29trip.html (June 10, 2009).

45   Steven Erlanger, "Obama Gets Europe's Ear, Pleasing Crowds without Specifics," *New York Times*, July 25, 2008, http://www.nytimes.com/2008/07/25/world/ americas/25iht-25assess.14778918.html (July 23, 2009).

46   Frank Rich, "How Obama Became Acting President," *New York Times*, July 27, 2009, http://www.nytimes.com/2008/07/27/opinion/27rich.html?r=2&scp=14 &sq=frank%20rich (July 23, 2009).

47   Barack Obama, "The American Promise," acceptance speech at the Democratic Convention, delivered in Mile High Stadium, Colorado, August 28, 2008, http://obamaspeeches.com/E10-Barack-Obama-The-American-Promise-Acceptance-Speech-at-the-Democratic-Convention-Mile-High-Stadium—Denver-Colorado-August-28-2008.htm (November 4, 2009).

48   Obama, "The American Promise."

49   Jeffrey M. Jones, "Race Tied as Democratic Convention Starts," *Gallup*, August 25, 2008, http://www.gallup.com/poll/109792/allup-daily-race-tied-democractic-convention-starts.aspx (July 24, 2009).

50   Jeffrey M. Jones, "Obama Acceptance Speech Gets High Marks From Public," *Gallup*, August 30, 2008, http://www.gallup.com/poll/109948/obama-acceptance-speech-gets-high-marks-from-public.aspx (July 24, 2009).

51   Paul Steinhauser, "CNN Poll: Obama 49, McCain 48," *CNNPolitics.com*, August 31, 2008, http://politicalticker.blogs.cnn.com/2008/08/31/cnn-poll-obama-49-mccain-48/ (July 24, 2009).

52   MSNBC, "VP Pick Palin Makes Appeal to Women Voters," *MSNBC*, August 28, 2008, http://www.msnbc.msn.com/id/25970882 (July 23, 2009).

53 MSNBC, "VP Pick Palin Makes Appeal to Women Voters."

54 Quoted in MSNBC, "VP Pick Palin Makes Appeal to Women Voters."

55 Elisabeth Bumiller, "Palin Disclosures Raise Questions on Vetting," *New York Times*, September 2, 2008, http://www.nytimes.com/2008/09/02/us/politics/02vetting.html (June 9, 2009).

56 Ewen MacAskill, "The Palin Effect: White Women Now Deserting Obama, Says Survey," *Guardian*, September 10, 2008, http://www.guardian.co.uk/lifeandstyle/2008/sep/10/women.uselections2008 (July 11, 2009).

57 Joe Klein, "Sarah Palin's Myth of America," *Time*, September 10, 2008, http://www.time.com/time/printout.0,8816,1840388,00.html (July 24, 2009).

58 MacAskill, "The Palin Effect."

59 Commission on Presidential Debates, "CPD Announces Formats for 2004 Debates," *Commission on Presidential Debates*, November 19, 2007, http://www.debates.org/pages/news_111907_p/html (July 24, 2009).

60 Evan Thomas, "The Great Debates," *Newsweek*, November 17, 2008, http://www.newsweek.com/id/167950/output (June 11, 2009).

61 Thomas, "The Great Debates."

62 Tom Baldwin and Alexi Mostrous, "John McCain Halts Presidential Campaign for Economy Crisis Talks," *Times*, September 25, 2008, http://www.timesonline.co.uk/tol/news/world/us_and_americas/us_elections/article4821236.ece (June 10, 2009).

63 Quoted in Baldwin and Mostrous, "John McCain Halts Presidential Campaign."

64 George Bishop, "Parsing the Instant Polls," *The Presidential Debate Blog*, September 29, 2008, http://presidentialdebateblog.blogspot.com/2008/09/parsing-instant-polls-on-first.html (July 23, 2009)

65 Jeffrey Jones, "Obama Viewed as Winner of Third Debate," *Gallup*, October 17, 2008, http://www.gallup.com/poll/111256/obama-viewed-winner-third-debate.aspx (June 14, 2009).

66 Gerald Pomper, "The Presidential Election: Change Comes to America," in *The Elections of 2008*, ed. M. Nelson, 45–73 (Washington, DC: CQ Press, 2010), 61–62.

67 Jones, "Obama Viewed as Winner of Third Debate."

68 Jeffrey Jones, "Bush's Approval Rating Drops to New Low of 27%," *Gallup*, September 30, 2008, http://www.gallup.com/poll/110806/bushs-approval-rating-drops-new-low-27.aspx (June 14, 2009).

69 Matthew Bigg, "McCain Gaffe over Houses Could Anger Voters," *Reuters*, August 22, 2008, http://www.reuters.com/article/newsOne/idUSN2229072120080822 (July 23, 2009).

70 Sam Stein, "McCain On 'Black Monday': Fundamentals Of Our Economy Are Still Strong," *The Huffington Post*, September 15, 2008, http://www.huffingtonpost.com/2008/09/15/mccain-fundamentals-of-th_n_126445.html (July 23, 2009).

71   Michael Scherer, "McCain's Struggles: Four Ways He Went Wrong," *Time*,
      October 17, 2008, http://www.time.com/time/politics/article/0,8599,1851400,
      00.html (June 11, 2009).
72   TUNC.biz, "How Katie Couric Destroyed Sarah Palin," *TUNC.biz*, http://
      www.tunc.biz/Katie_Couric_Destroyed_Sarah_Palin.htm (July 24, 2009).
73   Bob Unruh, "VP Debate Moderator Ifill Releasing Pro-Obama Book,"
      WorldNetDaily, September 30, 2008, http://www.worldnetdaily.com/index.
      php?fa=PAGE.view&pageId=76645 (June 12, 2009).
74   Michael Cooper and Michael Powell, "McCain Camp Says Obama is Playing
      'Race Card,'" *New York Times*, August 1, 2008, http://www.nytimes.com/2008/
      08/01/us/politics/01campaign.html (August 1, 2008).
75   Quoted in Cooper and Powell, "McCain Camp Says Obama is Playing 'Race
      Card'."
76   Quoted in Jonathan Martin and Ben Smith, "Race Issue Moves to Center of
      Campaign," *Politico.com*, August 1, 2008, http://dyn.politico.com/printstory.
      cfm?uuid=7b3aecc9-3048-5c12-00ba1e7bd09bdba5 (August 1, 2008).
77   Martin and Smith, "Race Issue Moves to Center of Campaign."
78   Sean Wilentz, "Race Man," *The New Republic*, February 27, 2008, http://www.
      tnr.com/story_print.html?id=aa0cd21b-0ff2-4329-88a1-69c6c268b304 (August
      1, 2008).
79   Alexander Mooney, "McCain Ad Compares Obama to Britney Spears, Paris
      Hilton," *CNN*, Politics, July 30, 2008, http://www.cnn.com/2008/POLITICS/
      07/30/mccain.ad/index.html (July 23, 2009).
80   Sam Stein, "Gergen: McCain Using Code Words to Attack Obama as 'Uppity,'"
      The Huffington Post, August 3, 2008, http://www.huffingtonpost.com/2008/
      08/03/gergen-mccain-is-using-co_n_116605.html.html (August 6, 2008).
81   Quoted in Thomas, "The Great Debates."
82   Quoted in Jason Horowitz, "Black Congressmen Declare Racism in Palin's
      Rhetoric," *The New York Observer*, Politics, October 7, 2008, http://www.
      observer.com/2008/politics/black-congressmen-declare-racism-palin-s-rhetoric
      (October 19, 2008).
83   Quoted in Horowitz, "Black Congressmen Declare Racism in Palin's Rhetoric."
84   Quoted in Jon Perr, "McCain's Supposed Adviser John Lewis Calls Him
      Out," *Crooks and Liars*, October 12, 2008, http://crooksandliars.com/jon-perr/
      mccains-saddleback-adviser-john-lewis-cal (June 12, 2009).
85   Quoted in Perr, "McCain's Supposed Adviser John Lewis Calls Him Out."
86   Quoted in Thomas, "The Great Debates."
87   Pomper, "The Presidential Election," 64.
88   Larry Rohter, "McCain is Faltering Among Hispanic Voters," *New York Times*,
      October 23, 2008, http://nytimes.com/2008/10/23/world/americas/23iht-23
      latino.17197720.html (July 23, 2009).
89   Quoted in Rohter, "McCain is Faltering Among Hispanic Voters."

90 Quoted in Rohter, "McCain is Faltering Among Hispanic Voters."

91 Frank Newport, "Obama Gains Among Former Clinton Supporters," *Gallup*, September 2, 2008, http://www.gallup.com/poll/109957/obama-gains-among-former-clinton-supporters.aspx (July 23, 2009).

92 John McCormick, "FEC Rules on Presidential Campaign Funding," *Chicago Tribune*, March 1, 2007, http://www.chicagotribune.com/news/nationworld/chi-070301elect,0,1248677.story (June 9, 2009).

93 Fairness and Accuracy in Reporting (FAIR), "Two Standards on Public Financing," July 3, 2008, http://www.fair.org/index.php?page=3569 (June 9, 2009).

94 Quoted in Daniel Dale, "Obama Splashes Money Across U.S.," *The Star*, October 28, 2008, http://www.thestar.com/printArticle/525710 (June 13, 2009).

95 Marian Currinder, "Campaign Finance: Fundraising and Spending in the 2008 Elections," in *The Elections of 2008*, ed. M. Nelson, 163–186 (Washington, DC: CQ Press, 2010), 173.

96 Currinder, "Campaign Finance," 174.

97 Currinder, "Campaign Finance," 174.

98 Currinder, "Campaign Finance," 174.

99 Jonathan Salant, "Spending Doubled as Obama Led First Billion-Dollar Race in 2008," *Bloomberg.com*, December 26, 2008, http://www.bloomberg.com/apps/news?pid=20670001&sid=aerix76GvmRM (June 14, 2009).

100 Pomper, "The Presidential Election," 64.

101 Jim Rutenberg and Christopher Drew, "National Push by Obama on Ads and Turnout," *New York Times*, June 22, 2008, http://www.nytimes.com/2008/06/22/us/politics/22obama.html (June 14, 2009).

7: Innovations in Technology and Media

1 Mel Watt, interview by author, Louisville, KY, December 19, 2008.

2 Quoted in Adam Nagourney, "The '08 Obama Campaign: Sea Change for Politics as We Know It," *New York Times*, November 4, 2008.

3 Steve Schifferes, "Internet Key to Obama Victories," *BBC News*, Technology Section, June 12, 2008, http://news.bbc.co.uk/2/hi/technology/7412045.stm (July 20, 2009).

4 Christi Parsons and John McCormick, "Obama's Formula: It's the Network—Technology Helped Campaign Take-Off and Change the Game," *Chicago Tribune*, May 24, 2008.

5 Frank Davies, "Web Politics Come of Age with Obama—Illinois Senator's Campaign Uses Internet Effectively for Fundraising and Communicating with His Supporters," *Contra Costa Times*, February 24, 2008, A1.

6 Davies, "Web Politics Come of Age."

7 Schifferes, "Internet Key to Obama Victories."

8 Catherine Holahan, "On the Web, Obama is the Clear Winner," *BusinessWeek Online*, The Primary Race, March 5, 2008, http://www.businessweek.com/technology/content/mar2008/tc2008035_280573.htm (July 22, 2009)

9 Davies, "Web Politics Come of Age."

10 Holahan, "On the Web, Obama is the Clear Winner."

11 Holahan, "On the Web, Obama is the Clear Winner."

12 Holahan, "On the Web, Obama is the Clear Winner."

13 Kenneth Vogel, "Money Bomb: Ron Paul Raises $6 Million in 24-Hour Period," *USA Today*, December 17, 2007, http://www.usatoday.com/news/politics/election2008/2007-12-17-ronpaul-fundraising_N.htm (July 22, 2009).

14 Schifferes, "Internet Key to Obama Victories."

15 Nagourney, "The '08 Obama Campaign: Sea Change for Politics."

16 Davies, "Web Politics Come of Age."

17 David Lightman, "Obama Backers Love Web, But Does It Give Him an Edge?," *Miami Herald*, June 16, 2008, 2A.

18 Lightman, "Obama Backers Love Web, But Does It Give Him an Edge?"

19 Tim Dickinson, "The Machinery of Hope: Inside the Grass-Roots Field Operation of Barack Obama, Who is Transforming the Way Political Campaigns are Run," *Rolling Stone*, March 20, 2008, 60.

20 Dickinson, "The Machinery of Hope," 60.

21 Quoted in Dickinson, "The Machinery of Hope," 65.

22 Quoted in Brian Stelter, "The Facebooker Who Friended Obama," *New York Times*, July 7, 2008.

23 Dickinson, "The Machinery of Hope."

24 Brian C. Mooney, "Technology Aids Obama's Outreach Drive, Volunteers Answer Call on Social Networking Site," *Boston Globe*, February 24, 2008, 1A.

25 Mooney, "Technology Aids Obama's Outreach Drive."

26 Stelter, "The Facebooker Who Friended Obama."

27 Mooney, "Technology Aids Obama's Outreach Drive."

28 Stelter, "The Facebooker Who Friended Obama."

29 Dickinson, "The Machinery of Hope," 62.

30 Mooney, "Technology Aids Obama's Outreach Drive."

31 Quoted in Dickinson, "The Machinery of Hope," 62.

32 Dickinson, "The Machinery of Hope," 62.

33 Stelter, "The Facebooker Who Friended Obama."

34 Quoted in Mooney, "Technology Aids Obama's Outreach Drive."

35 Dickinson, "The Machinery of Hope," 65.

36 Doug Abrahms, "Technology Keeps Supporters Connected," *USA Today*, April 2, 2008.

37   Quoted in Dickinson, "The Machinery of Hope," 65.

38   Mooney, "Technology Aids Obama's Outreach Drive."

39   Stelter, "The Facebooker Who Friended Obama."

40   Stelter, "The Facebooker Who Friended Obama."

41   Stelter, "The Facebooker Who Friended Obama."

42   Katharine Seelye, "The Million-Dollar Minute," *New York Times*, Politics, The Caucus, April 17, 2008, http://thecaucus.blogs.nytimes.com/2008/04/17/million-dollar-minute/ (July 22, 2009).

43   Carl M. Cannon, "The Facebook Election," *Reader's Digest*, June 2008.

44   Quoted in Stelter, "The Facebooker Who Friended Obama."

45   Kimberly Johnson, "Web Enabling More to Donate: Voters Can Pledge Their Support for Candidates from Virtually Anywhere," *The Denver Post*, March 3, 2008.

46   Quoted in Dickinson, "The Machinery of Hope," 64.

47   Davies, "Web Politics Come of Age."

48   Davies, "Web Politics Come of Age."

49   Schifferes, "Internet Key to Obama Victories."

50   Davies, "Web Politics Come of Age."

51   Quoted in David Schaper, "'Camp Obama' Trains Campaign Volunteers," *NPR*, June 13, 2007, http://www.npr.org/templates/transcript/transcript.php?storyId=11012254 (July 22, 2009).

52   Quoted in Schaper, "'Camp Obama' Trains Campaign Volunteers."

53   Quoted in Schaper, "'Camp Obama' Trains Campaign Volunteers."

54   Stelter, "The Facebooker Who Friended Obama."

55   Dickinson, "The Machinery of Hope," 65.

56   Dickinson, "The Machinery of Hope," 65.

57   Dickinson, "The Machinery of Hope," 64.

58   Virginia Heffernan, "Clicking and Choosing," *New York Times*, November 14, 2008, 22.

59   Barry Libert and Rick Faulk, *Winning Business Lessons of the Obama Campaign* (Upper Saddle River, NJ: Pearson Education, Inc., 2009).

60   Heffernan, "Clicking and Choosing," 22.

61   Heffernan, "Clicking and Choosing," 22.

62   Heffernan, "Clicking and Choosing," 22.

63   Heffernan, "Clicking and Choosing," 22.

64   Heffernan, "Clicking and Choosing," 22.

65   Heffernan, "Clicking and Choosing," 22.

66   Heffernan, "Clicking and Choosing," 22.

67   Marjorie Hershey, "The Media: Coloring the News," in *The Elections of 2008*, ed. M. Nelson, 122–144 (Washington, DC: CQ Press, 2010), 138.

68   Hershey, "The Media: Coloring the News," 139.

69   Libert and Faulk, *Winning Business Lessons of the Obama Campaign*, 101.

70   Jim Rutenberg, "Black Radio on Obama is Left's Answer to Limbaugh," *New York Times*, July 27, 2008.

71   Rutenberg, "Black Radio on Obama is Left's Answer to Limbaugh."

72   Rutenberg, "Black Radio on Obama is Left's Answer to Limbaugh."

73   Rutenberg, "Black Radio on Obama is Left's Answer to Limbaugh."

74   Ira Teinowitz, "African-American Media Waiting for Ad Spending by Obama Campaign," *targetmarketnews.com*, July 14, 2008, http://www.targetmarketnews.com/storyid07150801.htm (July 22, 2009).

75   Michael Luo, "Obama Recasts the Fund-Raising Landscape," *New York Times*, October 20, 2008.

76   Quoted in Johnson, "Web Enabling More to Donate."

77   Michael Luo, "Obama Hauls in Record $750 Million for Campaign," *New York Times*, December 4, 2008.

78   Johnson, "Web Enabling More to Donate."

79   Parsons and McCormick, "Obama's Formula."

80   AFP, "Obama Hits Back at Internet Slanders," *The Raw Story*, June 12, 2008, http://rawstory.com/news/afp/Obama_hits_back_at_Internet_slander_06122008.htm (July 22, 2009).

81   Stelter, "The Facebooker Who Friended Obama."

82   CBS/AP, "Obama's Prime-Time Appeal to Voters," *CBS News*, Politics, October 29, 2008, http://www.cbsnews.com/stories/2008/10/29/politics/main4557333.shtml (July 22, 2009).

83   Nagourney, "The '08 Obama Campaign: Sea Change for Politics."

84   Quoted in Nagourney, "The '08 Obama Campaign: Sea Change for Politics."

85   Libert and Faulk, *Winning Business Lessons of the Obama Campaign*, 95.

86   Quoted in Nagourney, "The '08 Obama Campaign: Sea Change for Politics."

87   Quoted in Nagourney, "The '08 Obama Campaign: Sea Change for Politics."

88   Quoted in Stelter, "The Facebooker Who Friended Obama."

89   Evan Thomas, *A Long Time Coming* (New York: Public Affairs, 2009), 163.

90   Quoted in Zach Baron, "Rappers for Obama, and Vice Versa," *Black Power*, Entertainment, Politics, January 23, 2009, http://www.blackpower.com/entertainment/rappers-for-obama-and-vice-versa/ (July 22, 2009).

91   Thomas, *A Long Time Coming*, 166–167.

92   Thomas, *A Long Time Coming*, 167.

93   AP, "Campaigns Uncork Get-Out-The-Vote Operations," *MSNBC*, Politics, Decisions '08 Archive, November 2, 2008, http://www.msnbc.msn.com/id/27483362/ (July 22, 2009).

94   Sarah Lai Stirland, "Obama's Secret Weapons: Internet, Databases and Psychology," *Wired*, Elections, October 29, 2008, http://www.wired.com/threatlevel/2008/10/obamas-secret-w/ (July 21, 2009).

95   Stirland, "Obama's Secret Weapons."
96   Quoted in Stirland, "Obama's Secret Weapons."
97   Nagourney, "The '08 Obama Campaign: Sea Change for Politics."
98   Cannon, "The Facebook Election."

8: Change Comes to America

1   Artur Davis, interview by author, Louisville, KY, November 18, 2008.
2   Kimberly Wilder, "Hofstra Presidential Debate Excludes 3rd Party Candidates: What Would Victoria Woodhull Do?," *OpEdNews*, September 25, 2008, http://www.opednews.com/articles/Hofstra-Presidential-Debat-by-Kimberly-Wilder-080924-580.html (July 22, 2009).
3   John McCormick and Christi Parsons, "Barack Obama to Visit Ill Grandmother Madelyn Dunham," *Chicago Tribune*, October 21, 2008, http://archives.chicago tribune.com/2008/oct/21/nation/chi-obama-grandmaoct21 (July 22, 2009).
4   Eric M. Appleman, "Election Day," *Democracy in Action: P2008*, November 4, 2008, http://www.gwu.edu/~action/2008/chrneday08.html (July 22, 2009).
5   Pearson Education, "National Student/Parent Mock Election To Give Students a Voice in 2008 Election," *Pearson*, Press Release, September 8, 2008, http://www.pearsoned.com/pr_2008/090908b.htm (July 22, 2009).
6   Appleman, "Election Day."
7   Quoted in Appleman, "Election Day."
8   Appleman, "Election Day."
9   Carrie Dann, "NBC Calls Ohio for Obama," *MSNBC*, First Read, November 4, 2008, http://firstread.msnbc.msn.com/archive/2008/11/04/1639565.aspx (July 22, 2009).
10 Quoted in B&C Staff, "Networks Call Election Simultaneously for Obama," *Broadcasting & Cable*, November 4, 2008, http://www.broadcastingcable.com/article/116172-Networks_Call_Election_Simultaneously_for_Obama.php (July 22, 2009).
11 NBC News, "NBC News Calls Election for Obama," *NBC News*, Transcript, November 4, 2008, http://icue.nbcunifiles.com/icue/files/icue/site/pdf/38832.pdf (July 22, 2009).
12 Gerald Pomper, "The Presidential Election: Change Comes to America," in *The Elections of 2008*, ed. M. Nelson, 45–73 (Washington, DC: CQ Press, 2010), 46.
13 Pomper, "The Presidential Election," 47.
14 Pomper, "The Presidential Election," 47.
15 Curtis Gans, *African-Americans, Anger, Fear and Youth Propel Turnout to Highest Level Since 1960*. American University, Center for the Study of the American Electorate, December 17, 2008, 2.

16 Pomper, "The Presidential Election," 48.

17 Pomper, "The Presidential Election," 48.

18 Pomper, "The Presidential Election," 48.

19 Mark Lopez and Paul Taylor, *Dissecting the 2008 Electorate: Most Diverse in U.S. History*, Pew Hispanic Center, April 30, 2009, http://pewhispanic.org/reports/report.php?ReportID=108 (June 17, 2009).

20 Lopez and Taylor, *Dissecting the 2008 Electorate*.

21 Lopez and Taylor, *Dissecting the 2008 Electorate*.

22 Lopez and Taylor, *Dissecting the 2008 Electorate*.

23 Lopez and Taylor, *Dissecting the 2008 Electorate*.

24 Lopez and Taylor, *Dissecting the 2008 Electorate*.

25 Appleman, "Election Day."

26 David Leip, "2008 Presidential General Election Results," *Atlas of U.S. Presidential Elections*, 2005, http://www.uselectionatlas.org/RESULTS/national.php?f=0&year=2008 (July 22, 2009).

27 Quoted in John Blake, "Obama's Victory Caps Struggles of Previous Generations," *CNNPolitics.com*, Election Center 2008, November 4, 2008, http://www.cnn.com/2008/POLITICS/11/04/obama.history/index.html (July 22, 2009).

28 Quoted in Blake, "Obama's Victory Caps Struggles of Previous Generations."

29 Eugene Robinson, "Stepping Into the Sunshine," *RealClearPolitics.com*, Elections 2008, November 6, 2008, http://www.realclearpolitics.com/articles/2008/11/stepping_into_the_sunshine.html (July 22, 2009).

30 Quoted in Barack Obama, "This Is Your Victory," acceptance speech delivered at Grant Park, IL, November 4, 2008, http://obamaspeeches.com/E11-Barack-Obama-Election-Night-Victory-Speech-Grant-Park-Illinois-November-4-2008.htm (July 22, 2009).

31 Essence Magazine, "Realizing the Dream," *Essence Magazine*, January 2009, 105.

32 Hill Harper, "I Want to Be Like Him," *Essence Magazine*, January 2009, 110.

Bibliography

Abrahms, Doug. "Technology Keeps Supporters Connected," *USA Today*, April 2, 2008.

AFP. "Obama Hits Back at Internet Slanders," *The Raw Story*, June 12, 2008, http://rawstory.com/news/afp/Obama_hits_back_at_Internet_slander_06122008. htm (accessed July 22, 2009).

Anderson, Eric. *Race and Politics in North Carolina: 1872–1901*. Baton Rouge: Louisiana State University Press, 1981.

AP. "Campaigns Uncork Get-Out-The-Vote Operations," *MSNBC*, Politics, Decision '08 Archive, November 2, 2008, http://www.msnbc.msn.com/id/2748 3362/ (accessed July 22, 2009).

Appleman, Eric M. "Election Day," *Democracy in Action: P2008*, November 4, 2008, http://www.gwu.edu/~action/2008/chrneday08.html (accessed July 22, 2009).

Ardon, Patricia. *Post-War Reconstruction in Central America: Lessons from El Salvador, Guatemala, and Nicaragua*. Oxford: Oxfam GB, 1999.

Asante, Molefi. "Barack Obama and the Dilemma of Power: An Africological Observation," *Journal of Black Studies* 38, no. 1 (September 2007): 105–115.

B&C Staff. "Networks Call Election Simultaneously for Obama," *Broadcasting & Cable*, November 4, 2008, http://www.broadcastingcable.com/article/116172-Net works_Call_Election_Simultaneously_for_Obama.php (accessed July 22, 2009).

Bai, Matt. "Is Obama the End of Black Politics?," *New York Times Magazine*, August 6, 2008, http://www.nytimes.com/2008/08/10/magazine/10politics-t.html (accessed July 21, 2009).

Baker, Peter, and Jim Rutenberg. "The Long Road to a Clinton Exit," *New York Times*, June 8, 2008, http://www.nytimes.com/2008/06/08/us/politics/08recon. html (accessed May 28, 2009).

Baldwin, Tom, and Alexi Mostrous. "John McCain Halts Presidential Campaign for Economy Crisis Talks," *Times*, September 25, 2008, http://www.timesonline. co.uk/tol/news/world/us_and_americas/us_elections/article4821236.ece (accessed June 10, 2009).

Barker, Lucius, Mack Jones, and Katherine Tate. *African Americans and the American Political System*, 4th ed. Englewood Cliffs, NJ: Prentice Hall, Inc., 1999.

Baron, Zach. "Rappers for Obama, and Vice Versa," *Black Power*, Entertainment, Politics, January 23, 2009, http://www.blackpower.com/entertainment/rappers-for-obama-and-vice-versa/ (accessed July 22, 2009).

BBC News. "Obama Fundraising Rivals Clinton," *BBC News*, April 4, 2007, http://news.bbc.co.uk/2/hi/americas/6527081.stm (accessed July 18, 2009).

Bell, Derrick. *Faces at the Bottom of the Well: The Permanence of Racism.* New York: Basic Books, 1992.

Bell, Derrick. *Race, Racism, and American Law*, 6th ed. New York: Aspen Publishers, 2008.

Bernstein, Robert, and Tom Edwards. "An Older and More Diverse Nation by Midcentury," *U.S. Census Bureau News*, Department of Commerce, Bureau of the Census, August 14, 2008, http://www.census.gov/Press-Release/www/releases/archives/population/012496.html (accessed July 17, 2009).

Bigg, Matthew. "McCain Gaffe over Houses Could Anger Voters," *Reuters*, August 22, 2008, http://www.reuters.com/article/newsOne/idUSN2229072120080822 (accessed July 23, 2009).

Bishop, George. "Parsing the Instant Polls," *The Presidential Debate Blog*, September 29, 2008, http://presidentialdebateblog.blogspot.com/2008/09/parsing-instant-polls-on-first.html (accessed July 23, 2009).

Black, Earl, and Merle Black. *The Rise of Southern Republicans.* Cambridge, MA: Belknap Press of Harvard University Press, 2002.

Blake, John. "Obama's Victory Caps Struggles of Previous Generations," *CNN Politics.com*, Election Center 2008, November 4, 2008, http://www.cnn.com/2008/POLITICS/11/04/obama.history/index.html (accessed July 22, 2009).

Bledsoe, Timothy. "A Research Note on the Impact of District/At-Large Elections on Black Political Efficacy," *Urban Affairs Quarterly* 22 (1986): 166–174

Blumenthal, Mark. "Ambinder: Race Over?," *Pollster.com*, January 7, 2009, http://www.pollster.com/blogs/ambinder_race_over.php (accessed July 20, 2009).

Bobo, Lawrence, and Franklin D. Gilliam, Jr. "Race, Sociopolitical Participation, and Black Empowerment," *The American Political Science Review* 84, no. 2 (June 1990): 377–393.

Bositis, David. Interview by author. Louisville, KY, October 23, 2008.

Broder, David. "Obama Gets Them Fired Up," *Real Clear Politics*, December 23, 2007, http://www.realclearpolitics.com/articles/2007/12/obama_gets_them_fired_up.html (accessed July 22, 2009).

Brownstein, Ronald. "Obama Buoyed by Coalition of the Ascendant," in *Annual Editions: American Government 09/10*, 39th ed., edited by B. Stinebrickner. New York: McGraw Hill, 2010.

Brunell, Thomas L. *Redistricting and Representation: Why Competitive Elections are Bad for America.* New York: Routledge, 2008.

Bruner, Nancy. Interview by author. Jeffersonville, IN, October 23, 2008.

Bullock, Charles S., and Susan A. MacManus. "Policy Responsiveness to the Black Electorate: Programmatic Versus Symbolic Representation," *American Politics Quarterly* 9 (1981): 357–368.

Bumiller, Elisabeth. "Palin Disclosures Raise Questions in Vetting," *New York Times*, September 2, 2008, http://www.nytimes.com/2008/09/02/us/politics/02vetting. html (accessed June 9, 2009).

Burke, Edmund. *Reflections on the Revolution in France* [1790]. Essex, England: Pearson Longman, 2006.

Butterfield, G. K. Interview by author. Louisville, KY, November 19, 2008.

Byassee, Jason. "Africentric Church: A Visit to Chicago's UCC," *The Christian Century*, May 29, 2007, http://www.christiancentury.org/article.lasso?id=3392 (accessed July 22, 2009).

Cameron, Charles, David Epstein, and Sharyn O'Halloran. "Do Majority-Minority Districts Maximize Substantive Black Representation in Congress?," *American Political Science Review* 90 (1996): 794–812.

Cannon, Carl M. "The Facebook Election," *Reader's Digest*, June 2008.

Canon, David T. *Race, Redistricting, and Representation: The Unintended Consequences of Black Majority Districts.* Chicago, IL: University of Chicago Press, 1999.

Carey, Charles W., Jr. *African-American Political Leaders: A–Z of African Americans.* New York: Fact on File, 2004.

Carroll, Susan. *Women as Candidates in American Politics*, 2nd ed. Bloomington: Indiana University Press, 1994.

CBS/AP. "Obama's Prime-Time Appeal to Voters," *CBS News*, Politics, October 29, 2008, http://www.cbsnews.com/stories/2008/10/29/politics/main4557333.shtml (accessed July 22, 2009).

Chambers, Julius. Interview by author. Louisville, KY, March 4, 2009.

Chang, Chingching, and Jacqueline Hitchon. "Mass Media Impact on Voter Response to Women Candidates: Theoretical Development," *Communication Theory* 7, no. 1 (March 1997): 29–52.

Clay, William. *Just Permanent Interests: Black Americans in Congress, 1870–1991.* New York: Amistad Press, 1992.

Clay, William Lacy. Interview by author. Louisville, KY, December 9, 2008.

Clayton, Dewey, and Angela Stallings. "Black Women in Congress: Striking the Balance," *Journal of Black Studies* 30, no. 4 (2000): 574–603.

Clines, Francis X. "The Powell Decision: The Announcement," *New York Times*, November 9, 1995, http://query.nytimes.com/gst/fullpage.html?res=9A06E5DB 1439 F93AA35752C1A963958260 (accessed June 29, 2009).

Clyburn, James. Interview by author. Louisville, KY, December 1, 2008.

CNN.com. "AmericaVotes2004: Election Results," Cable News Network, LP, http://www.cnn.com/ELECTION/2004/pages/results/states/IL/S/01/index.html (accessed July 19, 2009).

Cohen, Steve. Interview by author. Louisville, KY, December 19, 2008.

Commission on Presidential Debates. "CPD Announces Formats for 2004 Debates," *Commission on Presidential Debates*, November 19, 2007, http://www.debates. org/pages/news_111907_p/html (accessed July 24, 2009).

Cook, Charlie. "Time to Reassess the White House Race," *MSNBC*, National Journal, September 9, 2008, http://www.msnbc.msn.com/id/26625240/ (accessed July 23, 2009).

Cooper, Michael, and Michael Powell. "McCain Camp Says Obama is Playing 'Race Card,'" *New York Times*, August 1, 2008, http://www.nytimes.com/2008/08/ 01/us/politics/01campaign.html (accessed August 1, 2008).

Cose, E. "The 'Bradley effect,'" *Newsweek*, October 30, 2006, http://www.msnbc. msn.com/id/15366427/site/newsweek/ (accessed April 12, 2007).

Crowley, Candy. "Clinton Campaign Advisers: Bill Clinton 'Needs to Stop,'" *CNN Political Ticker*, January 8, 2008, http://politicalticker.blogs.cnn.com/category/ presidential-candidates/hillary-clinton/0politicalticker.blogs.cnn.com/category/ bill-clinton/page/6/ (accessed July 22, 2009).

Currinder, Marian. "Campaign Finance: Fundraising and Spending in the 2008 Elections," in *The Elections of 2008*, edited by Michael Nelson, 163–186. Washington, DC: CQ Press, 2010.

Dahl, Robert. *A Preface to Democratic Theory*. Chicago, IL: University of Chicago Press, 1956.

Daily Mail. "Obama's Presidential Bid Stutters as His Former Pastor Repeats the Claim: America Brought 9/11 on Itself," *Daily Mail*, April 29, 2008, http:// www.dailymail.co.uk/news/article-562716/Obamas-presidential-bid-stutters- pastor-repeats-claim-America-brought-9-11-itself.html;jsessionid=0217283AC 4E0147057553A129C7DB4F0 (accessed June 02, 2009).

Dale, Daniel. "Obama Splashes Money Across U.S.," *The Star*, October 28, 2008, http://www.thestar.com/printArticle/525710 (accessed June 13, 2009).

Dann, Carrie. "NBC Calls Ohio for Obama," *MSNBC*, First Read, November 4, 2008, http://firstread.msnbc.msn.com/archive/2008/11/04/1639565.aspx (accessed July 22, 2009).

Davies, Frank. "Web Politics Come of Age with Obama—Illinois Senator's Campaign Uses Internet Effectively for Fundraising and Communicating with His Supporters," *Contra Costa Times*, February 24, 2008, A1.

Davis, Artur. Interview by author. Louisville, KY, November 18, 2008.

Davis, George, and Fred Donaldson. *Blacks in the United States: A Geographic Perspective*. Boston, MA: Houghton Mifflin Company, 1975.

Dawson, Michael C. *Behind the Mule: Race and Class in African-American Politics*. Princeton, NJ: Princeton University Press, 2004.

Dickinson, Tim. "The Machinery of Hope: Inside the Grass-Roots Field Operation of Barack Obama, Who is Transforming the Way Political Campaigns are Run," *Rolling Stone*, March 20, 2008.

Dolan, Kathleen. "Do Women Candidates Play to Gender Stereotypes? Do Men Candidates Play to Women? Candidate Sex and Issues Priorities on Campaign Websites," *Political Research Quarterly* 58, no. 1 (March 2005): 31–44.

Du Bois, W. E. B. "Strivings of the Negro People," *Atlantic Monthly* 80 (1897): 194–198.

Elliot, Jeffrey M., and Sheikh R. Ali. *The Presidential-Congressional Political Dictionary.* Santa Barbara, CA: ABC-Clio Information Services, 1984.

Erlanger, Steven. "Obama Gets Europe's Ear, Pleasing Crowds without Specifics," *New York Times,* July 25, 2008, http://www.nytimes.com/2008/07/25/world/americas/25iht-25assess.14778918.html (accessed July 23, 2009).

Essence Magazine. "Realizing the Dream," *Essence Magazine,* January 2009, 67–135.

Fairness and Accuracy in Reporting (FAIR). "Two Standards on Public Financing," July 3, 2008, http://www.fair.org/index.php?page=3569 (accessed June 9, 2009).

Franklin, John Hope, and Alfred A. Moss, Jr. *From Slavery to Freedom: A History of Negro Americans,* 6th ed. New York: Knopf, 1988.

Fretland, Katie. "Obama Campaign Slams New Yorker Cover," *The Swamp,* July 14, 2008, http://www.swamppolitics.com/news/politics/blog/2008/07/printerbarack_obama_new_yorker_cover.html (accessed July 20, 2009).

Gans, Curtis. *African-Americans, Anger, Fear and Youth Propel Turnout to Highest Level Since 1960.* American University, Center for the Study of the American Electorate, December 17, 2008.

Green, Joshua. "The Front-Runner's Fall," *The Atlantic,* September 2008, http://www.theatlantic.com/doc/print/200809/hillary-clinton-campaign (accessed May 22, 2009).

Greenblatt, Alan. "Changing U.S. Electorate," in *Issues in Race and Ethnicity,* Congressional Quarterly Researcher, 4th ed., 25–47. Washington, DC: CQ Press, 2009.

Grofman, Bernard. "Expert Witness Testimony and the Evolution of Voting Rights Case Law," in *Controversies in Minority Voting,* edited by B. Grofman and C. Davidson, 197–229. Washington, DC: Brookings Institution, 1992.

Grofman, Bernard, and Chandler Davidson (eds.). *Controversies in Minority Voting: The Voting Rights Act in Perspective.* Washington, DC: Brookings Institution, 1992.

Hajnal, Zoltan L. *Changing White Attitudes towards Black Political Leadership.* New York: Cambridge University Press, 2007.

Harper, Hill, "I Want to Be Like Him," *Essence Magazine,* January 2009, 110.

Harrigan, John, and Ronald Vogel. "The City as a Place of Opportunity," in *Political Change in the Metropolis,* 146–159. New York: HarperCollins, 2000.

Healy, Patrick. "On Eve of Primary, Clinton Campaign Shows Stress," *New York Times,* Politics, January 8, 2008, http://www.nytimes.com/2008/01/08/us/politics/08clinton.html (accessed July 22, 2009).

Heffernan, Virginia. "Clicking and Choosing," *New York Times*, November 14, 2008, 22.

Herrnson, Paul S., and Jennifer Lucas. "The Fairer Sex? Gender and Negative Campaigning in U.S. Elections," *American Politics Research* 34, no. 1 (2006): 69–94.

Hershey, Marjorie. "The Media: Coloring the News," in *The Elections of 2008*, edited by Michael Nelson, 122–144. Washington, DC: CQ Press, 2010.

Holahan, Catherine. "On the Web, Obama is the Clear Winner," *BusinessWeek Online*, The Primary Race, March 5, 2008, http://www.businessweek.com/technology/content/mar2008/tc2008035_280573.htm (accessed July 22, 2009).

Horowitz, Jason. "Black Congressmen Declare Racism in Palin's Rhetoric," *The New York Observer*, Politics, October 7, 2008, http://www.observer.com/2008/politics/black-congressmen-declare-racism-palin-s-rhetoric (accessed October 19, 2008).

Ifill, Gwen. *The Breakthrough: Politics and Race in the Age of Obama*. New York: Doubleday, 2009.

Jamieson, Kathleen Hall. "Transcript," *Bill Moyers Journal*, December 7, 2007, http://www.pbs.org/moyers/journal/12072007/transcript1.html (accessed July 22, 2009).

Janda, Kenneth, Jeffrey Berry and Jerry Goldman. *The Challenge of Democracy*, 10th ed. Boston, MA: Wadsworth, 2009.

Johnson, Kimberly. "Web Enabling More to Donate: Voters Can Pledge Their Support for Candidates from Virtually Anywhere," *Denver Post*, March 3, 2008.

Johnson, Todd. "Obama Election Invigorates Black Lives, But Doesn't End Struggles, Some Caution," *Medill Reports Chicago*, December 16, 2008, http://news.medill.northwestern.edu/chicago/news.aspx?id=106519 (accessed December 16, 2008).

Jones, Jeffrey M. "Race Tied as Democratic Convention Starts," *Gallup*, August 25, 2008, http://www.gallup.com/poll/109792/allup-daily-race-tied-democractic-convention-starts.aspx (accessed July 24, 2009).

Jones, Jeffrey M. "Obama Acceptance Speech Gets High Marks From Public," *Gallup*, August 30, 2008, http://www.gallup.com/poll/109948/obama-acceptance-speech-gets-high-marks-from-public.aspx (accessed July 24, 2009).

Jones, Jeffrey M. "Bush's Approval Rating Drops to New Low of 27%," *Gallup*, September 30, 2008, http://www.gallup.com/poll/110806/bushs-approval-rating-drops-new-low-27.aspx (accessed June 14, 2009).

Jones, Jeffrey M. "Obama Viewed as Winner of Third Debate," *Gallup*, October 17, 2008, http://www.gallup.com/poll/111256/obama-viewed-winner-third-debate.aspx (accessed June 14, 2009).

Jones, Ricky L. *What's Wrong with Obamamania? Black America, Black Leadership, and the Death of Political Imagination*. New York: State University of New York Press, 2008.

Judis, John. "America the Liberal," in *Annual Editions: American Government 09/10*, 39th ed., edited by B. Stinebrickner, New York: McGraw-Hill, 2010, 109–111.

Judis, John, and Ruy Teixeira. *The Emerging Democratic Majority*. New York: Scribner, 2002.

Kantor, Jodi. "Disinvitation by Obama Is Criticized," *New York Times*, March 6, 2007, http://www.nytimes.com/2007/03/06/us/politics/06obama.html (accessed July 22, 2009).

Katel, Peter. "Race and Politics," in *Issues in Race and Ethnicity*, Congressional Quarterly Researcher, 4th ed., 1–24. Washington, DC: CQ Press, 2009.

Kennedy, Caroline. "A President Like My Father," *New York Times*, Opinion, January 27, 2008, http://www.nytimes.com/2008/01/27/opinion/27kennedy.html (accessed July 22, 2009).

Kernell, Samuel. *Going Public: New Strategies of Presidential Leadership*, 3rd ed. Washington, DC: CQ Press, 1997.

Key, V. O. *Southern Politics*. New York: Alfred Knopf, 1949.

Kilpatrick, Carolyn. Interview by author. Louisville, KY, December 19, 2008.

Klein, Joe. "Sarah Palin's Myth of America," *Time*, September 10, 2008, http://www.time.com/time/printout.0,8816,1840388,00.html (accessed July 24, 2009).

Kurtz, Howard. "For Clinton, a Matter of Fair Media," *Washington Post*, December 19, 2007, C01, http://www.washingtonpost.com/wp-dyn/content/article/2007/12/18/AR2007121802184.html (accessed July 22, 2009).

Large, Jerry. "A New Era Begins: The Significance of the Barack Obama Victory for America and the World," *BlackPast.org*, Perspectives on African American History, 2007–2008, http://www.blackpast.org/?q=perspectives/new-era-begins-significance-barack-obama-victory-america-and-world (accessed July 21, 2009).

Leip, David. "2008 Presidential General Election Results," *Atlas of U.S. Presidential Elections*, 2005, http://www.uselectionatlas.org/RESULTS/national.php?f=0&year=2008 (accessed July 22, 2009).

Lemon, Don. "Jackson Apologizes for 'Crude' Obama Remarks," *CNNPolitics*, July 9, 2008, http://www.cnn.com/2008/POLITICS/07/09/jesse.jackson.comment/ (accessed July 22, 2009).

Liasson, Mara, and Scott Simon. "Hillary Clinton Enters Race for President," *NPR*, January 20, 2007, http://www.npr.org/templates/story/story.php?storyId=6929745 (accessed July 22, 2009).

Libert, Barry, and Rick Faulk. *Winning Business Lessons of the Obama Campaign*. Upper Saddle River, NJ: Pearson Education, Inc., 2009.

Lightman, David. "Obama Backers Love Web, But Does It Give Him an Edge?," *Miami Herald*, June 16, 2008, 2A.

Lincoln, Eric C., and Lawrence H. Mamiya. *The Black Church in the African American Experience*. Durham, NC: Duke University Press, 1990.

Linkins, Jason. "Obama: Reverend Wright Made a 'Profound Mistake,'" *The Huffington Post*, March 18, 2008, http://www.huffingtonpost.com/2008/03/18/obama-reverend-wright-mad_n_92117.html (accessed July 22, 2009).

Lizza, Ryan. "Bill vs. Barack," *The New Yorker*, Campaign Journal, May 5, 2008, http://www.newyorker.com/talk/2008/05/05/080505ta_talk_lizza (accessed July 22, 2009).

Lopez, Mark Hugo. "How Hispanics Voted in the 2008 Election," *Pew Hispanic Center*, November 7, 2008, http://pewresearch.org/pubs/1024/exit-poll-analysis-hispanics (accessed July 21, 2009).

Lopez, Mark, and Paul Taylor. *Dissecting the 2008 Electorate: Most Diverse in U.S. History*. Pew Hispanic Center, April 30, 2009, http://pewhispanic.org/reports/report.php?ReportID=108 (June 17, 2009).

Lublin, David. *The Paradox of Representation: Racial Gerrymandering and Minority Interests in Congress*. Princeton, NJ: Princeton University Press, 1997.

Lui, Baodong. "Deracialization and Urban Racial Contexts," *Urban Affairs Review* 38 (March 2003): 527–591.

Luo, Michael. "Obama Recasts the Fund-Raising Landscape," *New York Times*, October 20, 2008.

Luo, Michael. "Obama Hauls in Record $750 Million for Campaign," *New York Times*, December 4, 2008.

MacAskill, Ewen. "The Palin Effect: White Women Now Deserting Obama, Says Survey," *Guardian*, September 10, 2008, http://www.guardian.co.uk/lifeandstyle/2008/sep/10/women.uselections2008 (accessed July 11, 2009).

Martin, Jonathan, and Ben Smith. "Race Issue Moves to Center of Campaign," *Politico.com*, August 1, 2008, http://dyn.politico.com/printstory.cfm?uuid=7b3aecc9-3048-5c12-00ba1e7bd09bdba5 (accessed August 1, 2008).

McClain, Paula, Niambi Carter, and Michael Brady. "Gender and Black Presidential Politics: 'From Chisholm to Moseley Braun,'" *Journal of Women, Politics, and Policy* 27, nos. 1–2 (2005): 51–68.

McClay, Wilfred. "The Weakness of Our Political Parties," *Society* 45, no. 5 (September 2008): 403–405.

McCormick, John. "FEC Rules on Presidential Campaign Funding," *Chicago Tribune*, March 1, 2007, http://www.chicagotribune.com/news/nationworld/chi-070301elect,0,1248677.story (accessed June 9, 2009).

McCormick, John. "Obama Marks '02 War Speech; Contender Highlights His Early Opposition in Effort to Distinguish Him from His Rivals," *Chicago Tribune*, October 3, 2007, 7.

McCormick, John, and Christi Parsons. "Barack Obama to Visit Ill Grandmother Madelyn Dunham," *Chicago Tribune*, October 21, 2008, http://archives.chicagotribune.com/2008/oct/21/nation/chi-obama-grandmaoct21 (accessed July 22, 2009).

Media Matters. "Tucker on Sen. Clinton: '[T]here's just something about her that feels castrating, overbearing, and scary,'" *Media Matters for America*, March 20, 2007, http://mediamatters.org/mmtv/200703200013 (accessed July 22, 2009).

Mendell, David. "Obama Routs Democratic Foes; Ryan Tops Crowded GOP Field," *Chicago Tribune*, Campaign 2004: Illinois Primary, March 17, 2004, http://www.chicagotribune.com/features/custom/fashion/chi-0403170332 mar17,0,47 16349. story (accessed July 21, 2009).

Mendell, David. *Obama: From Promise to Power*. New York: HarperCollins Publishers, 2007.

Merriner, James L. "The Friends of O," *Chicago* 57, no. 6 (June 2008): 74–99.

Milbank, Dana. "Still More Lamentations from Jeremiah," *Washington Post*, April 29, 2008, http://www.washingtonpost.com/wp-dyn/content/article/2008/04/28/AR2008042802269.html (accessed July 22, 2009).

Mishel, Lawrence, Jared Bernstein, and Heidi Shierholz. *The State of Working America Report 2008/2009*. Economic Policy Institute, State of Working America Series, 2006–2009, http://www.stateofworkingamerica.org/ (accessed July 21, 2009).

Misiroglu, Gina. *The Handy Politics Answer Book*. Canton, MI: Visible Ink Press, 2003.

Mooney, Alexander. "McCain Ad Compares Obama to Britney Spears, Paris Hilton," *CNN*, Politics, July 30, 2008, http://www.cnn.com/2008/POLITICS/07/30/mccain.ad/index.html (accessed July 23, 2009).

Mooney, Brian C. "Technology Aids Obama's Outreach Drive, Volunteers Answer Call on Social Networking Site," *Boston Globe*, February 24, 2008, 1A.

MSNBC. "VP Pick Palin Makes Appeal to Women Voters," MSNBC, August 28, 2008, http://www.msnbc.msn.com/id/25970882 (accessed July 23, 2009).

Nagourney, Adam. "The Pattern May Change If . . . ," *New York Times*, Week in Review, December 10, 2006, http://www.nytimes.com/2006/12/10/weekin review/10nagourney.html (accessed July 22, 2009).

Nagourney, Adam. "The '08 Obama Campaign: Sea Change for Politics as We Know It," *New York Times*, November 4, 2008.

Nagourney, Adam, and Carl Hulse. "Clinton Success Changes Dynamic in Delegate Hunt," *New York Times*, March 6, 2008, http://query.nytimes.com/gst/fullpage.html?res=9E05E0DA163BF935A35750C0A96E9C8B63 (accessed July 23, 2009).

Nagourney, Adam, and Jeff Zeleny. "Obama Chooses Biden as Running Mate," *New York Times*, August 24, 2008, http://www.nytimes.com/2008/08/24/us/politics/24biden.html?_r=1 (accessed June 8, 2009).

NBC News. "NBC News Calls Election for Obama," *NBC News*, Transcript, November 4, 2008, http://icue.nbcunifiles.com/icue/files/icue/site/pdf/38832.pdf (accessed July 22, 2009).

Nelson, Michael. "How the GOP Conquered the South," *The Chronicle of Higher Education*, *The Chronicle Review*, October 21, 2005, http://chronicle.com/free/v52/i09/09b01401.htm (accessed July 21, 2009).

Nelson, Michael. "The Setting: Diversifying the Presidential Talent Pool," in *The Elections of 2008*, edited by Michael Nelson, 1–21. Washington, DC: CQ Press, 2010.

Neustadt, Richard E. *Presidential Power*. New York: Wiley, 1980.

Newport, Frank. "Obama Gains Among Former Clinton Supporters," *Gallup*, September 2, 2008, http://www.gallup.com/poll/109957/obama-gains-among-former-clinton-supporters.aspx (accessed July 23, 2009).

New River Media. "Interview with: Christopher Jenks," *PBS Interviews*, no date, http://www.pbs.org/fmc/interviews/jencks.htm (accessed July 22, 2009).

Newton-Small, Jay. "Will Clinton's Obama Attacks Backfire?," *Time*, December 4, 2007, http://www.time.com/time/printout/0,8816,1690519,00.html (accessed July 24, 2009).

Nossiter, Adam. "For South, a Waning Hold on National Politics," *New York Times*, November 10, 2008, http://www.nytimes.com/2008/11/11/us/politics/11south.html?_r=1&scp=1&sq=for%20south%20a%20waning%20hold%20on%20national%20politics&st=cse (accessed November 11, 2008).

Obama, Barack. *Dreams from My Father: A Story of Race and Inheritance*. New York: Three Rivers Press, 2004.

Obama, Barack. "Keynote Address," delivered at the 2004 Democratic National Convention, Fleet Center, Boston, MA, July 27, 2004.

Obama, Barack. *The Audacity of Hope*. New York: Crown, 2006.

Obama, Barack. "Remarks of Senator Barack Obama: New Hampshire Primary," delivered in Nashua, NH, January 8, 2008, http://www.barackobama.com/2008/01/08/remarks_of_senator_barack_obam_82.php (accessed July 22, 2009).

Obama, Barack. "Obama's Father's Day Speech," *CNNPolitics*, delivered in Chicago, IL, June 15, 2008, http://www.cnn.com/2008/POLITICS/06/27/obama.fathers.ay/index.html (accessed July 22, 2009).

Obama, Barack. "The American Promise," acceptance speech at the Democratic Convention, delivered in Mile High Stadium, Colorado, August 28, 2008, http://obamaspeeches.com/E10-Barack-Obama-The-American-Promise-Acceptance-Speech-at-the-Democratic-Convention-Mile-High-Stadium—Denver-Colorado-August-28-2008.htm (accessed November 4, 2009).

Obama, Barack. "This Is Your Victory," acceptance speech delivered at Grant Park, Illinois, November 4, 2008, http://obamaspeeches.com/E11-Barack-Obama-Election-Night-Victory-Speech-Grant-Park-Illinois-November-4-2008.htm (accessed July 22, 2009).

Oinounou, Mosheh, and Bonney Kapp. "Michelle Obama Takes Heat for Saying She's Proud of My Country for the First Time," *FoxNews.com*, February 19, 2008, http://www.foxnews.com/printer_friendly_story/0,3566,331288,00.html (accessed July 20, 2009).

Orey, Byron D., and Boris E. Ricks. *A Systematic Analysis of the Deracialization Concept.* University of Nebraska: Faculty Publications, 2007.

Owens, Chris T. "Black Substantive Representation in State Legislatures from 1971–1994," *Social Science Quarterly* 86, no. 4 (2005): 779–791.

Parker, Jennifer. "Democratic Women Torn Between Clinton and Obama," *ABC News*, February 4, 2008, http://abcnews.go.com/print?id=4235711 (accessed July 17, 2009).

Parsons, Christi, and John McCormick. "Obama's Formula: It's the Network— Technology Helped Campaign Take-Off and Change the Game," *Chicago Tribune*, May 24, 2008.

Pearson, Rick. "Clinton: No Last Call at Maker's Mark," *The Swamp*, May 17, 2008, http://www.swamppolitics.com/news/politics/blog/2008/05/hillary_clinton_no_l ast_call_a.html

Pearson Education. "National Student/Parent Mock Election To Give Students a Voice in 2008 Election," *Pearson*, Press Release, September 8, 2008, http:// www.pearsoned.com/pr_2008/090908b.htm (accessed July 22, 2009).

Perr, Jon. "McCain's Supposed Adviser John Lewis Calls Him Out," *Crooks and Liars*, October 12, 2008, http://crooksandliars.com/jon-perr/mccains-saddleback- adviser-john-lewis-cal (accessed June 12, 2009).

Pitkin, H. F. *The Concept of Representation.* Berkeley: University of California Press, 1967.

Plano, Jack C., and Milton Greenberg. *The American Political Dictionary.* Fort Worth, TX: Holt, Rinehart, and Winston, Inc., 1993.

Pomper, Gerald. "The Presidential Election: Change Comes to America," in *The Elections of 2008*, edited by Michael Nelson, 45–73. Washington, DC: CQ Press: 2010.

Preston, Mark, and Robert Yoon. "Analysis: Sparks Fly in Most Contentious Debate to Date," *CNNPolitics.com*, January 22, 2008, http://www.cnn.com/2008/ POLITICS/01/22/sc.debate.anlysis/index.html (accessed July 22, 2009).

Putnam, Jackson. *Jess: The Political Career of Jesse Marvin Unruh.* Lanham, MD: University Press of America, 2005.

Raso, Anne. "His Early Life," *Today's Black Woman Presents: Barack Obama*, Collector's Edition #87, vol. 15, no. 5 (2008): 10–17.

Reid, Tim. "Hillary Clinton Gaffe over Martin Luther King May Cost Votes in South Carolina," *Times Online*, January 12, 2008, http://www.timesonline.co.uk/tol/ news/world/us_and_americas/us_elections/article3173652.ece (accessed July 22, 2009).

Reiter, Mark. "The Real Baracketology," *Washington Post*, April 3, 2009, http://www. washingtonpost.com/wp-dyn/content/article/2009/04/03/AR2009040303276. html (accessed July 22, 2009).

Ressner, Jeffrey. "Michelle Obama Thesis Was on Racial Divide," *Politico.com*, February 22, 2008, http://dyn.politico.com/printstory.cfm?uuid=42FC5818-3048-5C12-005E33B3C0F4E64B (accessed July 20, 2009).

Reyes, Robert. "Sharon Stone: Hillary Clinton Too Sexy To Run For President," *American Chronicle*, March 27, 2006.

Rich, Frank. "How Obama Became Acting President," *New York Times*, July 27, 2009, http://www.nytimes.com/2008/07/27/opinion/27rich.html?_r=2&scp=14&sq=frank%20rich (accessed July 23, 2009).

Ripley, Amanda. "A Mother's Story," *Time*, Special Commemorative Edition (April 21, 2008): 42–47.

Robinson, Eugene. "Stepping Into the Sunshine," *RealClearPolitcs.com*, Election 2008, November 6, 2008, http://www.realclearpolitics.com/articles/2008/11/stepping_into_the_sunshine.html (accessed July 22, 2009).

Roddy, Dennis. "Race on the Trail: Large Numbers of Voters Say Color of Skin Played a Role in Choice," *Pittsburgh Post-Gazette*, May 18, 2008. http://www.post-gazette.com/pg/08139/882900-176.stm (accessed May 28, 2009).

Rohter, Larry. "McCain is Faltering Among Hispanic Voters," *New York Times*, October 23, 2008, http://www.nytimes.com/2008/10/23/world/americas/23iht-23latino.17197720.html (accessed July 23, 2009).

Ross, Brian, and Rehab El-Buri. "Obama's Pastor: God Damn America, U.S. to Blame for 9/11," *ABCNews*, March 13, 2008, http://abcnews.go.com/Blotter/DemocraticDebate/story?id=4443788&page=1 (accessed July 22, 2009).

Rutenberg, Jim. "Pundits Declare the Race Over," *New York Times*, May 8, 2008, http://www.nytimes.com/2008/05/08/us/politics/07cnd-pundits.html (accessed July 23, 2008).

Rutenberg, Jim. "Black Radio on Obama is Left's Answer to Limbaugh," *New York Times*, July 27, 2008.

Rutenberg, Jim, and Christopher Drew. "National Push by Obama on Ads and Turnout," *New York Times*, June 22, 2008, http://www.nytimes.com/2008/06/22/us/politics/22obama.html (accessed June 14, 2009).

Salant, Jonathan. "Spending Doubled as Obama Led First Billion-Dollar Race in 2008," *Bloomberg.com*, December 26, 2008, http://www.bloomberg.com/apps/news?pid=20670001&sid=aerix76GvmRM (accessed June 14, 2009).

Schaller, Thomas. *Whistling Past Dixie: How Democrats Can Win Without the South*. New York: Simon and Schuster, 2006.

Schaper, David. "Camp Obama Trains Campaign Volunteers," *NPR*, June 13, 2007, http://www.npr.org/templates/transcript/transcript.php?storyId=11012254 (accessed July 22, 2009).

Scherer, Michael. "McCain's Struggles: Four Ways He Went Wrong," *Time*, October 17, 2008, http://www.time.com/time/politics/article/0,8599,1851400,00.html (accessed June 11, 2009).

Schifferes, Steve. "Internet Key to Obama Victories," *BBC News*, Technology Section, June 12, 2008, http://news.bbc.co.uk/2/hi/technology/7412045.stm (accessed July 20, 2009).

Schumpeter, Joseph. *Capitalism, Socialism, and Democracy.* New York: Harper and Row, 1942.

Seelye, Katharine. "Clinton-Obama Quandary for Many Black Women," *New York Times*, October 14, 2007, http://www.nytimes.com/2007/10/14/us/politics/14carolina.html (accessed July 22, 2009).

Seelye, Katharine. "Oprah May Campaign for Obama," *New York Times*, Politics, The Caucus, November 21, 2007, http://thecaucus.blogs.nytimes.com/2007/11/21/oprah-may-campaign-for-obama/ (accessed July 22, 2009).

Seelye, Katharine. "The Million-Dollar Minute," *New York Times*, Politics, The Caucus, April 17, 2008, http://thecaucus.blogs.nytimes.com/2008/04/17/million-dollar-minute/ (accessed July 22, 2009).

Shea, Danny. "Anna Wintour Takes Hillary Clinton to Task," *The Huffington Post*, January 18, 2008, http://www.huffingtonpost.com/2008/01/18/anna-wintour-takes-hillar_n_82132.html?view=screen (accessed July 22, 2009).

Smith, Ben. "Bill on Going Negative: Media Bias Made Her Do It," *Politico.com*, January 4, 2008, http://www.politico.com/blogs/bensmith/0108/Bills_reason_to_go_negative_media_bias.html (accessed July 22, 2009).

Smith, Ben. "Obama Campaign Learns from Others' Missteps," *Politico.com*, August 27, 2008, http://www.cbsnews.com/stories/2008/08/27/politics/politico/main4386932.shtml (accessed July 22, 2009).

Starks, Robert. "How He Did It: An Analysis of the Obama Tsunami," *N'Digo Profiles*, December 2008.

Stein, Sam. "Gergen: McCain Using Code Words to Attack Obama as 'Uppity'," *The Huffington Post*, August 3, 2008, http://www.huffingtonpost.com/2008/08/03/gergen-mccain-is-using-co_n_116605.html (accessed August 6, 2008).

Stein, Sam. "McCain on 'Black Monday': Fundamentals Of Our Economy Are Still Strong," *The Huffington Post*, September 15, 2008, http://www.huffingtonpost.com/2008/09/15/mccain-fundamentals-of-th_n_126445.html (accessed July 23, 2009).

Steinhauser, Paul. "CNN Poll: Obama 49, McCain 48," *CNNPolitics.com*, August 31, 2008, http://politicalticker.blogs.cnn.com/2008/08/31/cnn-poll-obama-49-mccain-48/ (accessed July 24, 2009).

Stelter, Brian. "The Facebooker Who Friended Obama," *New York Times*, July 7, 2008.

Stirland, Sarah Lai. "Obama's Secret Weapons: Internet, Databases and Psychology," *Wired*, Elections, October 29, 2008. http://www.wired.com/threatlevel/2008/10/obamas-secret-w/ (accessed July 21, 2009).

Sullivan, Amy. "A Star Is Born," *Time,* Special Commemorative Edition (2008): 64–65.

Swain, Carol M. *Black Faces, Black Interests: The Representation of African Americans in Congress.* Cambridge, MA: Harvard University Press, 1993.

Swarns, Rachel. "Could It Really Be Him? Yeah, Probably," *New York Times,* March 26, 2009, http://www.nytimes.com/2009/03/26/fashion/26washington.html (accessed July 21, 2009).

Swarns, Rachel. "Quiet Political Shifts as More Blacks Are Elected," *New York Times,* October 14, 2008, http://www.nytimes.com/2008/10/14/us/politics/14race.html (accessed July 1, 2009).

Sweet, Lynn. "Obama's NAACP Speech," delivered at the 99th Annual Convention of the NAACP in Cincinnati, Ohio, July 14, 2008, http://blogs.suntimes.com/sweet/2008/07/obamas_naacp_speech_cincinnati.html (accessed July 22, 2009).

Sykes, Patricia Lee. "Gender in the 2008 Presidential Election: Two Types of Time Collide," *PS: Political Science & Politics* (October 2008): 761–764.

Tate, Katherine. "Black Political Participation in the 1984 and 1988 Presidential Elections," *American Political Science Review* 84 (1991): 1159–1176.

Tate, Katherine. "The Political Representation of Blacks in Congress: Does Race Matter?," *Legislative Studies Quarterly* 26, no. 4 (November 2001): 623–638.

Tate, Katherine. *Black Faces in the Mirror: African Americans and Their Representatives in the U.S. Congress.* Princeton, NJ: Princeton University Press, 2003.

Teinowitz, Ira. "African-American Media Waiting for Ad Spending by Obama Campaign," *targetmarketnews.com,* July 14, 2008, http://www.targetmarketnews.com/storyid07150801.htm (accessed July 22, 2009).

Thomas, Evan. "The Great Debates," *Newsweek,* November 17, 2008, http://www.newsweek.com/id/167950/output (accessed June 11, 2009).

Thomas, Evan. *A Long Time Coming.* New York: Public Affairs, 2009.

Todd, Chuck, and Sheldon Gawiser. *How Barack Obama Won.* New York: Vintage Books, 2009.

Toner, Robin. "Obama Camp Thinks Democrats Can Rise in South," *New York Times,* June 30, 2008, http://www.nytimes.com/2008/06/30/us/politics/30south.html?scp=2&sq=Obama%20camp%20thinks%20democrats&st=Search (accessed June 30, 2008).

Tumulty, Karen. "The Five Mistakes Clinton Made," *Time,* Politics, May 8, 2008, http://www.time.com/time/politics/article/0,8599,1738331,00.html (accessed July 22, 2009).

Tumulty, Karen. "How Obama Did It," *Time,* Politics, June 5, 2008, http://www.time.com/time/politics/article/0,8599,1811857-2,00.html (accessed July 22, 2009).

TUNC.biz, "How Katie Couric Destroyed Sarah Palin," *TUNC.biz*, http://www/tunc.biz/Katie_Couric_Destroyed_Sarah_Palin.htm (accessed July 24, 2009).

U.S. Constitution, Article 1, Section 2.

U.S. Constitution, Article 1, Section 8.

Unruh, Bob. "VP Debate Moderator Ifill Releasing Pro-Obama Book," *WorldNet Daily*, September 30, 2008, http://www.worldnetdaily.com/index.php? fa=PAGE.view&pageId=76645 (accessed June 12, 2009).

Vanderleeuw, James, Baodong Lui, and Erica Williams. "The 2006 New Orleans Mayoral Election: The Political Ramifications of a Large-Scale Natural Disaster," *PS: Political Science and Politics* 41 (October 2008): 795–801.

Ververs, Vaughn. "Analysis: Bill Clinton's Lost Legacy," *CBS News*, January 26, 2008, http://www.cbsnews.com/stories/2008/01/26/politics/main3755521.shtml (accessed July 22, 2009).

Ververs, Vaughn. "Obama's Risky Denunciation of Rev. Wright," *CBSNews*, April 29, 2008, http://www.cbsnews.com/stories/2008/04/29/politics/main4056166.shtml (accessed July 22, 2009).

Vogel, Kenneth. "Money Bomb: Ron Paul Raises $6 Million in 24-Hour Period," *USA Today*, December 17, 2007, http://www.usatoday.com/news/politics/election2008/2007-12-17-ronpaul-fundraising_N.htm (accessed July 22, 2009).

Walton, Hanes, and Robert C. Smith, *American Politics and the African American Quest for Universal Freedom*, 5th ed. New York: Longman Publishing, 2010.

Watt, Mel. Interview by author. Louisville, KY, December 19, 2008.

Weathersbee, Tonyaa. "Commentary: Barack Obama's Decision to Leave Trinity Has Pros and Cons—But Ultimately, It Won't Matter," *Blackamericaweb.com*, June 4, 2008, http://www.blackamericaweb.com/site.aspx/sayitloud/weathersbee604 (accessed June 6, 2008).

Weissler, David. "Obama Raises $32.5 Million for White House Race," *Reuters*, July 1, 2007, http://www.reuters.com/article/politicsNews/idUSN0135051620070701 (accessed July 22, 2009).

Wenner, Jann. "A New Hope," *Rolling Stone*, Commemorative Edition 55, (March 20, 2008): 53–55.

Whitby, Kenny J. *The Color of Representation: Congressional Behavior and Black Interests*. Ann Arbor: University of Michigan Press, 2000.

Wilder, Kimberly. "Hofstra Presidential Debate Excludes 3rd Party Candidates: What Would Victoria Woodhull Do?," *OpEdNews*, September 25, 2008, http://www.opednews.com/articles/Hofstra-Presidential-Debat-by-Kimberly-Wilder-080924-580.html (accessed July 22, 2009).

Wilentz, Sean. "Race Man," *The New Republic*, February 27, 2008, http://www.tnr.com/story_print.html?id=aa0cd21b-0ff2-4329-88a1-69c6c268b304 (accessed August 1, 2008).

Williams, Erica N. Untitled Master's Thesis, Pan-African Studies, University of Louisville, 2009.

Wolffe, Richard, and Daren Briscoe. "Across the Divide," *Newsweek*, July 16, 2007, http://www.newsweek.com/id/33156/output/print (accessed July 19, 2009).

Woodward, C. Vann. *The Strange Career of Jim Crow*, 3rd ed. New York: Oxford University Press, 1966.

Yarmuth, John. Interview by author. Louisville, KY, February 4, 2009.

Zeleny, Jeff. "Burnishing Credentials, Obama Will Visit the Middle East and Europe," *New York Times*, June 29, 2008, http://www.nytimes.com/2008/06/29/us/politics/29trip.html (accessed June 10, 2009).

Index

Note: 't' following a page number refers to a table.

DATE DUE